C000213024

CHRISTOPHER SOMERVILLE'S

FIFTY BEST RIVER WALKS OF BRITAIN

CHRISTOPHER SOMERVILLE'S

FIFTY BEST RIVER WALKS OF BRITAIN

MICHAEL JOSEPH

To my mother

Frontispiece:
River Exe. Gleam of autumn sunshine below Nethercote

First published in Great Britain 1988 by
Webb & Bower (Publishers) Limited
9 Colleton Crescent, Exeter, Devon EX2 4BY
in association with Michael Joseph Limited
27 Wright's Lane, London W8 5TZ

Designed by Vic Giolitto

Production by Nick Facer/Rob Kendrew

British Library Cataloguing in Publication Data
Somerville, Christopher
Christopher Somerville's fifty best
river walks of Britain.
1. Walking—Great Britain—Guide-books
2. Rivers—Great Britain—Guide-books
3. Great Britain—Description and travel
—1971-—Guide-books
I. Title
914.1'04858 DA650
ISBN 0-86350-220-2

Typeset in Great Britain by
Keyspools Ltd, Golborne, Warrington, Lancs

Colour reproduction by Peninsular Repro Service Ltd, Exeter

Printed and bound in Spain by Graficromo SA

Contents

Acknowledgements

It is hard to know where to start in acknowledging all the help I received while walking, researching and writing more than 350 miles of river rambles in all parts of the kingdom. Although at times exhausted, thirsty, hungry, baffled, infuriated and terrified, I enjoyed every minute of it – in retrospect, at least! – and would not have done so without a mountain of freely-given assistance.

For invaluable information, much of it painstakingly written out by hand, I would particularly like to thank Joan Helliwell of the Hebden Bridge Literary and Scientific Society (Hebden Water); Hugh Trumper of Tunbridge Wells CHA/HF Rambling Club (River Medway); Molly Porter, the Speyside Way Ranger; Lilian Wright of Eynsham History Group (River Thames); Lt-Col Aidan Sprot (River Tweed); also Kathleen Pymm of the Friends of Morwellham, for whose letters and enthusiastic interest I am very grateful, even though the River Tamar didn't eventually find its way into the book.

I am also very grateful to the staff of Colchester Public Library for ferreting out and making available so many books of reference from all over the country; and to Regional Information Officers, Assistant Reference Librarians (Local Studies), Chief Development Officers, Bibliographical Officers and those other formidable titles behind which shelter so many kind and helpful people.

David Turner, Narborough's dedicated historian, cheerfully found time after a hard day's teaching to talk to me and show me his fascinating albums and other local material. Maurice Hanson, accompanied by his famous toad's-head stick, took me under the skin of the River Don countryside and shared some of his enormous knowledge of natural history. Dave Richardson first killed a bottle of Knockando with me, then showed me the plants along the Water of Leith in between chasing his daughter Megan.

Pat Bray patiently unlocked the riddle of my handwriting, and typed everything beautifully. Richard Scott Simon and Vivien Green encouraged me all along the line, as always, as did my family, who shared many of the walks with me.

Lastly, I wish I could thank in person all those people I met in pubs and farmyards, in lanes and churchyards, on river banks and over garden walls, who filled in my rough sketch of research with those vivid snippets of local detail that really made these walks come alive for me.

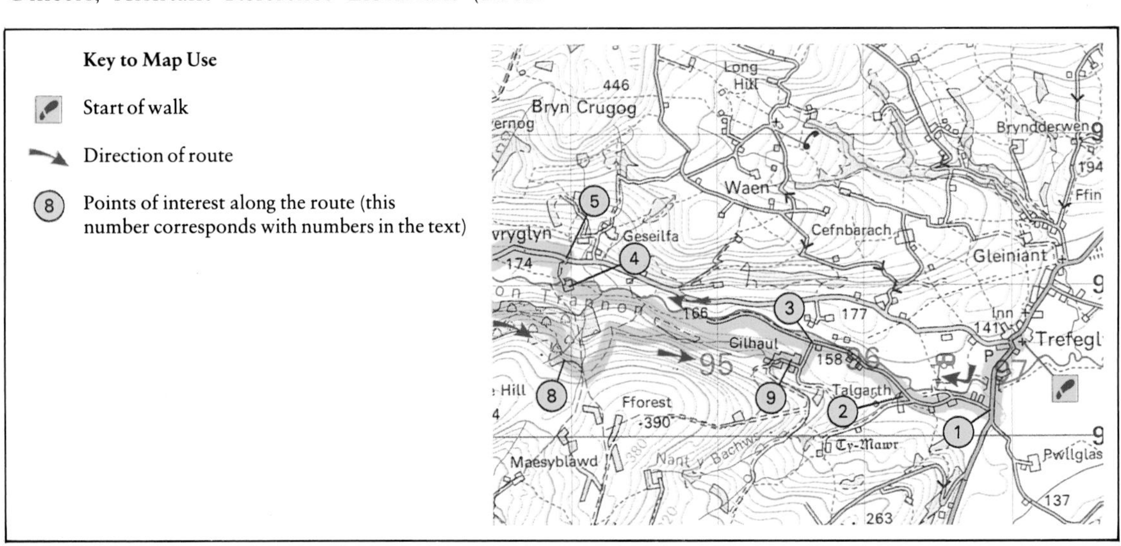

Introduction

When it comes to choosing somewhere to enjoy a ramble, more people make for the river bank than just about any other place. The rivers of Britain, whether tumbling out of the hills or winding slowly through the meadows, have such a lot to delight the walker. There is the attraction of the water itself, always changing colour, shape and sound in response to wind, weather and tide, crashing over rocks or trickling over pebbles. There are mountain rivers whose bright, clear waters, sparkling with oxygen bubbles, seem hardly to make contact with the channels down which they leap; and the ponderous green and grey depths of the same rivers in their sedate valley beds, different creatures entirely.

The landscape carved by rivers has a lot to do with their popularity with walkers: steep-sided valleys where one always has a ridge, a peak or a fold of ground to look up at; a lush water meadow with grazing cattle where the course of the river is marked by avenues of willows; the sweep of an estuary, broadening out to meet the flat line of the sea. Most river walking is level walking, too, always a bonus for a family ramble; though in the hills there is the contrasting challenge of scrambling up the rocky clefts down which waterfalls cascade.

The wildlife in, on and around rivers is another part of their allure. As we lose more and more of our plants, birds and animals to hedge-ripping, building, noise and pollution, the rivers play a vital part as refuges and sources of food. Many suffer from the effects of pesticides and fertilizers which drain into them from farmland, from the chemical outpourings of factories and from their ever-increasing leisure use by motor boats and anglers. Keeping our rivers clean is high on the list of conservation priorities, particularly as they support such a tremendous variety of wildlife. There is always something to see by the water. It might be a bright-green mat of moss around the source on some bleak moor in Devon or on the Pennines, or pale purple drifts of Himalayan balsam under a Kentish oak wood, or fragile blue gentians in Upper Teesdale. You never know if you are going to see herons, or curlew, or pintail ducks on a winter flood, or the white bibs of dippers on the stones in mid-river, or the blue flash of a kingfisher. You might spot water voles in a murky river in the industrial Midlands, or – if you're in luck – an otter flattening itself in a string of bubbles to the bed of some peaty water course in the Somerset Levels. And that's saying nothing of the fish!

Part of the charm of any walk lies in looking at, and wondering about, the houses, factories, churches, castles and other buildings you pass. River walks take in all these, and add to them the various kinds of buildings that are part and parcel of the life, past and present, of the river. Until the Industrial Revolution with its canals and railways, rivers were the only alternative method of inland travel and transportation to the muddy, dusty, pot-holed roads of pre-turnpike Britain. The modern tarmac network may have put them into retirement, but a surprising number of those old river-related buildings survive. Many water mills still stand, some converted into houses, others into restaurants or craft centres or museums, a large number derelict and overgrown with ivy, a few still turning their wheels and grinding corn or sawing timber. There are ornate boat houses built for colleges, clubs or rich men; lock-keepers' cottages with immaculate gardens; warehouses among the half-timbered pubs on Midland waterfronts; inns in shady backwaters that seem to have skipped a couple of centuries where you can while away the afternoon with a pint under the trees (the Harbour Inn at Arley on the Severn is my favourite); castellated pumping stations put up by some proud Edwardian water company; austere little fishing huts overhanging Scottish salmon pools. Then there are the bridges, carrying motorways on great concrete legs; or footpaths through miniature lattice-work suspension towers; or railway lines in plain cast-iron girders on fat cylindrical legs where every rivet stands out proudly as a testimony to the glory of the Victorian engineers who designed them.

Perhaps the best thing about river walking is that you don't need to be any kind of an expert to enjoy it. A good pair of boots will cope with the rough stuff up in the mountains, but on the vast majority of walks in this book there's not even a whiff of pack, compass and emergency rations. You can just get out there and enjoy it unencumbered, and so can your toddler.

Every walk in this book is on public rights of way, so you don't need to worry about whether you will be able to complete the course once you have set out. Ordnance Survey map references are included to locate points of interest, starting and finishing places and parts where there might be a question mark over the right route. However, no matter how sacrosanct rights of way are in law, or how clearly they are marked on the map, they are not always proof against the friction that does occur from time to time between ramblers and landowners. Experienced walkers know this well – if you are one, reader, bear with me through the following short summary of the situation.

England and Wales between them contain a network of public footpaths unequalled anywhere in the world. I am not referring to the great long-distance trunk routes such as the Pennine Way or the South Downs Way, but to those short stretches of path that connect village, field and farm as many of them have done since medieval times. Often the original purpose of these footpaths – to bring farm workers to the fields, say, or miners to the pit – has disappeared with changing circumstances, economic or social, down the centuries. But the paths remain, established by custom and perpetuated by law. To close or divert them requires a cast-iron case and the outlay of a good deal of time, effort and money – and quite rightly so: otherwise most of them would long ago have been sacrificed to the convenience of farmers and town planners, or the whims of landlords. Watchdogs like the Council for the Preservation of Rural England, the Ramblers' Association and the local authorities' footpaths officers keep a very close eye on their own patches; and farmers and landowners tend to respect the rights of walkers keeping to public footpaths across their territory.

However, the countryside is no more fixed or changeless than a town – it changes from day to day and from year to year, and so do its footpaths. Where today your path runs clear and unobstructed through a gap in the hedge, tomorrow the farmer may have fixed barbed wire. Today's wide strip of footway along the field edge can become next week's extra couple of feet of barley. Talking to the farmer, you usually find that these acts of obstruction are not just sheer bloody-mindedness – either so few people use the path that he can't see any good reason for maintaining it, or the inevitable 'mindless minority' have provoked him by walking across crops or leaving gates open. One fair-minded and courteous Cornish farmer told me that he welcomed ramblers anywhere on his land, adding mildly that he *had* had a bit of a problem recently when his neighbour's bullocks had got into his spring barley through a gate left open by a party of walkers. It had taken him all day and the following night to round the animals up, by which time they had done £1,000-worth of damage.

Poor waymarking and signposting and broken stiles are also responsible for a lot of bad feeling between those who work on the land and those who walk there. The farmer may be perfectly willing for you to follow the official line of a footpath through the middle of his farmyard, cornfields or hedges, but how are you to know that the path exists unless your way is marked by a clear sign or an unobstructed stile? Once the freelance detour has been made, damage done and the farmer's sympathies alienated, it can take months of negotiation and legal wrangling to restore the footpath—but the previous goodwill very often cannot be salvaged. Where the line of the path isn't clear, farmers and landowners are usually more than ready to point out an alternative route – after all, it's very much in their interest to keep walkers on the straight and narrow.

Scottish law on public rights of access has its own problems of interpretation. Here in theory, and for the most part in practice too, the walker is free to go where he will, provided that the landowner agrees. There are various exceptions to this general rule. For example, walking through deer forests and grouse moors in the shooting season, and along certain private stretches of river bank, will bring you at best a good ticking off, at worst a charge of buckshot in the breeches. On the whole, though, the countryside north of the Border is open to the rambler who takes the trouble to ask permission where it seems sensible, and follows the Country Code.

However, while all the Scottish landowners whom I approached were happy to allow individuals onto their property, none of them was willing to let me write about paths across their land. They feared that to enshrine such paths in print would give them the character of official walks which ramblers had the right to follow in any numbers and at any time. The Scottish river walks in this book, therefore, have had to be chosen from those sanctioned, set up and maintained either by local authorities or by the Forestry Commission. Some are nature trails with explanatory leaflets; others are walks beloved of generations of local inhabitants and safeguarded for them by official bodies. One is a rugged and spectacular section of the West Highland Way long-distance footpath; another is the existing half of what will soon be a sixty-mile trail beside the beautiful River Spey. These superb walks need no apology on my part – they are the cream of what is officially available to the general public. But there are hundreds more open to private enquiry and enterprise – I just can't write about them in this book!

Many of the English and Welsh walks in the book are similarly 'official'. These are ideal for family walking, or for the rambler who only wants a circuit of a few undemanding miles. They are usually clearly waymarked and free of obstructions, and in many cases you can buy for a few pence or pick up free a booklet or leaflet with information about what to look for on the walk – birds, butterflies, animals, insects, trees, plants, interesting buildings and so on.

The other variety – walks that I have put together by linking footpaths, tracks and lanes – may prove a bit more challenging. I have walked every inch of each one of them, and to the best of my knowledge none deviates at any point from public rights of way. However, as I have indicated, that's not to say that you may not meet with the occasional overgrown lane or strand of barbed wire along the way.

Most of the walks are circular, and those that are not offer public transport for the return routes (with one or two exceptions). In as many cases as possible these paths back to starting points contain a few plums: either a high-level view over the river valley which you have enjoyed from ground level, so to speak, on the outward half of the walk, or a pretty village, an interesting church or other building, a friendly pub – or just a contrasting view into another kind of landscape. I have indicated in the text pubs which welcome children, serve food and have outdoor facilities such as gardens or swings and slides. You will undoubtedly find others, and many gems of wildlife, architecture, historical detail and landscape that I have missed – in which case I would be very pleased to hear from you. All the walks of five miles or under should be suitable for children who are used to a bit of rough walking; and many are much smoother than that.

So here they are. Happy rambling!

SECTION ONE

West Country

River Hayle

OS 1:50,000 Sheet 203
$4\frac{1}{2}$ miles

'The bowels of the earth ripped open, turned inside out in the search for metal ore, the land defiled and cumbered with heaps and wastes of slags and rubbish, and the waters poisoned with tin and copper washings.'

Francis Kilvert, on holiday from his curacy at Clyro in 1870, found this part of Cornwall a pretty miserable place. His journey inland from Hayle among the 'bare bleak barren and ugly' villages, however, was a few miles from the little village of St Erth; so he missed the tall church tower, whitewashed cottages and narrow bridge that lie beside a river now recovered from its mineral poisoning from the mines in the hills behind. This area carries a very heavy concentration of tin and copper ores, which were washed in the nearest source of water – usually the river – to free the precious nuggets of metal-bearing rock from the gravel that was then left to clog up the waterway. The harbour a mile downstream of St Erth was killed off by this mine silt. Before then, travellers from St Ives Bay to Mount's Bay could avoid a nasty brush with the rocks off Land's End and the Lizard by taking ship as far up the River Hayle as St Erth, then switching to a coach for the three short miles overland to Marazion.

Nowadays the River Hayle runs crystal clear under the three low, round arches of St Erth bridge[1] (550351). The only visible reminder of industrial pollution is the speckled black and gold gravel of its bed. The origins of the bridge lie back in the fourteenth century: in 1538 Leland recorded that it had been made 'a 200 yeres syns and hath a three arches. Afor ther was a fery'. Most of the present structure dates from the seventeenth century, and once sheltered a smuggler, hiding under its arches from an exciseman who had chased him all the way from Redruth. When the villain emerged from the river, he discovered that his horse and the barrels of brandy roped to its back had gone; but on getting home to Redruth he found the faithful nag outside his door, complete with cargo. These days the bridge is a favourite place for local lads to swim, fish and swing across the narrow span of the river on Tarzan ropes. Above it stands the pink granite church of St Erc, whose fourteenth-century tower of three stages, adorned with weathered gargoyles of devils and a wild boar, dominates the valley. The church contains a very beautiful wagon roof, painted black and gold in the chancel, and plain wood, carved with flowers, leaves and faces, above the south aisle.

Cross the bridge from the church and turn left along the path beside the river, which soon branches out into a wide, reed-fringed pool over which there is a striking view of the church tower among its surrounding trees. After this

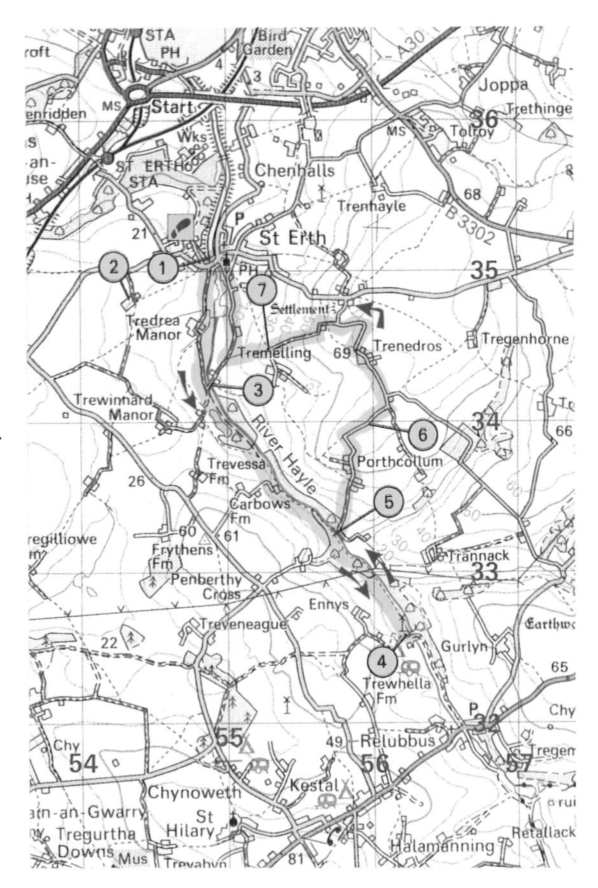

Bright-green water plants gleam through the clear water of the River Hayle above the bridge at St Erth.

tranquil spot the Hayle narrows again to a clear channel of fast-moving water a few feet wide, full of bright-green and red water weeds trailing in the current. For the full length of this walk the course of the river is marked by a winding avenue of reeds, whose gentle whispering is a constant companion. The wooded valley broadens out as it approaches St Ives Bay, studded at regular intervals by grey-roofed, granite-built farmhouses, barns and mills. The hillside behind is cut about by the tin and copper mines and the open wounds of granite quarries, but down here it is an agricultural scene of cornfields, hedges and dark stands of trees.

Over on the right are the roof and chimneys of Tredrea[2] (543348), in 1767 the birthplace of a famous Cornishman, Davies Gilbert. Born Davies Giddy, and rather understandably changing his name, he became MP for Helston, and later for Bodmin; but his real interest lay in mathematics, a recondite pleasure in Regency days. He wrote, practised and theorized the subject to such effect that he finally became President of the Royal Society. As MP for two mining constituencies, however, he also gave the district practical help in promoting and backing the experiments of Cornwall's greatest engineer, Richard Trevithick, who was struggling to get acceptance for his notions of putting the power of steam to use in pumping engines that would drain the ever-sodden mines. In 1797 Gilbert – then still plain Mr Giddy – had a visit from a young curate from another mining parish. John Skinner was an enthusiastic twenty-five-year-old who at that stage in his life would probably have enjoyed taking advantage of a time-warp to have a lark and a few glasses of sherry with Francis Kilvert. Skinner was just ordained and fresh from Somersetshire, enjoying a trip through Cornwall with no shadow on him of the agonized and lonely man he later became, his copious diaries his only solace. Skinner had heard Davies Giddy talked of at Oxford as a 'Ralph' or scruffy individual, but defended his host hotly and prophetically in his journal:

> '*... this Ralph may chance to have his name remembered when the fine gentlemen who were so proud of their fancied superiority are no more heard of, as he is generally esteemed a good scholar, and turns his studies chiefly to the mathematics, and possesses the greatest collection of books on that science I ever saw in a private library.*'

Skinner, to be sure, found Giddy's dress and manners 'not very prepossessing', but would have liked to have spent the day with him if time had allowed.

Bracken and gorse, those twin clothiers of Cornwall's landscape, line the rough ground each side of the river as it winds its way past a sluice and bridge[3] where Tremelling Mill once stood (549343) – a busy place of industry where a furnace smelted the tin from the ore brought down here from the moorland mines, and a waterwheel drove the stamps that shaped the metal. The Hayle ripples onward, flanked each side by fields of grazing cattle and corn, under electricity cables to the little single-arch stone bridge at the River Valley Caravan Park[4] (563326). Twenty years ago this was a derelict site of weeds and slag from the disused mine up on the hillside above the river. Since then the owner of the caravan park has cleared the ground, laid out a neat camping site with a shop, built himself a bungalow by the Hayle and even installed a small waterwheel in the river just upstream of the bridge to make his own electricity.

From the bridge you retrace your steps under the power lines to another bridge[5] (558332), where you cross the river and walk up a shady lane between trees to pass the cluster of old stone buildings at Porthcollum Farm (559337). There was once a sizeable settlement here with its own Bible Christian Chapel, but today the farm stands alone overlooking the valley. Continuing up the lane you reach a magnificent viewpoint[6] at the top over the narrow neck of Cornwall: northwards to St Ives Bay and the Atlantic spaces beyond, southwards over Marazion to Mount's Bay in the throat of the Channel – the two seas bridged by a six-mile swell of smoothly rolling, green and yellow quilted farmland.

The brambly lane, thick with foxgloves and ragged robin, curves on between the buildings at Trenedros Farm, past which you leave the lane at the second sharp right-hand bend (558347) to walk down stony Trevellin Lane, bounded with high hedgebanks several centuries old that give a U-shaped view ahead of hills, fields, woods and sea. The lane dog-legs past Porthmelling bungalow, then bends left towards Tremelling Farm. Here you are faced with a junction of several lanes and tracks[7] (553345); keep straight ahead down the field edge to the path by the River Hayle (550344) which takes you in half a mile back to the bridge at St Erth. Just up the hill from the bridge is the seventeenth-century Star Inn, opposite an ancient Cornish cross, where you can drink good beer on a terrace overlooking the river valley.

West Looe River

OS 1:50,000 Sheet 201
4½ miles

This walk takes you along a chain of narrow little lanes linked together in a deep, wooded valley by the West Looe River. The West Looe is no mighty torrent; it curves peacefully under Forestry Commission spruce, oak and silver birch, winding down the steep-sided cleft it has carved out of the downland a few miles west of the Tamar. Two villages mark the high and low points of the ramble, Duloe sitting up on top of the ridge and Herodsfoot lying in a sheltered angle of the valley floor. Duloe has shops, a good pub, a fourteenth-century church full of history, and a far older monument to man's religious feelings in a field beside the road. Herodsfoot has just a post office, and the memory of a devastating accident that killed its staple industry.

St Cuby was a Cornishman who travelled far and wide to bring the Word into remote areas of Britain. The church at Duloe[1] (234581) is dedicated to him, and contains many stone carvings and slate memorials. Its greatest treasure is an ancient font consecrated by the saint which was once placed to hold the waters of a holy well nearby. This low, round stone bowl was renewing souls through water and the spirit long before St Cuby's ministry in the fifth century; it was probably used before Christianity came to Britain for washing away men's imperfections, and its makers cut suitable symbols into its sides – a winged and beaked gryphon, and a dolphin, both symbols of the evil which would disappear with the cleansing water. The font is a rare survival, a link between an old faith and an even older one.

Just above the road north of the church stands the monument that continues that thread of faith back into unrecorded history. A sign points up a side track and over a gate into a field, on the far side of which stand the Duloe Stones[2] (235583), eight white quartz slabs of differing heights and shapes in a circle thirty-eight feet across. They look more impressive now than they did in early Victorian days, when they lay flat where they had fallen during the long centuries. In 1863 they were raised to their proper stature, an operation so clumsily carried out that one of the stones was broken, and another toppled over while it was being lifted, shattering into smithereens a cremation urn that had lain safely underneath for nearly 3,000 years.

Back on the B3254 road, walk on to the top of the village and keep straight ahead where the main road bends right (232589). Take the first turning on the left, signposted 'Church Bridge', and in one hundred yards go right (230590) into a narrow lane that leads towards the river, its course between high hedges visible far ahead as it climbs over the shoulders of Black Down. Honeysuckle trails over the tops of the hedges, which dip every so often to allow glimpses down to your right of the trees lining the rounded valley sides below and the large fields sprawling up and over the opposite ridge. A tall ivy-covered chimney pokes up out of the tree tops, the relic of the engine house that once

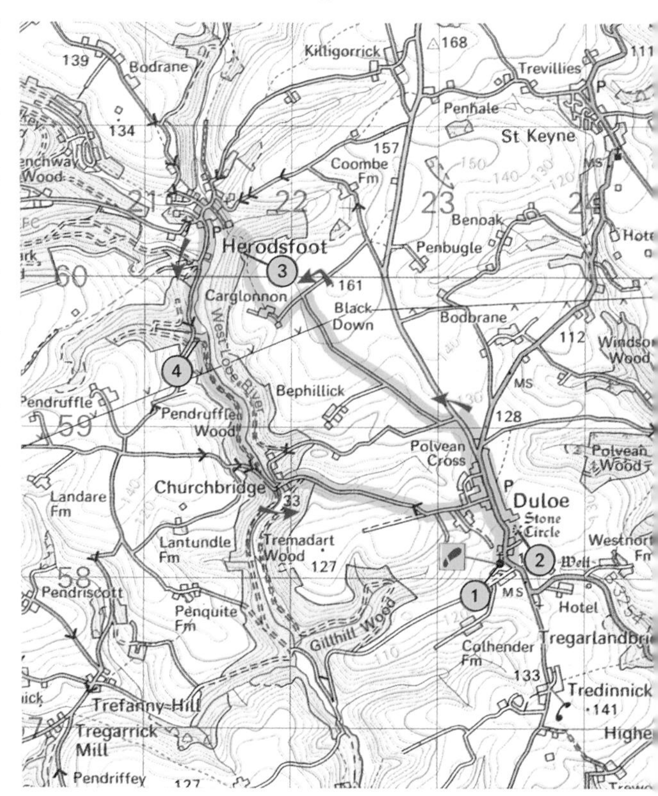

Symbols of a thread of faith 3,000 years long – the Duloe Stones and St Cuby's Church.

pumped water out of a silver-lead mine.

Turn left at a T-junction (221599) to drop down a track to Carglonnon Farm (218598). The path runs across the farmyard and on diagonally down a field to a gate, beyond which you bear to the right along the top of the Forestry Commission wood and around the bottom edge of a cornfield to a wooden stile into the trees[3] (217602). From here a path runs steeply and muddily down under the dark spruce branches to the hamlet of Herodsfoot at the bottom of the valley (214605).

The houses are scattered along the road through the village, a small group of them standing beside a little green by the bridge under which flows the shallow West Looe River. It is a pretty and peaceful scene; but peace and quiet have only recently come to the hamlet. Herodsfoot was a busy industrial community until the 1860s, mining silver-lead in the hills above the river. Silver-lead was a vital component of explosives before modern manufacturing methods outdated it; and Herodsfoot could also rely on its woodlands to provide the charcoal necessary to make the black gunpowder used in the Royal Navy's guns. Locals were proud of the fact that their charcoal played its part in the victory at Trafalgar. In 1846 the East Cornwall Gunpowder Company built a powder mill at Herodsfoot, so when the silver-lead industry came to an end local men and women stayed in work. It was a dangerous business; only four years after the company established its works an explosion killed two men. However, explosives continued to be milled and cartridges to be made, filled and dipped in wax for waterproofing until 1963.

Local people can tell you the full story of that Sunday when thirty pounds of explosives went up. The magazine at the works held up to one hundred tons of the stuff, so at least the worst didn't happen; but what did was bad enough. The explosion tore through the building, killing one man, injuring others, blowing all the doors out of their frames and sending the corrugated iron walls flying in all directions. When these were picked up and examined later, they had

A long lane rises from the West Looe River towards Duloe on its ridge.

been smoothed into flat sheets by the tremendous concussion. One of the two iron milling wheels was hurled so high into the air that on landing several hundred yards away it embedded itself completely in the earth, only the shaft sticking up above the ground. The family that owned the works, appalled at the tragedy, sold up, and the place was closed down within a year. Nearly a hundred people lost their jobs, a hammer-blow for such a small community. Nowadays a holiday chalet park stands on the site, but nothing can wipe away the local people's memories of that terrible sound and of the wreckage that littered the area after the echoes had died away.

Cross the bridge by the green and turn left past the telephone box down a lane (213604) that runs above the West Looe River and below the old silver-lead mine chimney. The cows far above you on the grass slopes seem to balance one above another as they move slowly along, nose to ground. The banks of the lane – apparently not worth the attentions of the council's hedge-slasher – are a mass of cow parsley, ragged robin and coltsfoot. The lane drops sharply to cross a stream, where you bear left[4] (213596) onto a good, firm track through the Forestry Commission's Pendruffle Wood plantation. Under the Norway spruce and tall silver birch trees the river flows on the left of the path, half-hidden in a thick mat of undergrowth. Few people walk this quiet track, where wood-pigeons murmur in the tree tops and wrens dart about at lower level beside the water.

The forestry track meets a road which descends to cross the river (219586). From here you climb a steep, leafy lane with a brook rushing noisily down beside it. In the bank grow saplings of beech and oak, between whose slim trunks are views into sloping fields as you mount the hillside. At the top, Duloe church is framed by the hedges of the lane, which runs up to meet the B3254 road through the village (233585). A short way along the street towards the church is Ye Olde Plough House, a comfortable slate-floored pub with old upright wooden chairs, draught beer and a little garden terrace.

East Dart River

OS 1:50,000 Sheet 191
4 miles

Be careful coming to Postbridge over the moor, midear! Being in one of those newfangled motor cars won't help you if the Hairy Hands of Dartmoor are abroad. You'll find the steering wheel suddenly wrenched from your grasp, the sweat will pour from your flesh as you wrestle unavailingly with the irresistible power of the Hands, and the next thing you know you'll be upside-down in the ditch. So drive slowly and keep your eyes on the road, and you *may* be all right – with luck.

Dartmoor is full of legends, most of them older than the Hairy Hands of the Postbridge road. There are only two roads crossing the moor, and hundreds of square miles of lonely peat bogs, tors and tiny streams. It's hard enough for an experienced walker with map and compass to find his way in this landscape of endlessly repeated, empty horizons – most visitors to the area don't even try, but stick to the roads and the outskirts of the moor. Out among the sedges and granite boulders the everlasting silence can play on your nerves until black hounds, malevolent pixies and will-o'-the-wisps – not to mention Hairy Hands – seem nearer than the nearest pub or post office. The moor is full of mysteries, not least of which are the leavings of primitive man that litter the tors and valleys. Very little is known of the day-to-day lives of those hardy dwellers in the wilderness – an approximate dating of their huts, circles, granite monuments and broken shards of pottery, and a more or less informed guess as to the state of their toolmaking expertise. How they cheered themselves up in the bitter Dartmoor winters, what religious experiences they had, how they looked after their sick, the games their children played – we can only speculate about the substance of the lives these remote ancestors of ours led out there in the wastes of Dartmoor.

Postbridge, the straggling roadside hamlet along the moor road where this walk begins, lies at the centre of what was once a busy Bronze Age collection of settlements. On the tors and beside the streams in every direction stand enclosed stone stockades containing the circular remains of huts, rings of standing stones (many now fallen and half buried in the peat), burial chambers and stone avenues. There were just a couple of farms at Postbridge until the road was turnpiked in the late eighteenth century. A bridge of three arches was built across the East Dart River and a small village grew up around it, taking its name from the posting coaches that stopped at the Greyhound Inn by the bridge on their long, lonely journey across the moor. Miners from the nearby tin mines came in to spend their money in the Greyhound; the tin industry had been centred here in the Middle Ages, and now revived the hamlet. By the time the new tin boom was over the charabancs were already spluttering into Postbridge to disgorge crowds of tourists for a picnic by the famous clapper bridge just below the road.

Beehive hut beyond Broad Down, spartan dwelling of an Iron Age family.

From the car-park (646788) with its excellent Information Centre (leaflets, books, exhibition and advice all available), walk down the road past the Greyhound (now a private house) and the post office to the turnpike bridge in the centre of Postbridge. The old clapper bridge[1] (648788) stands a few yards downstream, two piers of granite blocks supporting a decking of

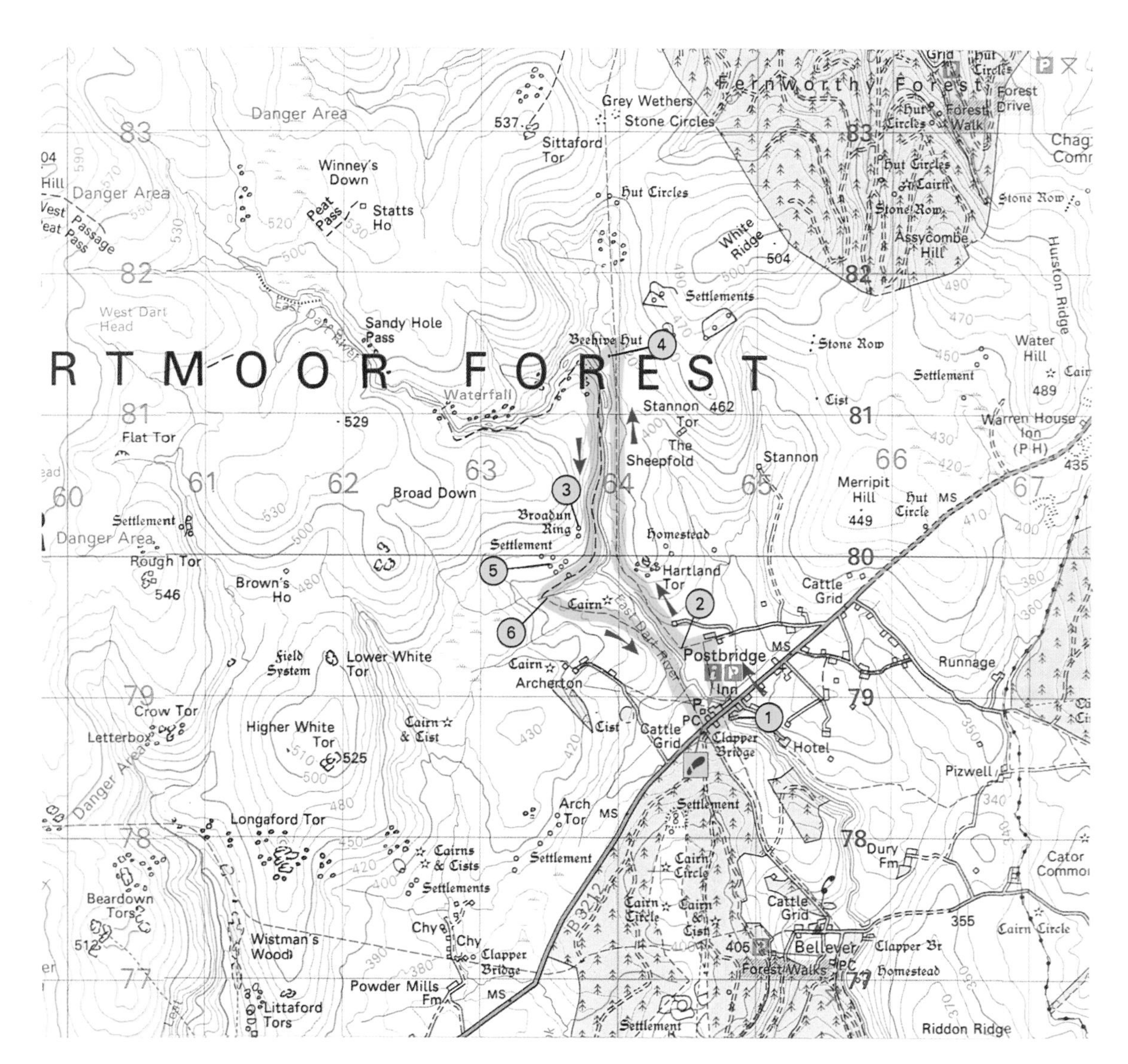

slim slabs of the same stuff. Local legend says it's a prehistoric structure, but it was probably built in the fourteenth century to carry the ancient trackway from Tavistock to Moretonhampstead, forerunner of the present B3212 road, across the river at this point. It's a popular place to be photographed swinging your legs above the river and waving at the camera. The grassy banks of the East Dart each side of the bridge are trodden flat by boots and stiletto heels during the summer season, and nibbled short by sheep at other times.

On the north side of the turnpike bridge a bridlepath notice on a gate leads into The Drift, a rough track still used to move cattle to and from their summer pastures on the moor. Follow The Drift up the side of a wall and round the edge of a large, boggy field where blue arrow waymarks direct you down to the path on the east bank of the river[2] (645794). It runs through a shallow valley below old stone walls, its cold brown waters tumbling around granite boulders under bushes of willow. The view ahead rises over rough slopes lumped with mossy, lichened stones towards the high back of Broad Down filling the cleft cut into the moor by the river. On the infrequent days of clear sunshine Broad Down shines out in green and brown; very often it is a grey, misty bulk under a leaden sky. Soon the track leaves the river, climbing up the hillside to skirt round the sodden slides by which streams flow down to join the East Dart. Here the sloppy black peat can go down several feet, so beware! These detours may be a nuisance, but you will spend far more time cursing and scraping muck off your legs if you go for a bold short cut across the wet peat.

The river bends briefly to the left before taking a sharp turn to the right under Broad Down (638799). Again the path climbs high to the stonier, firmer ground above the peat bogs, leading up into a silent valley whose coarse brown grass and granite outcrops might never have echoed to a human voice. Just across the river, however, clear evidence of a vanished civilization stands out starkly on the skyline of Broad Down – the encircling wall of Broadun Ring[3] (637802). The return route to Postbridge passes through the enclosure, but here in the valley bottom you can admire the clever positioning of this Bronze Age settlement – high enough to see all round, yet less than a minute's downhill scramble from a permanent source of water.

The 1,700-feet hump of Sittaford Tor stands over the top of the valley, where the East Dart River swings to the left among low hummocks. Keep straight ahead here, walking due north for a few yards, and you will come suddenly upon the remnants of one early Iron Age farmer's carefully constructed house[4] (639814), hidden by a swell of ground until you are only a few steps away. This hut was probably built 500 years before the birth of Christ, shaped like a beehive with its walls of granite boulders sloping gently inwards and upwards to give the structure enough strength to support a stone roof. Two and a half thousand years have reduced the hut to a horseshoe of walls about three feet high, but you can still make out the depression where the floor was sunk below ground level, and the doorway facing south-west away from the worst of the Dartmoor weather. People were quitting the moor by the time this householder built his hut by the stream under Sittaford Tor. His would have been a lonely existence, the nearest neighbours several minutes' walk away. Not so lonely, perhaps, if his family was a large one – the whole building measures just ten feet by six.

If the East Dart River is swollen by rain (and it's quite likely to be – over one hundred inches fall every year on Dartmoor), you will have to

retrace your steps from the beehive hut back to Postbridge. If the river is low enough you can ford it just upstream from the hut and take the path which runs halfway up the western slope of the valley. From this track it's a short and stiff climb to the top of the ridge and the great circular enclosure of Broadun Ring.

This settlement was constructed in the early Bronze Age, maybe 1,500 years before the isolated dwelling down below. That keen archaeologist (and mythologist, and novelist, and collector of folk songs, and writer of hymns), the Rev Sabine Baring-Gould, excavated Broadun Ring in 1893 with his colleague Robert Burnard. They found at least fifteen 'inclosures' or hut circles inside the surrounding wall. These im-

A stream trickling near scattered granite boulders is typical scenery in the wide wastes of Dartmoor.

prints of ancient dwellings can be seen in the grass, some recognizable from the shallow indentations of their floors, others still walled around with a jumbled ring of stones. Many are built hard against the encircling wall of the ring, especially on the south side where their entrances could be burrowed out of the wall itself and share its strength. From the Ring there is a long view southward down the winding East Dart River to Postbridge and the Tors beyond.

Bear diagonally to your left down the slope of the hill to regain the track, along which you turn to your right. All around the path, above and below, are the tiny circles of Bronze Age huts which together made up the huge enclosed settlement of Broadun Pound[5]. This is the largest enclosure on Dartmoor, incorporating more than 1,700 separate dwellings – though you will need sharp eyes to spot them. Baring-Gould estimated that 2,000 people were living within a mile of Postbridge during the early Bronze Age.

The path reaches a stile, where it drops straight down the hillside to cross a stream[6] (634797). From here you follow a stone wall across the moorland slope above the river to a line of trees below Archerton, and keep straight ahead to reach the car-park at Postbridge.

River Exe

OS 1:50,000 Sheet 181
7 miles

The River Exe creeps modestly from the flanks of eastern Exmoor, a slender flow wide enough to jump over in summer as it winds down its steep valley above Winsford. There is no hint here of the great river that cleaves through Devon towards Exeter and the sea. In winter the Exe can put on a different face altogether, tearing down the valley in turbulent, elephant-grey sheets of foam, whirling whole trees and boulders along and threatening the narrow-arched bridges in the villages along its course. Autumn sees this walk along the upper reaches of the river at its best when the larches shine out in pale gold, contrasting with the long-lasting green of alders overhanging the water. A pretty village as a starting point; a deep, winding valley above which buzzards wheel; centuries-old farmsteads joined by a hedge-banked lane that climbs 450 feet to the top of the moor; a view of Dunkery Beacon, the highest point of the moor at 1,704 feet – this is the cream of Exmoor poured out over seven miles of exhilarating walking.

Winsford won the Best Kept Village competition of 1982, deservedly so. The thatched, whitewashed cottages are grouped charmingly along the lanes and footways crossing the Exe and the Winn Brook by eight bridges that vary from old pack-horse crossings to stone and wooden footbridges. There were few settlements of any size on Exmoor in the Middle Ages when Winsford was an important centre where pack-horse traders and other travellers descended from the ridges of the moor to cross the river. Ernest Bevin, who was to become in turn

Winsford, as pretty as a picture.

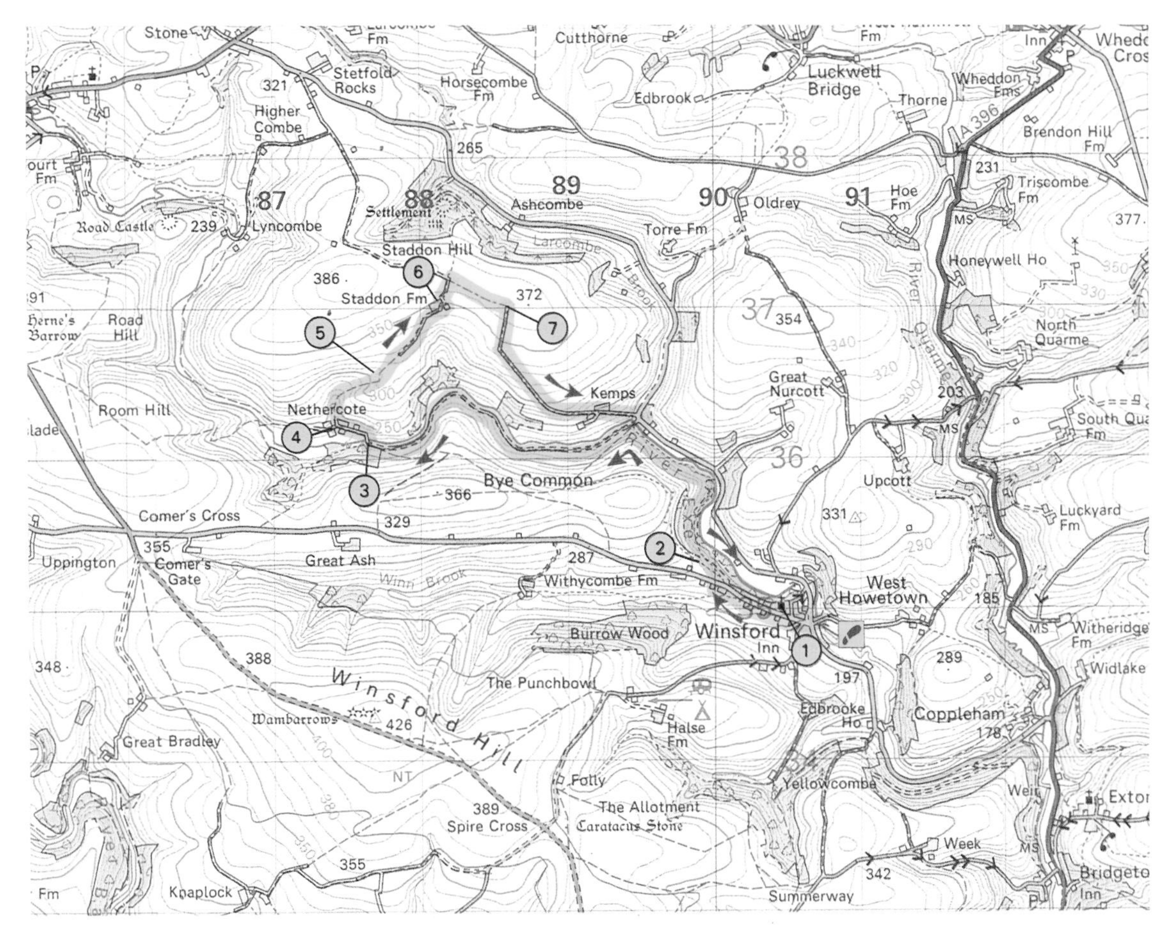

the first General Secretary of the TGWU, Churchill's wartime Minister of Labour and Attlee's Foreign Secretary, was born in a cottage here in 1881, stepson of a mole-catcher. His birthplace (907348) stands just down the road from the bridge in the centre of Winsford where our walk begins.

Follow the 'Withypool' sign across the ford over the Winn Brook and climb the lane to reach the church of St Mary Magdalene on the right[1] (904350). A Norman doorway leads through a gnarled old wooden door whose iron strap hinges are probably 700 years old. Inside the church hangs a beautifully painted coat of arms of James I, one of only four in the country. Dated 1609, it features a colourfully masculine lion and unicorn, and a warning to peasants to know their place typical of that dour, suspicious Scot:

'Curfe not the king noe not in thy thought, neither curfe ye rich in thie bed-chamber, for the fowle of heaven fhal cary ye voice and that which hath wings fhall declare the matter.'

The piers of the south aisle, all leaning five degrees out of the perpendicular, lead up to the east window where a fourteenth-century Madonna in a gold crown and blue robe, surrounded by stars, gazes enraptured at the tiny Christ child on her shoulder.

Walk on up to the top of the lane, where a green signpost 'Path to Exford $4\frac{1}{2}$' (901352) points down a muddy path[2] descending the steep combe side to reach the River Exe trickling at the bottom of the cleave. There are fine views back to Winsford church tower framed in the dip of the valley as you walk north-west, curving with the river to a lonely house at a meeting-place of combes (900359) where the river swings round to the west. The green top of the ridge ahead stands out above the beeches and

The Exe below Nethercote, overhung by glorious autumnal trees.

alders by the water, barring the view forward until the Exe takes another westward bend (895362) under the hillside farm of Kemps. Here the river runs in a tunnel of trees into the ever-tightening arms of the valley. Crossing the water by a footbridge[3] (876361) the path reaches Nethercote Farm[4], isolated and utterply quiet in its crevise in the valley bottom.

You pass between farmhouse and stone barns, one with an arched doorway and dovecote holes high up in the wall, and turn right (874362) to climb a steep lane which centuries of feet have trodden from earth to bare rock, sunk deep between hedge banks and rising along the stony spine of the hill. After rain this track takes on the character of a moorland stream, alive with bubbling water through which you squelch to a dog-leg on the left by the tumbledown buildings of Middle Nethercote[5] (877366) – snowdrops still star the banks here in early spring, a legacy of the old farmhouse garden. The path goes through a gate and climbs on up to Staddon Farm[6] (881370), which like Nethercote has kept its name since Plantagenet days. Staddon is sheltered in its windy position by a few tall beech trees and stone walls, but its inhabitants still lead a rough and lonely life, separated from the nearest road by two miles of muddy hilltop track.

Above the farm you turn right at a T-junction of tracks (882372) to walk along the ridge, looking north towards the purple-brown swell of Dunkery Beacon and south into the folds of the Exe valley where the river, seen from this height of over 1,100 feet, looks like a thread of silver wire among the trees. Soon the path turns right[7] (886370) and drops down past Kemps Farm to the entrance to the Nethercote farm road and the riverside path back to Winsford. Here the Royal Oak, dating back in part to Norman times, will serve you good food and beer in front of a roaring log fire.

River Carey and King's Sedgemoor Drain

OS 1:50,000 Sheet 193/182
13 miles

The surroundings for this walk are quite unlike any other countryside in Britain, for the two rivers which merge one into the other flow through the flat peatlands of the remote and haunting Somerset Levels, which lie at or below sea level for much of their 500 square miles. These low-lying marshlands are rich in wet-land plants and birds, a rare storehouse in a Britain rapidly losing such marsh sites to the plough. The Levels were not tamed and drained until the monks of Glastonbury and Muchelney built dykes and sea walls and opened up the land for agriculture. After the Dissolution of the Monasteries in 1539 the Levels reverted to a boggy morass, and only became fairly passable again during the last century when the peat companies and the withy-gatherers took them in hand.

The walk begins at the old market cross in Somerton[1], the small ridge-top town that was one of a few places above the waters when King Alfred established a centre of operations here in his struggle against the invading Danes. Somerton became the capital of Wessex during the Dark Ages, and the focus for merchants and marketeers in the area. The covered market cross is dated 1673 and carries a fine group of gargoyles, one apparently a monkey wrenching open a giant's jaws, another shaped like a grotesque winged frog, and a third a Frankenstein figure with a bolt through its cheeks.

From the market place (491285) you walk down West Street, cross over the Frome to Taunton railway line, and fork right along the Langport road. At a roundabout turn right up Pound Pool[2], and keep straight on past the fire station and infant school to walk down Brockle Hill and into a narrow lane that winds between hedges to Etsome Farm (482308). Ahead is the rounded bulk of Dundon Hill, and on your right lines of willows hedge in the small fields by the River Carey. At the farm you cross an old arched bridge[3], just upstream of which is a sluice gate crowned with large unguarded cog-wheels, and turn left onto the far bank of the river at a green public footpath sign.

The river is shallow and gravelly where it can be seen through the mats of thick green weed. The footpath crosses rickety wooden fences and squeezes across narrow stone parapets over the many drainage ditches that bring water off the fields into the river. Some of the large, geometrically squared-off fields are under crops, but most are pasture for sheep and cows whose hooves have hollowed out boggy drinking places at the water's edge. Crowds of lapwings tumble upwards from the grass, and you will be unlucky not to spot at least a couple of herons lifting themselves laboriously away from the river bank with great, slow wing flaps.

At Somerton Door the low bridge of dark stone is covered with lichen and ivy (470303). Beyond the bridge large willows lean and trail from the bank – there is a really fine specimen beside a curious humpback bridge[4] (460304) made of a single layer of stones set on end to give purchase to the hooves of animals crossing the river.

At Pitney Steart Bridge (453308) a tumbledown farm is crumbling into its trees, the red-tiled roofs sagging and windows gaping. The pretty village of High Ham sits comfortably on top of Sedgemoor Hill to the left, and can be reached by crossing the River Carey at the next bridge[5] (449311) and walking up a lane to turn right at the road and climb steeply up the hill. The village green in front of the church is a fine place to rest, but for beer and good company turn right and walk down to the shabby old Kings Head pub[6] (425314). In the dark, green-painted and panelled bar the Somerset accents are as thick as the tobacco smoke, and the landlord reckons up pints and shorts with a piece of chalk on his wooden bar-top. The road carries you down the hill again with wide views over the Levels, to rejoin the river at Cradle Bridge (426333)[7]. Above here it bends for the last time

Sutton Fm
Fursland Fm
Knoll Hill
Mount Close Batch
Fowler's Plot
Sutton Hams
Sutton Mallet
Pit Hill
Moorlinch
Sharpenton Hill
Greinton
Lang Moor
Sedgemoor 1685
Westonzoyland
King's Sedgemoor Drain
Greylake Fosse
Briarwood Fm
Bussex
Liney
Penzoy Fm
Burdenham Fm
Cemy
Inn
Greylake Br
King's
South Moor
Weston Level
Langmead
Wr Twr
Greylake
Moorland Fm
Owery Fm
Green
Middlezoy
A372
A361
Hoopers Elm Fm
Thorngrove
Nether Moor
Shride Fm
Aqueduct
Horlake Moor
Moorland House Fm
Turn Hill
Earlake Moor
Othery
Beer Door
Beer
Manor Fm
Saltmoor Fm
Hunter's Lodge
Aller Wood
Breach Wood
Burrow Bridge
Burrow Mump
Pathe
North Moor
Lower Salt Moor
Stanmoor Br
Southlake Moor
Danger Area
Burrowbridge
Longstone
Athelney Hill
Mon
Stan Moor
Aller Hill
Aller
Athelney
Stathe
Aller Moor
Aller Court Fm
Stathe Court
Curload
Stanmoor
Mead
Middle Moor
Parsonage Fm
Holly Moor
Oath Lock
Sowy River
River Parrett
Sluice
Slough Court
Dykes Fm
Moat
Woodhill
Oath
Oath Hill
Meads

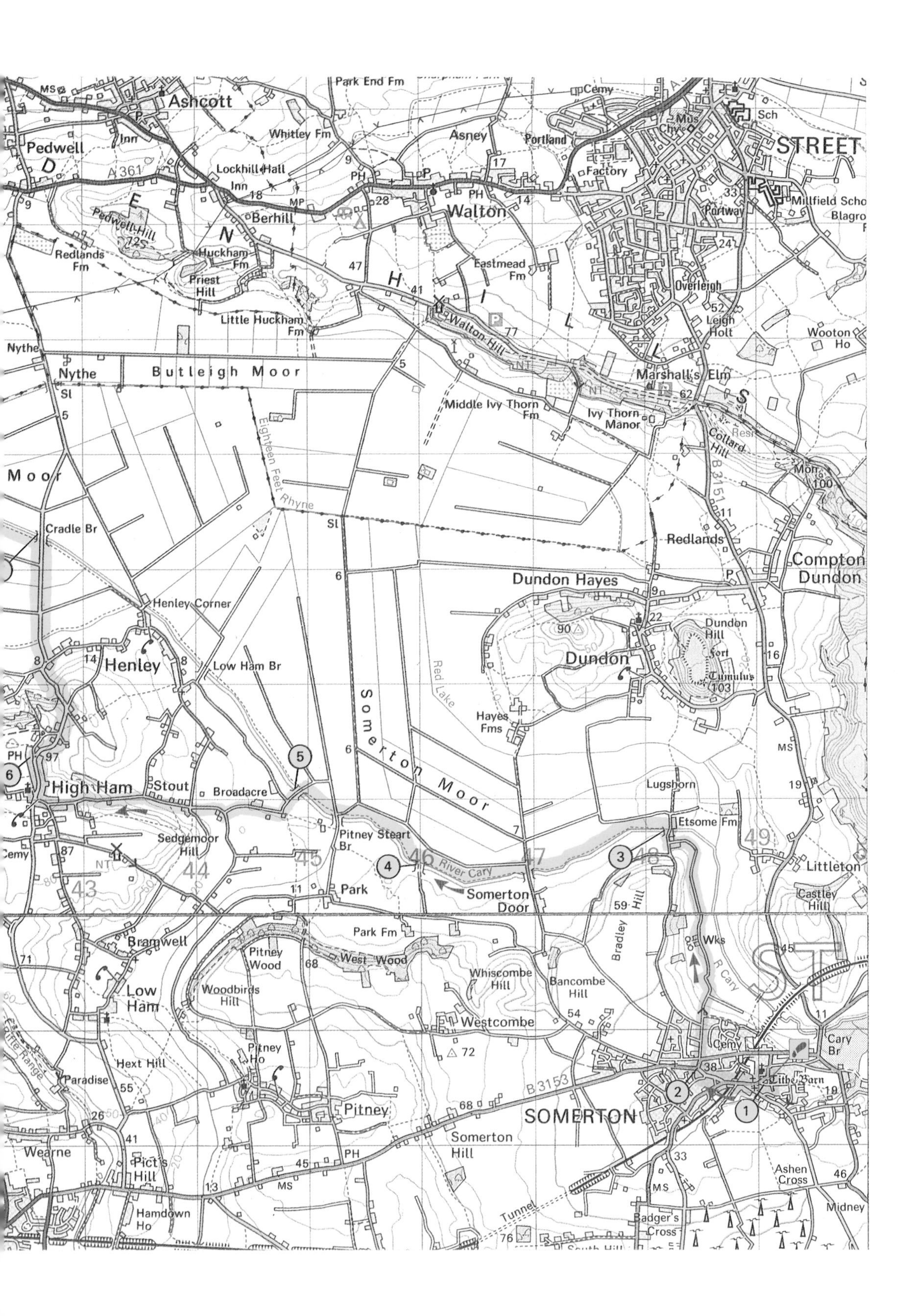

Park End Fm
Ashcott
Pedwell
Whitley Fm
Asney
Portland
STREET
Sch
Factory
Lockhill Hall
Inn
Berhill
Walton
Millfield Scho
Portway
Pedwell Hill
Redlands Fm
Huckham Fm
Priest Hill
Eastmead Fm
Overleigh
Little Huckham Fm
Walton Hill
Leigh Holt
Wooton Ho
Nythe
Butleigh Moor
Marshall's Elm
Middle Ivy Thorn Fm
Ivy Thorn Manor
Collard Hill
Moor
Eighteen Feet Rhyne
Cradle Br
Redlands
Compton Dundon
Dundon Hayes
Henley Corner
Dundon Hill
Fort
Tumulus
Henley
Low Ham Br
Dundon
Red Lake
Somerton Moor
Hayes Fms
Lugshorn
High Ham
Stout
Broadacre
Etsome Fm
Sedgemoor Hill
Pitney Steart Br
River Cary
Littleton
Somerton Door
Park
Castley Hill
Bradley Hill
Bramwell
Park Fm
Wks
Pitney Wood
West Wood
Whiscombe Hill
Bancombe Hill
R Cary
Low Ham
Woodbirds Hill
Westcombe
Cary Br
Cemy
Pitney Ho
Hext Hill
Paradise
Tithe Barn
Pitney
SOMERTON
Somerton Hill
Wearne
Pict's Hill
Ashen Cross
Midney
Hamdown Ho
Badger's Cross
Tunnel
South Hill

before running under the name of King's Sedgemoor Drain for five ruler-straight miles to Westonzoyland. The footpath runs on the left bank of the river among more large flat fields, black under the green grass with the rich peat which many local people stack in huge piles in their back gardens and sell on the roadside.

Beyond Greylake Bridge (397344) the flatness of the landscape is emphasized by the descent of the Polden Hills ridge, which has accompanied the walk all the way, to the level of the fields. The tall tower of St Mary the Virgin at Westonzoyland comes into view over the trees ahead and to the left. Two side rhynes are crossed[8] (380351), and at the next footbridge[9] (372354) – a favourite haunt of swans – you leave the river and walk over the slight embankment of a former flood barrier to join a rough drove road a few hundred yards to the south (372353). After a mile this lane bends to the right where a side drove leaves it on the left[10]. You continue ahead to turn at right angles (357362) down towards Westonzoyland.

The fields on the right[11] were the scene of the Battle of Sedgemoor in the early hours of 6th June, 1685, in which an efficient force of King's men led by Lord Faversham thoroughly routed a ragged army of 3,500 peasants assembled by the Duke of Monmouth. Monmouth, the illegitimate son of King Charles II, had come from Holland by way of Lyme Regis, hoping to force his way to London and challenge the newly proclaimed James II, King Charles's unpopular Roman Catholic brother. Instead, cornered in the Somerset Levels, he staked everything on a night attack on the King's army; but he was delayed by a muddle over the crossing place of Langmoor Rhyne and lost the element of surprise when one of his supporters let off his pistol by accident. The King's men, forewarned, stood to and cut Monmouth's pathetic army to pieces, losing only sixteen men while slaughtering at least 300 of the rebels, most of these shot without mercy when daylight came and they could be driven by 'beaters' from the cornfields where they were hiding, more like pheasants than men.

An open-air service is held each year on the anniversary of the battle at the monument which stands in Burial Field (350356) to the right of the drove road, where the corpses of the dead rebels were dug unceremoniously into the peat – the King's men who fell were buried with honours, five in the church and eleven in the churchyard. Such is the number of American tourists who come to view the battlefield that the farmer who owns the land has half-seriously considered advertising '6 foot burial plots in Sedgemoor's historick Burial Grounde' in the Yankee papers.

King's Sedgemoor Drain arrows towards the sea through the flat peat moorlands of the Somerset Levels.

The village of Westonzoyland is reached by turning left at the bottom of the drove, then right. The church[12] contains a small exhibition of documents about the battle, recording that 500 prisoners were brought to the church, seventy-nine of them wounded, of whom five died there in St Mary's. Twenty-two rebels were hanged in the village, part of the example made of local participants during the infamous

'Bloody Assize' conducted by Lord Chief Justice Jeffreys. Altogether about 330 were executed, and 849 transported to Barbados. Pieces of the hanged men's bodies were displayed in towns and villages all over the West Country to warn presumptuous yokels of the consequences of challenging the status quo.

Monmouth himself escaped during the battle, leaving his followers to their horrible fate, and got nearly to Ringwood in Hampshire before being captured, sent to London to plead on his knees for mercy from King James, and summarily executed the following day.

St Mary the Virgin has a store of more pleasant exhibits however, chief among them the superb tower (from which Monmouth reconnoitred the ground before the battle with the aid of a 'perspective glass'), the beautifully carved rood screen and loft, and especially the wonderful 'angel roof' with its ranks of carved angels staring down at the floor of the nave where the rebels were herded to await the Bloody Assize. The massive south door contains a round hole supposed to have been caused by a bullet fired during the battle.

Next door to the church is the ancient and friendly Sedgemoor Inn, over whose front door is a fine painted board depicting scenes from the battle –

'Night attack by Monmouth's army.' (Bill-hooks by moonlight.)
'Surprised, drums sound the alarm.' (King's drummers in their nightshirts.)
'Caught, recognised, detained.' (Two red-coats threatening a bedraggled Monmouth in a ditch.)
'Sentenced by Judge Jeffreys.' (Monmouth wilting under an accusing finger.)

River Otter

OS 1:50,000 Sheet 192
$7\frac{1}{2}$ miles

NB: This is a one-way walk from Ottery St Mary to Otterton. Return transport should be thought about in advance – either by car, taxi (Ottery St Mary 5115 or 2223) or bus (Devon General: Sidmouth 4948).

This walk passes down one of the loveliest and most peaceful valleys in East Devon, following the broad curves of the River Otter. This is quintessential Devon of apple orchards and dairy farms, wide skies and woodland. It's easy walking, too; mile after mile of grassy riverside path, well signposted and level, leading on from one eye-catching view to the next.

Ottery St Mary's narrow streets of seventeenth- and eighteenth-century buildings are crowned by the finest parish church in Devon[1] (098956), a miniature cathedral built in 1260 and extended by Bishop Grandisson of Exeter when he founded a college in the town sixty years later. His workmen placed the weathercock on top of the stumpy herringbone-patterned spire, where it still rules the roost. The interior of the church is tall and grand in white stone, with many arches adding to the sense of space and light. The memorials include a splendid life-size gentleman in full colour Stuart dress, and several Coleridges – the poet who became the best friend of the Wordsworths was born here in 1772, thirteenth son of the parson. The south transept contains an Elizabethan clock, clicking and clanking in the silence of the church. This transept is tiled in high Victorian style like an ornate railway booking hall – not surprisingly, as the work was carried out by the railway designer Butterfield. There is also a superb square Victorian font of local marble and Cornish serpentine, and some modern decorations that include a ceramic plaque of the great Ottery fire of 1866, made by local schoolchildren.

The churchyard wall holds a bronze tablet to Samuel Taylor Coleridge, depicted by his great-great-nephew Gilbert as young and handsome before opium and nervous exhaustion had reduced him to a physical and spiritual wreck. From here you walk down the sloping streets of Ottery St Mary to pass Otter Mill, now turning out electrical switchgear, and reach the iron bow girder bridge over the river[2] (093951). A wooden fingerpost points over the flat meadows along the west bank of the Otter, flowing in its red channel between the red and green hills. Herons flap heavily up from their fishing posts on the grassy ledges by the river, trailing their long green toes in the water as they struggle to gain height before lumbering away to settle in nearby trees and wait for you to leave them in peace. On your right is the line of the disused railway[3] that was opened in 1897 to connect the

Old water mill above Tipton St John.

Exeter main line with the South Devon coast. It lasted for seventy years until its closure in 1967, and now runs as a green track accompanying the river down the valley.

The path passes a weir and a half-ruinous old red brick mill[4] (092924); here you cross the railway track and walk up to the road, turning left to reach the river bridge at the little village of Tipton St John (091918). Seagulls from the coast seven miles to the south join the herons in looking for river pickings as you walk through a shanty town for pigs and onwards, recrossing the old railway[5] (090911) and following the red-brown Otter towards the slender tower of Harpford church. The view in front is closed by the houses of Newton Poppleford on their hill, round which the river flows to the east. The crumbling platform of the old railway station stands above the A3052 road (089898) where you turn right, then left in a hundred yards up Millmoor Lane[6] among the pampas grass and flowering cherries of the village gardens.

Where the path forks among trees, bear right up the bank to walk along the top of the sandstone river cliff, looking out over the curving Otter towards the enclosing hills to the east. From up here you can see the old railway crossing the river on rusty iron bridges, and the bright-purple patches of Himalayan balsam along the banks interspersed with yellow splashes of ragwort. Soon the path drops to the end of a lane[7] (085871) which leads off to the right into Colaton Raleigh; cross the railway line here and walk on beside the river under a curious footbridge[8] (084861), its top end springing out of the bank under Anchoring Hill and curving down over the Otter into the water meadows. The arched white gatehouse of Bicton House[9] stands among the outer line of trees in the famous gardens here, followed by the stone needle of an obelisk. Soon the river path passes another weir and cream-coloured thatched house behind an apple orchard to come to the three-arched stone bridge at Otterton[10] (079853).

This sleepy little village was a thriving salt-making and shipping community in medieval times when the Otter estuary extended this far inland. The Saxons settled here, and before the Norman invasion King Harold's mother Countess Gytha owned Otterton manor and most of

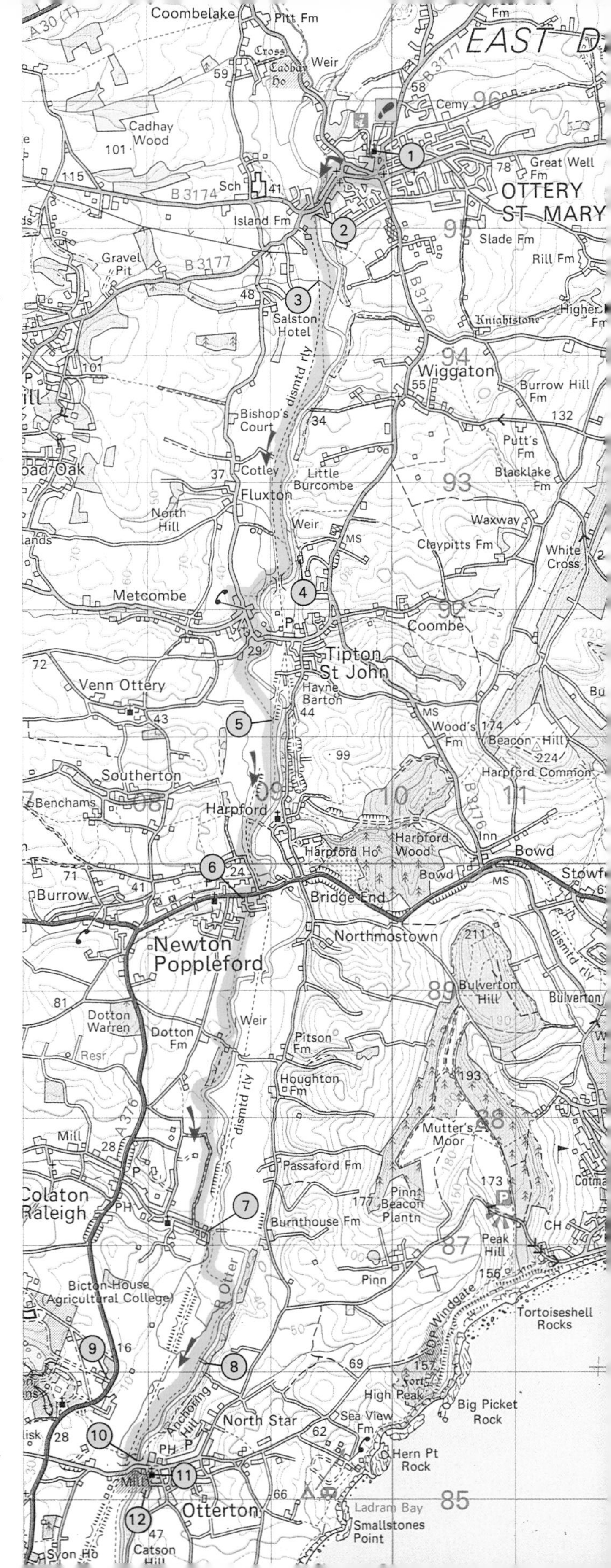

Red earth and lush green meadows of the wide Otter Valley.

the surrounding area. After her son's defeat and death at Hastings the Countess fled over the Channel to Flanders, leaving her Devon possessions to the tender mercies of the new king. He handed them over to one of his French backers, the Abbey of Mont St Michel, which set about building a Benedictine monastery on the knoll above the river where the present church of St Michael[11] now stands. Old and more recent ecclesiastical architecture stand side by side here: the remnants of the monastery's visitors' hall, incorporated into a fine red stone house by the Duke family that took over the property after the Dissolution in 1539; and the church, completely rebuilt in one year between 1870 and 1871. It's a heavy and solid reconstruction, but a harmonious one, with white freestone arches and a bulky, ornate wooden nave roof.

Below the church, Otterton Mill[12] stands by the river bridge on a site where milling has gone on since Countess Gytha's day. In contrast with the dereliction of most of Britain's water mills, this one positively throbs with life. It mills its own flour using water power, and bakes its own bread and cakes; craftsmen and women weave, print, paint and make toys in co-operative workshops set up in the mill buildings; others produce iron-work, pottery and quilts. There are exhibitions of lace-making, 'folklore' weeks of music and dancing, teas and lunches. The mill is open from 10.30 am to 5.30 pm daily during the summer, and for a shorter time during the winter (*Tel*: 0395 68031). It is a heartening scene of optimism and industry, restoring life and bustle to the village which had almost died the commuter and retirement death a few years ago.

Just up the street is the Kings Arms pub (bar food, children's room and beer garden) where you can restore the tissues before wending your way by bus, taxi or co-driver back up the lovely Otter valley to Ottery St Mary.

River Piddle

OS 1:50,000 Sheet 194
8 miles

Apart from the signs outside the Piddle Inn (a man clutching a chamberpot, and a pixie in another potty sailing down the river) Piddletrenthide and the other villages of the Piddle Valley have managed to refrain from cashing in on the naughty name of their river. Quite an act of self-restraint, situated as they are in the heart of Dorset's tourist country. That name was too much altogether for the Victorians, who rechristened the river 'Puddle' or 'Trent'. Nowadays, no one locally calls it anything else but Piddle.

The names of the villages along the Piddle have a Betjemanic ring: Piddletrenthide, Piddlehinton, Puddletown, Tolpuddle, Affpuddle, Briantspuddle and Turners Puddle. At Puddletown Thomas Hardy's grandfather played bass viol in the church orchestra; while from Tolpuddle came the celebrated martyrs—agricultural labourers transported in 1834 in a shamelessly fixed trial for daring to combat wage cuts by setting up their own Friendly Society. This walk, however, connects the first two in the Piddle/Puddle chain, returning via the downland to the east.

All Saints Church[1] (702008) stands on the northern edge of Piddletrenthide, signposted off the B3143. Cars can be parked on the grass verge up the lane. As you walk across the bridge over the little River Piddle, on your left is a grassy area, once the mill-pond for Piddletrenthide Mill, whose wheel was powered by spring water from the hillside beyond. Mill Cottage, with an old stone wheel outside, stands just beyond the bridge below the church.

All Saints' is built of Portland stone, faced with golden hamstone. It is rich in gargoyles; some leering devils cling to the fifteenth-century tower, and snarling lions crouch on the buttresses of the south wall. The doorway is a Norman design, ornamented with dog-tooth chevrons. Inside you can buy a booklet of *Poems from the Piddle Valley Parsonage* by Mrs Heather Parry, which includes 'Paddling in the Piddle', 'Piddletrenthide Church Fete', 'The Bishop's Wife' and 'The Vicar's Farewell' – your money will help maintain the Piddle Valley churches.

A network of disused lanes radiates outwards from the church, which was the centre of the village in medieval times. Variously known down the years as Uppidelen, Pidrie and Pudletrenthead, the village's name derived from its assessment of value in Domesday Book at thirty hides. It was given to Winchester College in 1543, and stayed in their hands until the 1950s.

Turn right up the lane from the church, and left (702006) just before a rough track leading up to Kiddles Farm. Our path runs southwards behind the straggly village[2], parallel with the B3143. It was the main road to Dorchester until the seventeenth century, and was probably abandoned after a disastrous fire in 1654 which burned most of the village. The thatched, whitewashed cottages among their apple orchards are strung out along the valley, built close to the river for necessity's sake in an age when water could not be made to travel uphill. There was little room, anyway, to expand sideways up the steep sides of the narrow Piddle valley.

At the road from Cerne Abbas (702998) you turn left, and right down a short lane[3] which ends at a farm. Go over a gate at your right and follow the edge of the fields, parallel with the river. The old houses of Piddletrenthide are succeeded by the new until the village comes to a stop. Above the beautiful copper beeches around South House you meet a farm road[4] (707991), which becomes a rough lane through gates and along fields where the farmer has thoughtfully left a strip of earth in his crops to show the line of the path. The river, hitherto winding invisibly a few yards to the left, suddenly decides to make itself known and approaches to run right beside the path, five feet wide and fast-flowing over its weedy bed. Folded valleys, their green grassy sides marked with white scars of chalk, run down to the river from the west, and the trees which shade the path are shaggy with lichen.

Bear left under an old chalk quarry (708982) above White Lackington, an intermediate settlement halfway between Piddletrenthide and Pid-

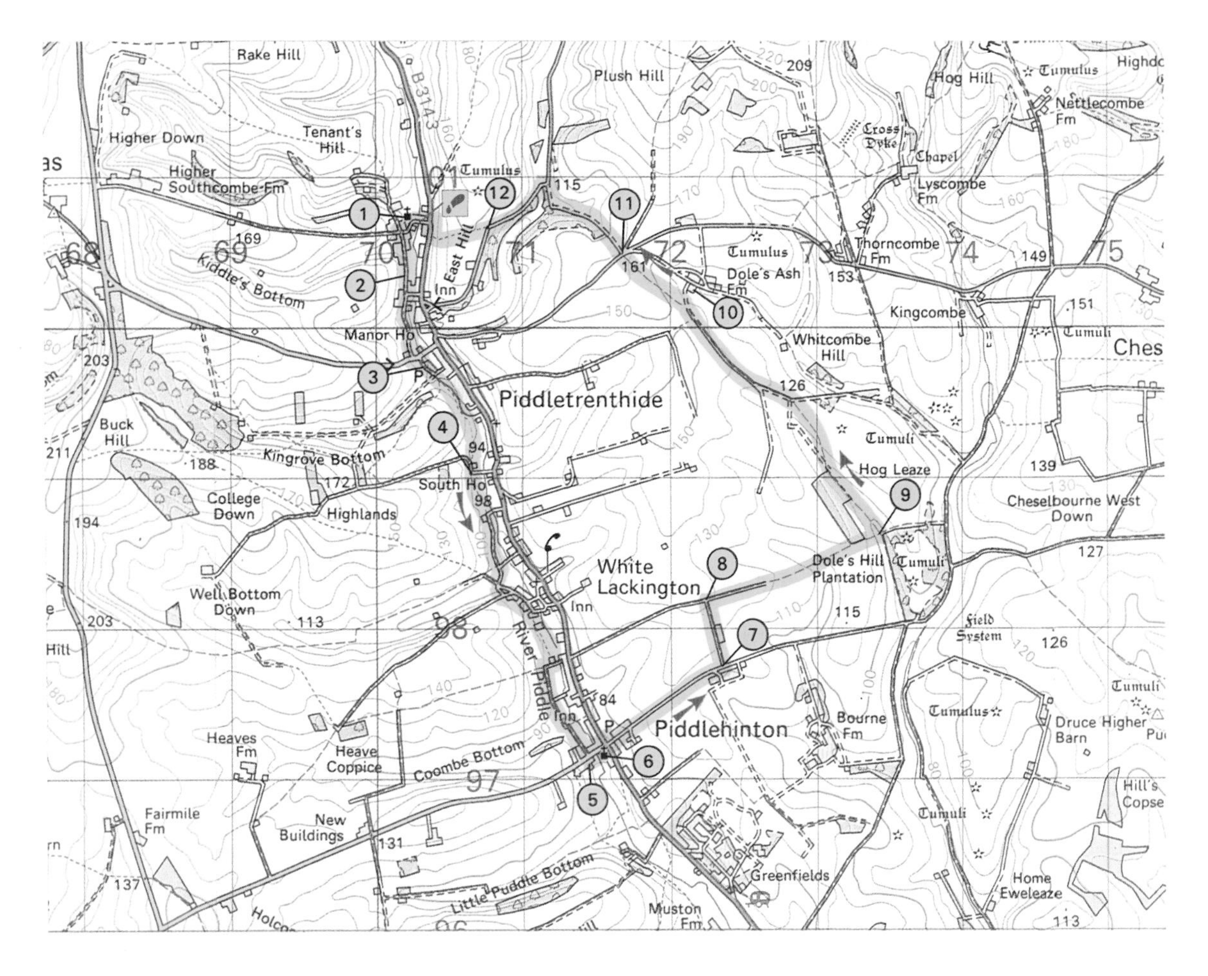

A lion of golden hamstone guards a buttress of All Saints Church at Piddletrenthide, witness to a medieval mason's skill.

dlehinton, and less well-groomed than either with its ramshackle corrugated iron sheds, ancient tractors rotting away in nettle patches and old box-bodied trucks entwined in the hedges. The valley becomes wider and shallower as you reach the road at Piddlehinton (714971) opposite a long wall of plastered stone with a hat of mossy tiles. It guards the Old Rectory[5], built like most of the district's large houses of alternating bands of flint and brick. Like Piddletrenthide, Piddlehinton village was owned by a great public school, in this case Eton. The ownership lasted more than 500 years, from 1442 until 1966.

Turn left down the road to the church of St Mary the Virgin[6] (715971), which stands by the main road shaded by magnificent beeches and limes. The church contains some splendid memorials. In the chancel there is a narrow brass one inscribed:

> *'Here lyethe the bodye of Master Wyllyam Goldynge somtyme parson of thys paryshe wyche decesyd the XV day of Maye in the yere of Ovre Lorde God 1562.'*

On the opposite wall Thomas Browne, Rector of Piddlehinton from 1590–1617, stands engraved on brass in a coat with long puffed sleeves, wearing a hat and carrying a stick. He died aged 'sixtie and seaven yeares old.'

The chancel also holds a memorial in Latin to Martha Clavering, wife of another Rector, who was tending victims of the plague in 1664 when she succumbed to the same disease. Her grieving husband wrote her inscription:

> *'She was a cheerful housewife, a matron of spotless chastity, most prudent, calm and gracious. In beauty of bodily form and of mind she was lovely and loveable . . . In bereavement he is forlorn, rendered inevitably a sorrowing mourner: like the night raven wakeful in the house, or as the sparrow left alone upon the housetop . . .'*

From the church you cross the B3143 road (carefully! lorries come very fast round the bend), and turn right up London Row, signposted 'No Through Road.' There is a good view behind of the Piddle valley as you climb up for nearly a mile into the heart of the downs. Just past the roaring chimney of an animal feeds factory, turn left[7] (723977) past a farmhouse and large brick and flint barn to reach a T-junction[8] (722982), where you turn right. This lane was an old drove road running east-west across the downs; its hedges may be 600 years old or more. The view is over twenty miles of corn, trees, yellow oil-seed rape and chalk ploughland the colour of milky coffee.

Turn left at Doles Hill Plantation[9] (734986) to walk along the floor of a shallow upland valley between two swells of downland. The path, surfaced with chalk and lumps of flint, runs with a curve or two north-west to Dole's Ash Farm[10], a substantial house in brick and flint with a salmon-pink plastered facade backed by a cluster of barns and fronted by a meadow with some

shapely old oaks and beeches, tucked away in a sheltered crevice out of the worst of wind and weather. Evidence of early settlement here has been unearthed in the shape of Roman tiles and Samian pottery. Carry straight on through a curlicued iron gate (720002) and across a field to the road and a stony lane opposite[11] (717005), which rounds the corner of a wood to meet another road (712009). Here you turn left, and climb uphill to a left-hand bend[12]. Go through the gate on your right (707007) and follow the field edge over the ridge, keeping a hedge on your right. Gradually the valley ahead deepens until the tower of Piddletrenthide church pops into view, snugly set below the fields and trees of the downs rising behind it.

All Saints standing like a shepherd over its flock of cottages at Piddletrenthide.

Plenty of these in springtime on the field slopes above the Piddle Valley.

A stile leads into a nettle-smothered, jungly old lane, badly in need of trampling, which drops downhill to a gate on to the B3143 just above the church lane.

The Piddle Inn and the Poachers Inn at Piddletrenthide both serve food and have beer gardens fronting on to the river; the 'Poachers' has a sign bravely proclaiming 'Children welcome'.

SECTION TWO

Southern England

River Avon (Bath)

River Itchen

River Misbourne

River Arun

Cuckmere River

River Rother

River Medway

River Avon (Bath)

OS 1:50,000 Sheet 172
8 miles

Ever since King Bladud, the swineherd outcast from his father's court, cured his pigs and himself of leprosy with a dip in a nearby healing swamp, Bath has attracted sufferers from disease, especially rheumatism, to take the curative waters and relax among the hills and valleys of this gateway area to the West Country. The *Aquae Sulis* of the Romans who built the first formal baths here, it was a centre of pleasure to Beau Nash and the eighteenth-century nobility and squirearchy who saw the spa city rebuilt in new splendour. Bath still attracts millions of visitors, both native and foreign, who come to marvel at he crescents, squares and streets built during that Georgian revival, and looked after with jealous care by Bath's numerous civic and architectural societies.

Our walk forms part of the Avon Walkway, a path based on the river which runs from Pill on the Severn estuary under the Clifton Suspension Bridge to the centre of Bristol. From there it goes through open countryside to Bath and the tall Dundas aqueduct on the Kennet and Avon canal – in all, some twenty-five miles.

We start at the eighteenth-century New Bridge[1] (otherwise known as Newton Bridge) on the western outskirts of the city (717658), whose arch crosses the River Avon in a single one hundred-foot span of creamy oolite stone. You climb down to the river bank over a stile on the western side of the bridge, and walk away from the city of cures and pleasures with the pale yellow walls and grey roofs of Kelston Park[2] ahead, perched among trees on the end of its ridge (702661).

Soon the river is crossed by a long girder bridge which carries the now disused railway line from Mangotsfield into Bath Green Park Station – this wonderful Palladian building was saved from demolition and is now a J Sainsbury's store. A cycleway and footpath have been established along the old railway[3], which provides a flat, firm surface for cyclists, joggers and walkers passing under the ash wood of Kelston Park. The present house was designed in about 1770 by John Wood, the junior of the father-and-son partnership whom we can thank for many of Bath's finest eighteenth-century buildings. It replaced an Elizabethan country house of 1587 where lived Sir John Harington, godson of Queen Bess and as often in her bad books as in her favour – his witty tongue or saucy poetry usually the cause.

After a mile on the old railway line, a stile on the left takes you down to the river again at Kelston Lock (689669), where a notice warns canoeists of the hazards of shooting the weir's rapids. Files of young canoeists follow their leader like cygnets in the wake of a mother swan past the ranks of moored cruisers here, passing his words of wisdom down the line: 'Keep to the left! Oi, John! Keep in to the side!'

The path goes under another girder railway bridge with the flat top of Little Down and the clump of trees on Kelston Round Hill marking the ridge of the bowl of hills that sweeps down towards Bath away to the south. Soon you come opposite the Jolly Sailor pub overlooking another lock, where you bear right up the bank and across a stile to go in front of a terrace of stone cottages, built for the workers at Kelston Brass Mills.[4] The twin pyramids of the smelting ovens still stand beside the river (693679). In this peaceful spot they are a reminder of the small industries that sprang up all over the country before the Industrial Revolution got under way. Now the only sounds to be heard are cocks crowing, the rush of the water over the weir and the chink of ice in the gins and tonics of the boat owners moored by the river bank.

The path goes left-handed between two houses and crosses a field to a stile twenty yards up from the river. You cross a brook by a plank bridge and go up the hedge to another stile on the A431 road. Cross with care (sharp corner, fast cars!), turn right for a few yards and then left up a steep lane signposted 'North Stoke $\frac{3}{4}$' (697682). This little narrow road rises sharply up to the top of the downs and comes to a full stop at the delightful village of North Stoke, full of

The Avon curves to leave Bath under green ridges – a view from New Bridge.

well-preserved old houses and barns. Our walk continues to the right at the T-junction, but by turning left you reach the little church of St Martin[5] (703691), sitting four-squarely at the top of the lane, which has a raised footway to avoid the stream that floods it in wet weather. Crooked old steps bring you to the Norman doorway and the tiny interior, hung about with memorial slabs. One, to the Lawrence family, details the illustrious service performed by five brothers in India – all military men and all successful – including the 1st Lord Lawrence of Punjab and Viceroy of India (buried in Westminster Abbey); and Brigadier-General Sir Henry Lawrence, who was nominated as Governor-General of India but fell defending the Residency at the siege of Lucknow. Their sister's service was nearer home – she married the Rector of North Stoke. There is also a gruesome epitaph of 1774:

> *'O Reader ftay and here behold*
> *How we lay here inclofd in mould*
> *Think how by wormes we daily waft*
> *So will they do by you at laft*
> *Repent in time prepare to die*
> *That thow maift live Eternaly.'*

Back at the T-junction, a walled, stony lane goes gently up towards the ridge ahead, becoming more boggy underfoot as the cobbles (laid down when this was a favourite walk for the eighteenth-century Bath fashionables) give way to mud churned up by horses. You walk up between wire fences to an immense view at Prospect Stile[6] (712681). The outskirts of Bath are in sight ahead, the red and white sprawl of Bristol behind you to the west, the Cotswolds marching away to the north and Mendip to the south, and on a clear day in the east the edges of Savernake Forest and the outliers of Salisbury Plain. From Prospect Stile you turn right at the green 'public footpath' sign, passing behind the crown of trees on Kelston Round Hill through more hoof-trodden quagmire, which is soon divided by a fence from the rather drier and easier pedestrian path. Now the track begins to

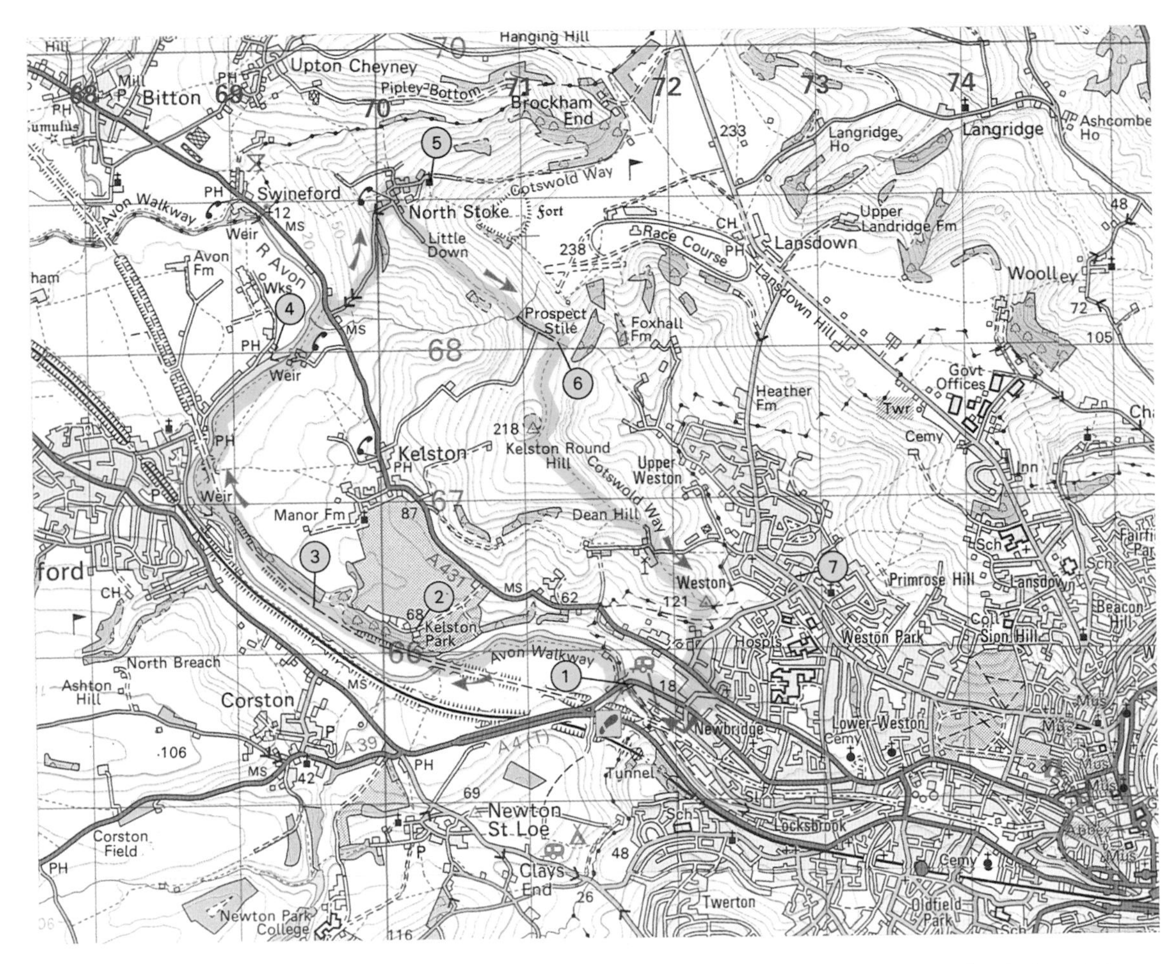

The hundred-foot span of New Bridge leaping the River Avon on the western outskirts of Bath.

drop downhill, and comes to the isolated Pendean farmstead (718667). Here you can carry on straight ahead to meet the road which takes you back to New Bridge, or, if thirsty, you can swing left through the farm gate and continue your descent down a tarmac lane which brings you out into Weston. Turn right at the road to reach the Crown and Anchor pub[7] 300 yards further on (728664) – a plain locals' pub with draught beer, bar food and a small paved garden behind.

From the pub turn right up Anchor Road, past the hospital and the Italianate bell tower of Oldfield Girls' School to come to the A431 road opposite Newbridge House. Turn left here, then sharply right in 200 yards down Old Newbridge Hill with a view ahead of the river and bridge. At the bottom of the hill turn right to reach the bridge. If you did not visit the Crown and Anchor, the Riverside Cafe beside the bridge serves grills, snacks and teas.

River Itchen

OS 1:50,000 Sheet 185
6 miles

The Itchen is a fisherman's delight. It is crammed with trout – not that they are easy to catch, as the clear water of the river running over its chalk bed gives them an excellent view of what's going on on the banks and bridges. Unless you move stealthily, they are more likely to spot you than vice versa; but in season you will see the fishermen under the willows, flaying the air with their long casts.

The Hampshire village of Itchen Abbas lies about four miles north-east of Winchester in the shallow valley that the Itchen has smoothed out of the chalk downland. The church of St John the Baptist[1] (534327) is a Victorian reconstruction, heavy and sombre, of the Norman church that was demolished in 1863, using the original doorway and part of the chancel arch. A yew tree in the churchyard may date back to the building of the old church, and under it is the grave of the last man to be hanged for horse-stealing, the gipsy John Hughes. He went to his death in silver buttons and with head held high, and his burial site is a memorial to forgiveness – the owner of the horse was the vicar of Itchen Abbas.

The footpath runs from the lychgate into the fields above the Itchen, then drops beside the river which flows west in a greenly-lit tunnel of oaks and poplars. At handsome red-brick Chilland Place (524326) you cross a lane and carry on up a path that crosses the meadows, looking over the river to a low ridge of chalk downland, to emerge opposite St Swithun's church at Martyr Worthy[2] (nothing to do with martyrs, but the homestead of the Norman Lord Henri la Martre). The church (515328) was built less than a century after the Conquest, and its north wall contains a slate tablet that makes you long to know more about the five spinster sisters it commemorates. The splendidly-named daughters of the vicar of Easton – Agnes, Euphemia, Eva, Jessica and Margaret – lived their long lives together at the Manor House in Martyr Worthy and all died there in the space of six years between 1952 and 1958. 'They devoted their lives,' says the plaque, 'to their Church, their country and this valley.'

Turn down the lane, bearing left up the bank at the bottom through the cottage fruit gardens into a path through the fields above the flat bends of the Itchen, with a fine view to your left of the massive walls and little pointed bellcote of Easton church across the river. You go under the motorway and reach Abbot's Worthy by way of the B3047 road and a path dropping to a kissing gate above the site of the village's mill (498325). Turn left here to cross a bridge from which you look downstream to the houses by the mill race half hidden by weeping willows, with green bushes of weed on the river bed trailing out with the current, providing cover for the trout that swirl after the flies on the surface.

The path runs through patches of buttercups and marigolds across low, marshy ground to a peaceful spot[3] where more water courses approach and diverge (499321). The gardens of the house on the bank here are loud with birdsong and the splashing of water through a sluice under willows and horse chestnuts. How the owner must have cursed when the motorway was extended to run right above the back of his secluded property. The path goes through his garden and bears left to go under the road, then runs up through the fields to the Church of St Mary at Easton[4] (509322). The church was built at about the same time as St Swithun's across the river, and also has five daughters to be proud of. The offspring of Agatha Barlow, who died in 1595, they each married a bishop – Coventry and Lichfield, Hereford, Durham and two Winchesters.

Follow the lane from the church to turn right, then left by the Cricketers Inn (511320) through the village. The road runs through classic Hampshire countryside of cornfields and downland to reach a splendid view (527321) of Avington Park[5] standing in red brick magnificence at the far end of the long ornamental water, dammed into position from the Itchen. This must have been the view the architect had in mind for the

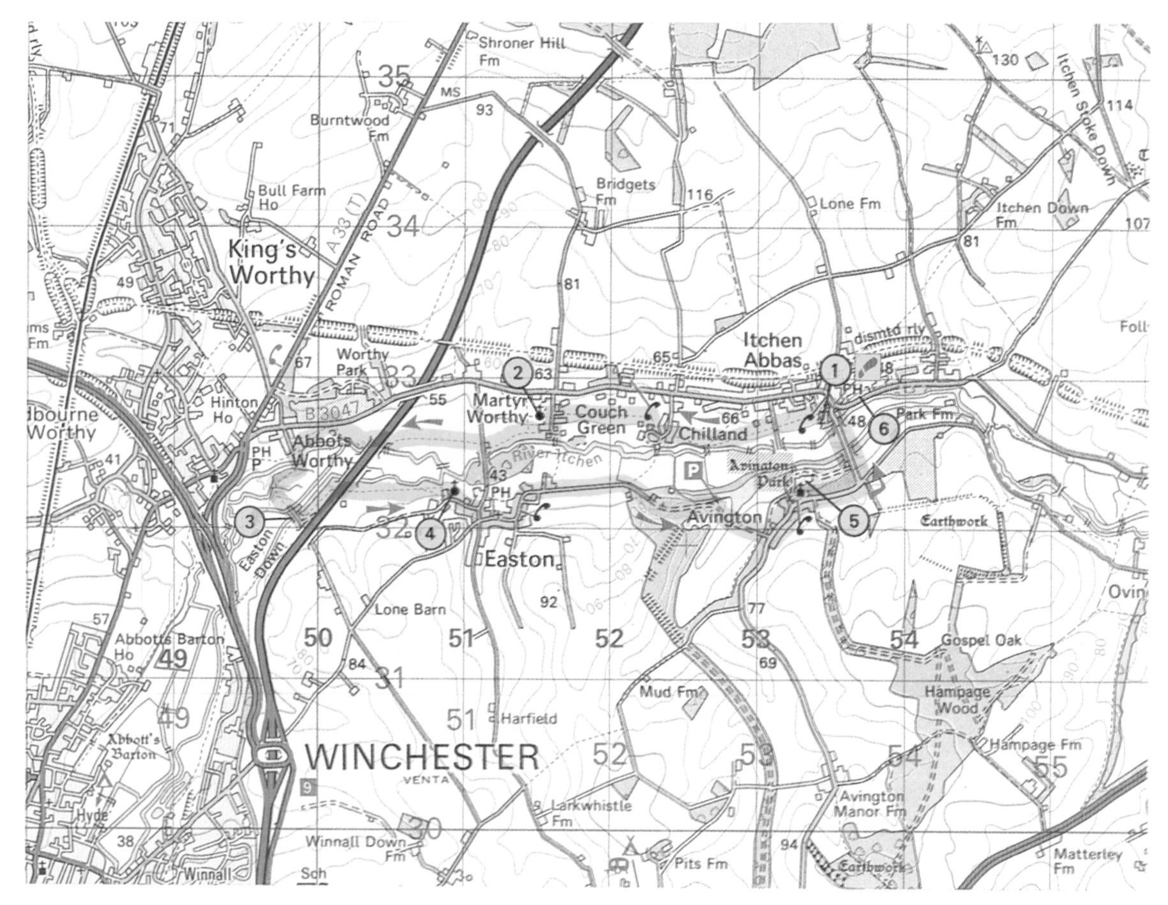

house, seen far off among trees and over water. The road curves through the estate hamlet and round the edge of the park to reach the gates of the house (536324), open to the public on summer afternoons at the weekend.

Avington Park has had a long and chequered history. Its two wings were added during the reign of Charles II to a Tudor centre, and succeeding owners have added library, orangery, ballroom and beautiful wall paintings and furnishings, as well as the brick Georgian church in the grounds which replaced a Saxon one. Kings and their queens (and mistresses) have stayed at Avington along with statesmen and more riotous company – Bacchus and Pan are well represented among the trimmings of house and park. On 6th August, 1823 William Cobbett rode to 'the Duke (of Buckingham)'s mansion-house at Avington and the little village of that name, both of them beautifully situated, amidst fine and lofty trees, fine meadows and streams of clear water.' Cobbett, however enchanted by Avington, had no time at all for its owner, Richard Brydges-Chandos, who had been created 2nd Marquess of Buckingham the previous year by his friend King George IV. Cobbett had heard how the Duke had been persecuting a local farmer, Mr Deller, for allegedly poaching the great man's game, and delivered a round ticking-off in his journal:

> 'Hobbies, *my Lord Duke, ought to be gentle, inoffensive, perfectly harmless little creatures. They ought not to be suffered to kick and fling about them: they ought not to be rough-shod, and, above all things, they ought not to be great things like those which are ridden by the Life-guards: and, like them, be suffered to dance, and caper, and trample poor devils of farmers under foot.*'

From the gates of Avington Park it's a short step back to Itchen Abbas, where you can enjoy a meal and a pint of Marston's excellent ale at the

Plough Inn[6] (536329) on the B3047. The pub succeeded another of the same name where Charles Kingsley, inspired by the quiet waters of the Itchen, wrote part of *The Water Babies*.

Nature not exactly rampant in this quiet backwater of the River Itchen below Abbot's Worthy.

Architect's dream view – Avington Park over its lake, dammed from the Itchen.

River Misbourne

OS 1:50,000 Sheet 176
3 miles

When John Milton arrived in Chalfont St Giles in July 1665 at the invitation of his admirer Thomas Ellwood, that stout-hearted Quaker was not on hand to welcome the blind poet. Having hoisted a flag of principle by attending the funeral of another Quaker, Ellwood was spending a short but uncomfortable week or two in Aylesbury gaol. Those were awkward times for people who had nailed their colours to the Parliamentary mast during the Civil War, including Milton himself, a staunch supporter of Oliver Cromwell throughout the eleven-year existence of the Commonwealth which had been brought to an end only five years before. The poet who came with his family to the leafy depths of the Buckinghamshire countryside to escape the plague raging in London had no illusions about his popularity in a country still tickled to death with its newly-restored Merry Monarch. Here in his 'Pretty Box at Giles Chalfont' he lay low, working on and finally finishing *Paradise Lost.* By the time of his return to a plague-free London the following year he was already juggling with the sequel, *Paradise Regained*, an idea sparked off by Thomas Ellwood's chance remark.

Milton's cottage[1] (988937) stands on the village street a couple of hundred yards up the hill from the church. It's a cramped little dwelling of red bricks and timber beams with a neat cottage garden in front, its door flanked by a vine on one side and a pear tree on the other. If you wanted to reach the upstairs rooms in Milton's day you had to do so by way of a ladder, so it's likely that the blind and gouty tenant slept in his workroom on the ground floor. The cottage is a museum nowadays, open most days during the spring, summer and autumn, with an exhibition of portraits, letters and rare Milton editions as well as a little coiled lock of his lank white hair.

This walk begins with a stroll along the ridge of the Misbourne's valley, looking down between hedges and copses into the watermeadows by the river. Turn left at a green public footpath sign opposite the Milton's Head pub just above Milton's cottage into a narrow lane running in the shade of bushy hedges. It passes the village playing fields, dipping into a green dell between oak and beech woods before curving round the edges of orchards, with yellow archangel growing under the hedges and long views out over the wide, shallow river valley towards the massed tree-tops on the far rise. Beside the orchards you bear left[2] (990920) to reach a lane opposite Grove Cottage, turning left again here to the grand brick entrance to Windmill Farm (992918). Another green footpath takes you round stables and paddocks and down across hay meadows on the outskirts of Chalfont St Peter to reach the bank of the mysterious Misbourne[3] (997914) – mysterious because there's a chance the river may not be there at all.

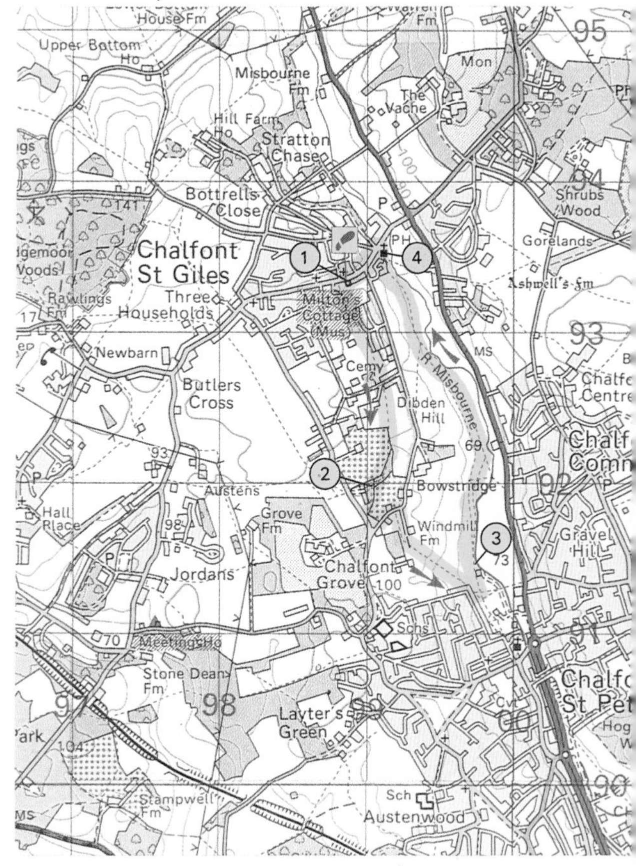

Nobody really knows why the Misbourne simply vanishes from time to time. Tradition says it's a sign of impending war. The old *Sunday Referee* had fun with a story headed 'Women Pray On Banks of Hoodoo River', quoting one of them as saying:

> *'The river's always right. It's always an ill omen when it dries up. At the beginning of the Great War it vanished ... now it's vanished completely again. We don't like the looks of it.'*

That report was printed on 29th January, 1939. The cause of the Misbourne's periodic disappearing act has been attributed at various times to cracks in its bed, overgrowth of weeds, droughts and cesspit excavation. A more likely explanation is that the river simply mirrors the level of the water table under the nearby Chiltern Hills. Another factor could be the ten million gallons extracted from the Misbourne every day by the line of pumping stations along the valley. The river wildlife has certainly been affected by sewage, though not in the way one might think. Far from being poisoned, the fish, birds and plants of the Misbourne valley thrived on the enriched water until the sewage plant at Amersham a few miles upriver closed in 1950, so local naturalists claim.

Even if the river is not in hiding, it's hard to spot in places as it winds in a channel you could easily jump across round the contorted trunks of a line of willows once pollarded but now shooting up thirty and forty feet high. There are charming views under the crooked elbows of their branches over the broad meadows of the Misbourne, with thick stands of beech and oak running away to the crown of the ridge. The path goes through a silver birch thicket and out into buttercup-freckled fields where horses and cows graze. Here on the commuter fringe of London you are rarely out of sight of houses or the sound of traffic, but the riverside path threads

Ancient, unpollarded willow split under its own weight.

The River Misbourne snaking through its meadows. Now you see it, now you don't.

its way peacefully down the green centre of the valley. Soon it passes apple orchards – none of your stunted little commercial runts of convenience trees here, but proper apple trees twenty feet high that you have to climb into from a ladder. The hawthorn hedges bend over into a shady tunnel where familiar garden birds – chaffinches, sparrows, thrushes, blackbirds – dash about among the greenery.

The muddy lane under the bushes reaches Chalfont St Giles beside the church[4] (991935), a flint building with some marvellous fourteenth-century wall paintings inside. In faded colours but undiminished vigour they show Biblical scenes from Genesis to the New Testament. Creation has a deer and leopard that might have leaped straight off a cave wall cavorting under what looks like a magpie; Adam and Eve are being seen off, stark naked, by an angel with a fiery sword; there is a Crucifixion scene full of expressive faces; and Salome admiring the head of John the Baptist on her charger and doing some energetic aerobics in front of Herod.

The church also contains a striking set of 147 individually and lovingly worked kneelers (a booklet describes each one, illustrated with a colour photograph), and some fine brasses. Sir Thomas Fleetwoode and his two wives, Barbara and Bridget, kneel rather po-faced and formal at their prayers, but there must have been more relaxed moments in their lives according to the inscription below:

> *'He had eightene children, foure by the fyrst wife and fouretene by the seconde.'*

There they all are in ranks behind their respective mothers, hands meekly folded and no fidgeting, the boys in starched collars and the girls in stiff little caps.

From St Giles's you go under a beamed archway among the old red-brick houses and shops on the village street. There are plenty of good pubs in Chalfont St Giles, or you can have a blow-out at Milton's Restaurant just across the road from the poet's rural retreat.

River Arun

OS 1:50,000 Sheet 197
5 miles

The famous view confronts you as you come out of the railway station at Arundel – the castle in its collar of trees[1], the steeply sloping houses of the little town running along to the pinnacles and buttresses of the Roman Catholic church[2]. So often reproduced on postcards and in magazines, it really is a stirring view, and one to stop and savour before walking across Arundel Bridge and starting this ramble beside the River Arun.

The gap in the wall of the downs, carved by the river, needed plugging well before the Norman Conquest, and some kind of keep stood up there on a mound before Roger Montgomery, Earl of Shrewsbury, extended it into a proper motte-and-bailey castle at the end of the twelfth century. His son was one of the rebel barons challenging the king, and thereby forfeited his castle to the Crown. In 1580 the recusant Howards, Dukes of Norfolk, married into the castle and it has remained in their staunchly Catholic hands ever since – apart from during the Civil War when Sir William Waller

Arundel – the picture postcard view. Catholic cathedral church on the left, St Nicholas's in the centre and the castle on the right.

besieged it for Parliament and forced the Royalist garrison to surrender.

What you see from the station road is all late eighteenth-century rebuilding by the 10th Duke of Norfolk, which hides the more modest and older structure from view. The fine Catholic church of St Philip Neri was consecrated in 1873.

Walk straight ahead to Arundel Bridge (020070); the irregular flint shell on the far side was the Maison Dieu almshouse[3], founded in 1395. On the town side of the bridge, turn right up Mill Road past the towers of Arundel Castle gatehouse (the castle and grounds are open to the public) and walk along in a double avenue of lime trees to the bridge below Home Farm[4] (018077). The flint buildings are set back from the road below the white scar of an old chalk quarry at the foot of Swanbourne Lake. The massive farmhouse is connected by a covered way to the octagonal dairy building. On the far side of the bridge – not as old as it looks, as it was built in 1892 – turn right along the side of the outlet stream of Swanbourne Lake. This path, of grey-white chalky clay laced with knotted tree roots, can be slippery after rain.

Soon the stream meets the River Arun (023077), and you turn left along the bank with the honking, quacking, screeching reed-beds of Sir Peter Scott's Wildfowl Trust on your left[5] – Slimbridge's younger brother, and very popular with visitors. The Arun is wide and slow, moving seaward between muddy banks in its broad, flat flood-plain, well separated from the downland cliffs it has carved out. The downs sweep in a semicircular bowl round from the east to north, their green sides cut by white splashes of chalk quarrying. The chalk was burned in

Ruins of Maison Dieu almshouse, the towers of Arundel Castle peeping over the treetops behind.

kilns to make lime, which was spread on the fields to fertilize the heavy local clay soil.

The path reaches the Black Rabbit at Offham[6] (027085), a popular pub on summer evenings with river, downs and castle all laid out in front of its beer garden. Near the pub a right-of-way through the castle grounds was disputed by the mid-nineteenth-century Duke of Norfolk. His villagers' hackles went up, they took him to court – and he lost! Beyond the pub the river splits into two. The Arun Navigation was undertaken between 1785 and 1790 to bring sea-going cargoes further upriver than Arundel; and in 1813–1816 it was extended northwards to join the River Wey as the Wey and Arun Canal, giving a through route from London to the Channel without having to go round by the Thames Estuary and Dover. Too many locks and tolls made it unsuccessful, and the Arun Valley Railway killed it off. It closed in 1871, eight years after the trains arrived in the valley. It is the original course of the river that swings off to the east[7] to run under Burpham village; our path continues by the Arun Navigation's short cut, whose banks are thick with kingcups, yarrow and yellow flags.

The hamlet of South Stoke[8] is a huddle of flint and brick among trees in a salient of the river – actually the 'new cut' of the Arun Navigation, which closed the neck of the great horseshoe sweep taken by the river close under the downs. It is a peaceful place at the end of a road going nowhere. The little church (027100) contains a modern treasure – a book of poems and photographs by a local man, Mr P M Dyson, about South Stoke and its environs, generously left in the church by the author for the pleasure of visitors.

The tow-path bends with the River Arun around the red-roofed church at South Stoke.

Cross the footbridge below the church and turn left over a stile (signposted 'North Stoke') to reach the course of the old river in 150 yards, striking off at right angles from the top of the new cut (025102). You walk on its right bank among trees on a raised flood embankment – between the path and the weed-choked river bed is a jungle, left to grow unmolested since the new cut was built – fallen tree trunks, fungi, undergrowth, mosses, ferns and birdsong.

Soon the path crosses the old river by a miniature Severn Bridge (023105), and strikes uphill to reach North Stoke, like its sister village marooned in the crook of the river's elbow. The road curves down through the village, but before taking it turn left down a cul-de-sac lane to reach North Stoke Church[9] (020108), a jewel not to be missed. It is cruciform – unusual enough in a small village church – and the main body of the church dates from about 1200. There are many ancient and well-preserved features in the building, as the excellent guide-notes explain: in particular a blissful stained-glass Virgin Mary being crowned – the blues, reds and ochre yellows still fresh and vivid after seven centuries of existence. See if you can find a hand holding up an arch, a yellow hen standing on her head, and a pop-eyed ram with donkey's teeth!

Back on the road, walk down to the valley bottom, turning left through a gate (024109) opposite a pair of tile-hung flint cottages to rejoin the river bank and walk on to Houghton bridge and the Bridge Inn's draught beer and little walled garden. Behind it is Amberley Station – and behind that a lane leads to the open-air chalk pits museum[10], which is well worth a visit before taking the Arun Valley railway line back to Arundel.

Cuckmere River

OS 1:50,000 Sheet 199
8 miles

Alfriston, all narrow streets and half-timbered inns, is a crossing place for walkers on the South Downs Way striding east-west, and tourists sauntering north-south. Bed, breakfast and beer for the walkers – hotels and antiques for the tourists – Alfriston provides all of these, and its streets become very crowded in high summer. Our walk starts at the free car-park on the northern edge of the village (521034), from which you cross the road onto a signposted path to the Cuckmere River.

The Cuckmere Valley southwards from Alfriston is one of Sussex's best-kept secrets – four miles of broad, windswept meadows well away from the tourist beat, its remote interior unpenetrated by any motor road. The Cuckmere River widens as it goes south to meet the sea, its water often driven back on itself by wind and tide. It is a haven for wildlife, jealously preserved from building or development by local conservationists.

The path runs on the west bank of the river on a raised causeway, constructed to defend the surrounding pasture land from flooding. It passes beneath the stumpy spire and tower of Alfriston's church of St Andrew (521030), behind which stands the National Trust's Clergy House whose tiled roof is surmounted by a crown of thatch. The valley broadens out as it approaches the sea, the high downland ridges sweeping down to the cliffs at Cuckmere Haven. A large colony of swans inhabits the river, its members sailing downriver with the ebb tide and beating back upstream with the flow.

The barns, houses and tiny church at Litlington are grouped attractively among trees a little way from the river on the east bank, backed by the swelling ridges of the downs. The tall trees of the village are not just ornamental – they protect the houses from the strong sea wind which blows constantly inland. The path curves east and south with the river, which has scoured away the down into the escarpment of High and Over (510011), rearing above the valley on the right and decorated with a white horse[1]. In fact he's a coffee-coloured beast, stained with the chalky clay washed over him by the rain. The swans and herons are joined by shelduck, oyster-catchers and gulls as the influence of the sea

Swans of the Cuckmere River at ease: St Andrew's Church at Alfriston beyond them.

becomes stronger, and the banks of the river slope further back to make room for the tidal surges.

Nearing Exceat Bridge, the Cuckmere meanders away to the east while the path keeps close to the hillside, running on a broad billiard table of short turf on top of the flat ledge of hard-packed silt deposited by the river. The water gives off a salty smell and strands of seaweed lie on the banks, which are fortified with lattices of twigs and stakes pushed deep into the mud.

Barbed wire and corrugated iron block off the path just above the Boat House, and you climb up to the road and turn left to follow it down to Exceat Bridge (513993). Cross the A259 into the car-park of the Golden Galleon pub (food, olde worlde garden and Harvey's beer, brewed nearby in Lewes), from which stiles take you away from the river into Seaford Haven Nature

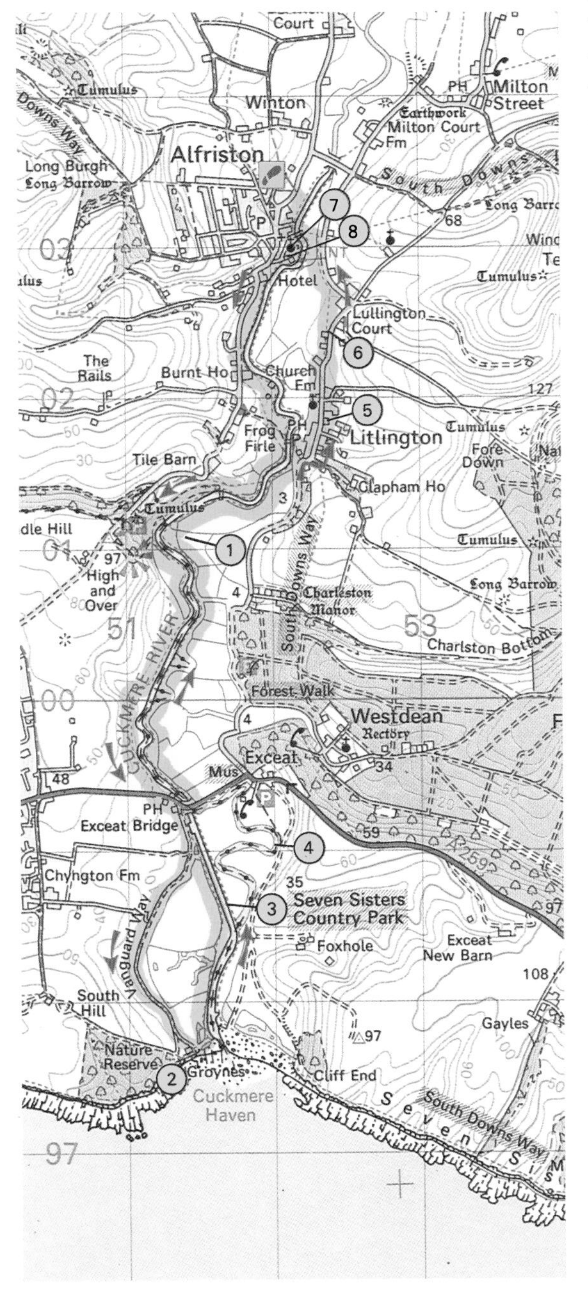

Reserve. The Reserve protects the three kinds of habitat present here – wet pasture, foreshore and the precious remnants of the Sussex downland, most of which has gone under the plough since the Second World War. The path leads on towards the chimneys and solid, square walls of the coastguard cottages on the cliff[2] (513977), built here to keep an eye on the ships that ran smuggled cargo into Cuckmere Haven during the eighteenth century. Smuggling was a profitable business then; brandy, lace and tobacco were brought up the Cuckmere River to Alfriston, where they were hidden away for onward transportation. The coastguard cottages were a constant threat to the smugglers from their position overlooking the bay, but now they themselves are threatened by the natural enemy of both coastguard and smuggler – the sea. Their gardens drop abruptly away into the waves, and it is only a matter of time before they tumble down the cliff into oblivion.

From the cottages, walk down the slope and across the shingle to the mouth of the Cuckmere River. Beyond it rise the sheer white cliffs of the Seven Sisters, and in the distance the whale's jaw of Belle Tout, crowned by a disused lighthouse. The path leads back to Exceat Bridge beside the river – this is the New Cut[3], built in 1846 to avoid the sharp bends of the Cuckmere River's natural course[4] to the east. Grey-green mats of sea purslane knit the banks together with their long roots.

Cross the bridge and walk back inland up the right-hand bank of the river, with High and Over ahead to the left and the bare shoulder of Windover Hill to the right. The fishing-reel clicking of grasshopper warblers comes from the extensive reed beds to your right. At Litlington take the tarmac path from the footbridge (521017) and walk up to the road, where you turn left to go through the village (teas on the lawn and a variety of plants at the nursery)[5]. At the top of the road turn down a waymarked track beside North Ham House[6] (524024), over stiles and across fields to the footbridge (521031) opposite Alfriston church.

St Andrew's[7] is known as the 'Cathedral of the Downs'. It was built in 1360, all of it at the same time with no later additions, in the form of a cross, whereby hangs a tale. The original plan was to erect the church in a nearby meadow, but

Alfriston Clergy House is over 600 years old. In 1896 it was the first building to be acquired by the National Trust.

Opposite: Litlington, sheltered by trees and the swell of the downland.

to the builders' consternation the foundation stones kept mysteriously shifting to the present site on the Tye, Alfriston's village green. Someone noticed a group of four oxen lying down there rump to rump in the shape of a cross, and put two and two together. The builders took the heavenly hint, and St Andrew's went up with no more trouble.

Beside the church is the Clergy House[8], the first building acquired by the National Trust in 1896. It dates from 1350, 200 years before the Reformation, and contains a magnificent medieval hall with a carved roof and a floor of four inches of rammed chalk, sealed with thirty gallons of sour milk – rather hard on the priests in hot weather. By 1885 the house had become so dilapidated that the vicar decided to have it pulled down. However, he agreed to a stay of execution to allow the tenant, an old lady, to die under her own roof; and in 1889 a new vicar was appointed. He quickly realized the uniqueness of the treasure on his doorstep, and he carried out repairs which kept the ancient house standing until the National Trust took it over. The house is open to the public in the spring and summer.

Alfriston has several interesting old pubs, including the Market Cross House (now Ye Olde Smugglers Inne) where Stanton Collins, leader of an eighteenth-century smuggling gang, lived and planned 'runs'. There is also the Star, reputed to have an underground passage going all the way to Cuckmere Haven for the transport of illicit goods. The Star is decorated with carvings, including a St George and dragon, a double-headed monster and a bear holding a ragged staff – the arms of the Dudley family – and is guarded on its southern corner by a splendid red-painted wooden lion, grinning conspiratorially. He was probably the figurehead of a seventeenth-century ship, wrecked on the coast, and perhaps was brought here through the secret passage – if it exists!

River Rother

OS 1:50,000 Sheet 189
$12\frac{1}{2}$ miles

No wonder the French gave Rye such a hard time during the turbulent fourteenth century. The town sits cockily up on top of its hill above the flat marshlands of West Kent, an open invitation to any invader to come and cut it down to size. Those medieval French raiders made several unwelcome visits, finishing off the job in 1377 by burning the whole place to the ground. It was a shrewd blow, as Rye had been admitted to the Cinque Ports trading confederation along with neighbouring Winchelsea by Henry II, and had grown into a major port. The Great Storm of 1287 had proved an ill wind that blew Rye a lot of good. In its fury it swamped Winchelsea and pushed the River Rother westward to flow right at the feet of Rye. But the increased prosperity brought by sea up Rye's new river didn't last long. By Tudor times the water approaches were well silted up, and Rye's golden age of trade was over.

The town where the playwright John Fletcher was born in 1579, where Henry James came to live for the last eighteen years of his life, and where E F Benson wrote many of his 'Lucia' novels (and was mayor for three years) is all crooked, climbing streets, charming alley views and splendid houses. If, having arrived, you decide to spend the day exploring and give this walk a miss, I won't blame you! If you can tear yourself away, however, make for the A259 bridge over the Rother (925206), below which fishing boats and their nets hung out to dry line the muddy banks of the river under the high red-brick houses of Rye. Turn left and walk along the raised flood wall on the east bank, passing under the railway line by way of a stile. On the far side the view eastward stretches away over the sheep-dotted marshes towards a distant line of downs that was the sea cliff until the Romans, and after them the monks, completed the drainage of the marshland. Only careful maintenance of the sea wall keeps the sea out of these fields; in places you are walking twenty feet below sea level.

The river rounds the wooded bluff of Playden and runs north under bridges and through sluices where black-headed gulls and herons cruise overhead. Until the Great Storm the Rother flowed in a wide estuary to the east, and the humps and ridges of land that rise out of these fields were islands in mid-river. Once the ground had been reclaimed from the sea it proved wonderfully fertile, but the great dry apron of fields gave a potential landing ground to any invader. This threat disturbed the government so much when Bonaparte was assembling his invasion barges across the Channel that they decided to create a water barrier right round the inland perimeter of the Walland and Romney Marshes from below Rye in the west to Hythe in the east. Soon you come to the junction of the river with the Royal Military Canal[1] (936244), which heads off through a lock to the right. As a military defence it was just another white elephant, but local fishermen nowadays reap the benefit of that Napoleonic scare.

Cross the canal by the lock (day fishing permits obtainable at Lock Cottage), and carry on along the Rother. Inland the long ridge of the Isle of Oxney fills the horizon, patched with woods and the large yellow blocks of oil-seed rape fields. Oxney was an island in the middle of the Rother's original estuary, and even after the river shifted its course the main means of communication between island and mainland was by ferry between Stone and Appledore. A look at the map illustrates how Oxney can still be cut off during particularly bad winter floods.

Just beyond New Bridge[2] (914253) a series of helpful, well-sited yellow arrow waymarks points you north-west away from the river across the sheep pastures to climb the flank of the Isle of Oxney to Budd's House[3] (902265), a lovely mellow red-brick building on your left as you reach the top of the rise. The path dog-legs round the property to reach Wittersham village beside the church of St John the Baptist[4] (897270), a wide and spacious building under a massive stone tower of the early sixteenth century. In the south aisle there is a memorial

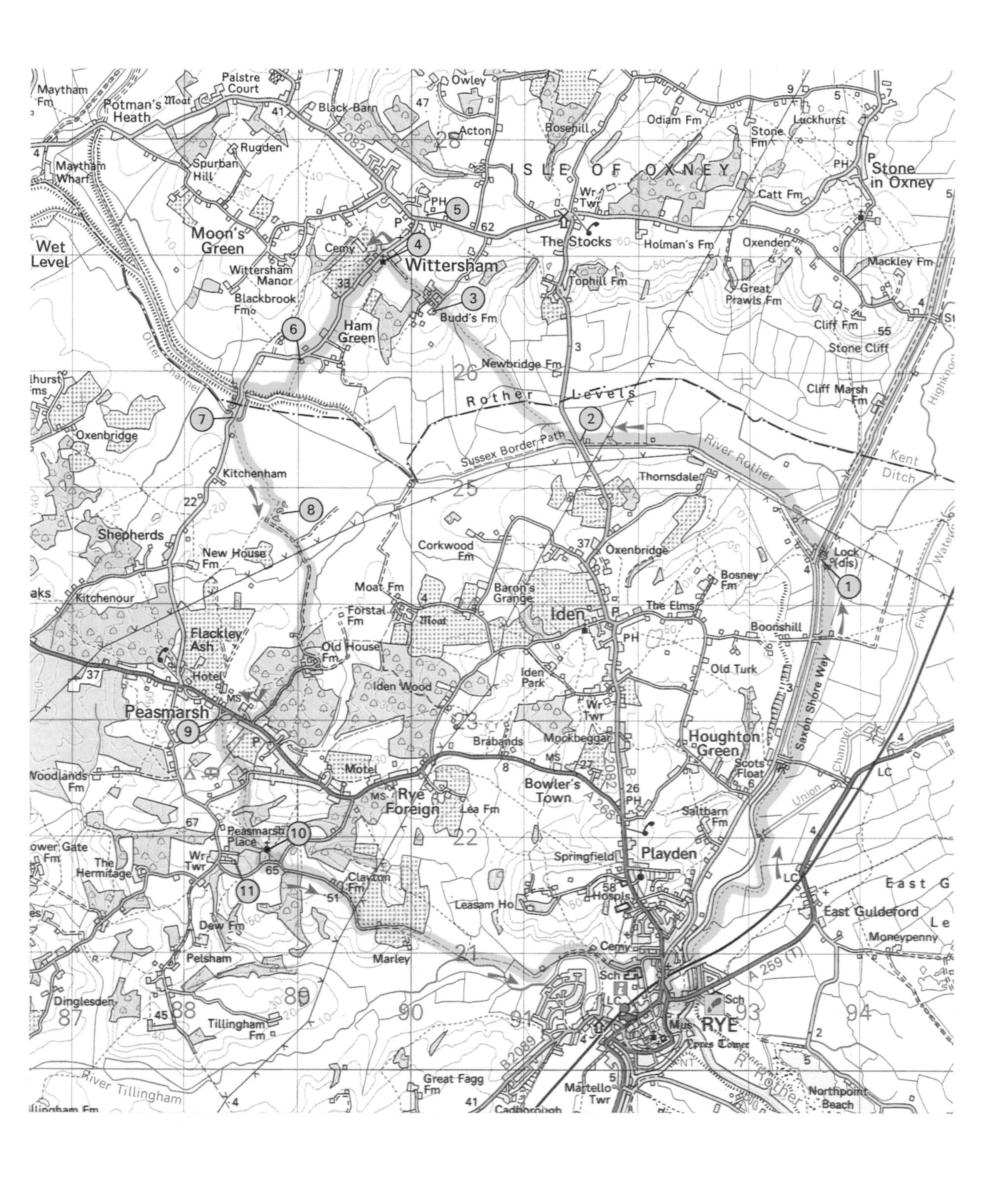
Wittersham
ISLE OF OXNEY
Stone in Oxney
Rother Levels
River Rother
Sussex Border Path
Saxon Shore Way
Iden
Peasmarsh
Playden
RYE
Rye Foreign
Houghton Green
East Guldeford
The Stocks
Moon's Green
Ham Green
Kitchenham
Oxenbridge
Flackley Ash
Bowler's Town
Isle of Oxney
Potman's Heath
Wet Level
River Tillingham
Otter Channel
Kent Ditch
Union Channel

tablet to the cricketer and MP Alfred Lyttleton, who lived at Wittersham and died in 1913 – 'Athlete, Lawyer, Statesman: a man greatly beloved'.

Turn right along the street from the church to reach the Lamb and Ewe pub[5] (draught bitter, food and beer garden), left to continue the walk down into the Rother Valley, with wide views ahead. By Barn Cottage[6] (890261) a stile and field path lead to the river, where you turn westward. Cross the Rother over Blackwall Bridge (885258), followed by the Otter Channel[7], after which a footpath strikes out across the fields to the left (884255). Aim for the top corner of a group of bushy dells, marked as ponds on the map[8] (888247), to reach a stony farm track running through the yard of Old House Farm and then through oak and beech woods up to the A268 road (886230). You turn right here past the Cock Inn, then immediately left past Jempson's bakery, which together with a caravan park has swallowed the network of footpaths here. A stile on the left one hundred yards up the lane[9] (883229) leads to a path which runs over fields and a road, then dives through a wood (885222) to climb to the little Norman church of St Peter and St Paul at Peasmarsh[10] (887219).

The round-headed and narrow red standstone chancel arch in the church is smaller and slimmer by far than the arch under the bell tower, and proved too small for the congregation in the nave to see what was going on up there at the altar – so in the fourteenth century a squint or peep-hole was added to lay the mysteries bare. Above the chancel arch is an Elizabethan tablet displaying the Ten Commandments, the Lord's Prayer and the Creed; it is flanked by two much older figures (probably carved at the same time as the arch was built) of leopards swallowing their own tails. Before leaving the church, go to the south-east corner of the exterior and lift the wire netting over the drain hole there to see something slipped into the architecture by a mason with pagan affinities – an antlered beast from an older sylvan tradition.

Just to the west of the church stands Peasmarsh Place[11], the home of the Liddell family. Young Alice Liddell enjoyed her father's appointment as Dean of Christ Church in Oxford, for it was there that nice Mr Dodgson wove her into such a thrilling story. Later on, under the name of Lewis Carroll, Mr Dodgson had quite a success with his little tale.

From the church you turn left along the road, then right in one hundred yards into a pebbly track (888218) that passes Clayton Farm and Marley through apple orchards to drop down the slope to marsh level (902211). A straight walk through the sheep-grazing meadows runs beside the winding River Tillingham into the tight red sprawl of Rye across its hilltop.

Opposite: Seagoing boats moor in the muddy banks of the River Rother under Rye's elegant huddle of houses.

River Medway

OS 1:50,000 Sheet 188
7 miles

The Weald of Kent has more than its share of beautiful stately houses, but none is more beautiful or stately than Penshurst Place[1] (528440). 'A very fair and sportelyke park as any in this parte of England' was the verdict of its Steward in 1611, and there are few great houses with more history crammed inside their walls. The house was built in 1341 for Sir John de Pulteney, a rich London merchant who chose a marvellous site on the banks of the River Medway. The original solar, buttery and pantry still surround the fourteenth-century great hall, considered the finest in Britain. The Black Prince stayed here, as well as Elizabeth I and the Earl of Dudley; also James I, and the children of Charles I, who, poor mites, were bundled off to Kent by Cromwell after he had got rid of their father. Perhaps the brightest star in Penshurst's crown was Sir Philip Sidney, courtier, soldier and man of all talents, who was born here. The house, still belonging to his descendants, is open to the public in summer.

The River Medway runs below Penshurst Place under the second of the two bridges (529437) as you leave the great house. Cross the bridge past the tile-hung Bridge House and walk up the hill for one hundred yards to turn off to the right along a rough lane signposted 'Poundsbridge' (530435). Below the path the river has carved out a wide valley of gently rounded, wooded hills with red-brick and timber buildings set among the trees, many with conical, white-tipped oast-houses beside them. Hops are grown all over this part of Kent, and the path soon runs along the top of a hop field set with a maze of tall wooden posts supporting a cat's cradle of wires and strings up which the growing hops climb. Sheep graze under the trellises, nibbling away the weeds and leaving the hops alone – an economical way to farm in two ways at once. In summer the sweet, tangy smell of the hops is overpowering.

Trees come down to the path on your left, and a few yards further on you bear right[2] around the bottom edge of the hop field to cross the Medway (530427) and turn left along the bank. Bushes of may grow thickly along the river, and each ridge of hills carries a line of houses, seemingly placed there just to look good! The red tiles and dark beams of Old Swaylands (534426) stand across the river below a red wall which encloses a garden.

Recross the river by a gated footbridge[3] (533421) and walk straight ahead beside a ditch to go through a gate to the hedge facing you. Ignore a tempting stile and turn right up the hedge to reach the road by a little chapel[4] at the top of the field (538418). Turn right here past the roadside oast-house at Hansell Farm for a long half-mile to a lane on the right (532411), marked by a tall old signpost: 'Public footpath through

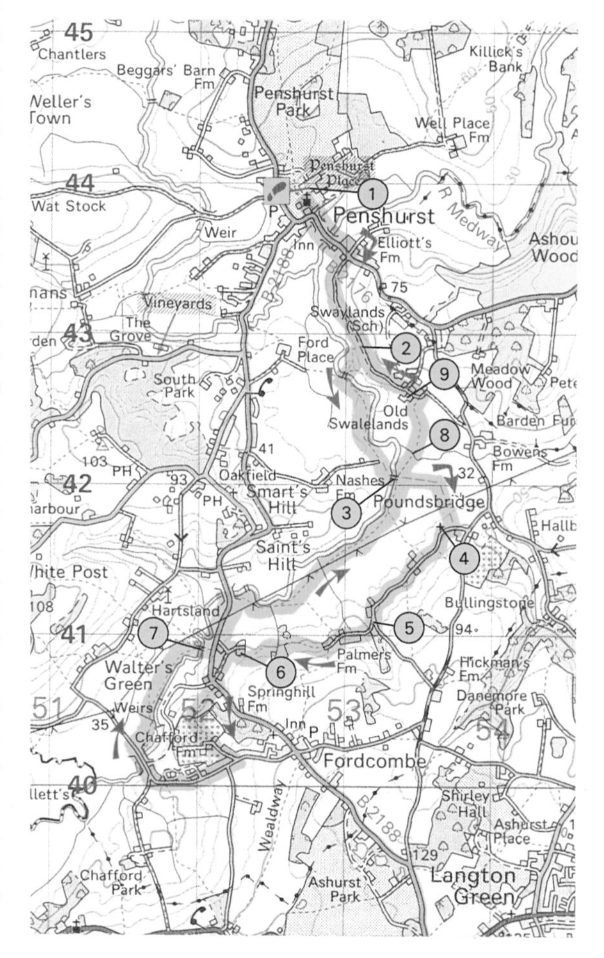

Meadows of the River Medway below the walls of the 'fair and sportelyke park' of Penshurst Place.

Holt Farm to Fordcombe and Springhill'[5]. The age of the lane can be judged by the oak and ash trees which are rooted at the bottom of the ten-foot banks trodden out by centuries of farm-workers' boots.

The lane goes through a long, dilapidated farmyard, swinging right where it ends through a grove of trees and across a field to a stile half-way up a wood (526409). Cross the stile and walk across the waist of the wood, emerging above the two capless oast-houses of the complex of buildings at Fordcombe Manor[6] (523409). At the time of writing (May 1986) the path went just to the left of the Manor and down the drive; plans were being finalized to divert it down the right-hand edge of the property.

Fordcombe Manor is magnificently situated on a crest overlooking the valley. The sixteenth-century house was extended during the seventeenth century, and at one time was a coaching inn for the old road whose double hedge can still be seen crossing the drive below the house.

Turn left on reaching the B2188, and walk up the hill to go right beside a wooden fence (521406) just up from the entrance to Fordcombe Manor – *not* down the private road immediately opposite the manor drive. The path goes down wooden steps and up a slope, over stiles and between fences, turning left to cross the bottom of an orchard and reach a roughly surfaced lane (521403) by Chafford Farm. The lane runs left to the road, where you turn right to walk down to Chafford Bridge, dated 1881 (516402). The Medway has been out of sight for some time, but here you turn right on the far side of the bridge and walk along the river bank for half a mile to the next footbridge[7] (520409), which you cross to the B2188 and turn left to the road bridge (522413). Here you follow the footpath on the south bank of the river for another mile in a tranquil stretch of grazing meadows, where recent history is crumbling away in the shape of the red-brick Second World War pill-boxes placed along the Medway in 1940 to guard the hinterland from Hitler's anticipated invasion.

Pass the footbridge at 533421 and take the right-hand of two bridges[8] (534422) over a tributary stream around the edge of a hop field. Cross a stile and go up the hedge to the lane at the top (535426), where you turn left to reach Old Swaylands[9].

The central part of this fine old timber and plaster house dates from Plantagenet days. It was once the home of an ironmaster – the local clay is full of iron nodules, and there was a thriving iron-founding business in the area.

From Old Swaylands the path leads ahead to the rough lane back to Penshurst Place.

SECTION THREE

Eastern England

River Granta (or Cam)

River Chelmer

River Stour (Constable Country)

River Blyth

River Nar

River Witham

River Humber

River Granta (or Cam)

OS 1:50,000 Sheet 154
$4\frac{1}{2}$ miles

'... stands the Church clock at ten to three?
And is there honey still for tea?'

The present-day inhabitants of the Old Vicarage at Grantchester must wish they had a pound for every time that nostalgic couplet is murmured by literary pilgrims gazing in at their front gates. The shade of Rupert Brooke pervades this green and gorgeous stroll through the riverside meadows where he lazed, bathed and ran during his golden undergraduate years before the First World War. He adored his 'lovely and dim and rustic life' in the peaceful little village a couple of miles out of Cambridge, writing in a letter to a friend in 1910, 'I love being there so much – more than any place I've ever lived in. I love the place and especially the solitude so much.' Sitting on a window seat in the Café des Westens in Berlin in May 1912, he poured out his fond memories of his rural haven in the long and gently mocking poem *The Old Vicarage, Grantchester*, catching its middle-class donnishness as well as its beauty:

'In Grantchester their skins are white;
They bathe by day, they bathe by night;
The women there do all they ought;
The men observe the Rule of Thought.'

Undergraduates still bicycle, punt and stroll out to Grantchester from Cambridge to spend summer afternoons splashing about by the mill pool on the Granta (435551) where –

'... laughs the immortal river still
Under the mill, under the mill...'

A book, a bike and Grantchester Mill – still heaven for Cambridge undergraduates.

Walking up the village street from the mill bridge you pass the Old Vicarage[1] (434552) where Brooke lodged with the Neeves in 1911 – Mr Neeve kept bees, memories of whose honey inspired that famous last line. A handsome brick building behind wrought-iron gates, it has been smartened up since Brooke's time, when it was described as a 'long, low, ramshackle, tumble-down one-storied house'. Next door is The Orchard,[2] Brooke's lodgings between June 1909, when he had moved here from rooms in King's College, and December 1910 when he shifted his belongings into the Old Vicarage. In summer you can take tea in the garden at The Orchard where Brooke and his friends would lie out on the grass talking nonsense in the manner of undergraduates down the ages.

The church of St Andrew and St Mary[3] stands on the other side of the road, its little brick and timber porch under a short, square tower leading into a cool interior where there's a very discreet Rupert Brooke industry in the shape of a few typewritten and hand-sketched pamphlets on the poet and his celebrated poem. Near the gate stands the war memorial, Brooke's name squeezed in between those of Walter Bolton and Alfred Cutter. He died, not in the glorious heat of battle, but of septicaemia in the Mediterranean on 23rd April, 1915, and was buried under an olive tree on the island of Skyros.

Opposite the church – whose clock keeps perfect time – turn right down a tarmac alleyway (433555) which brings you out below the garden of the Green Man pub[4] (excellent food

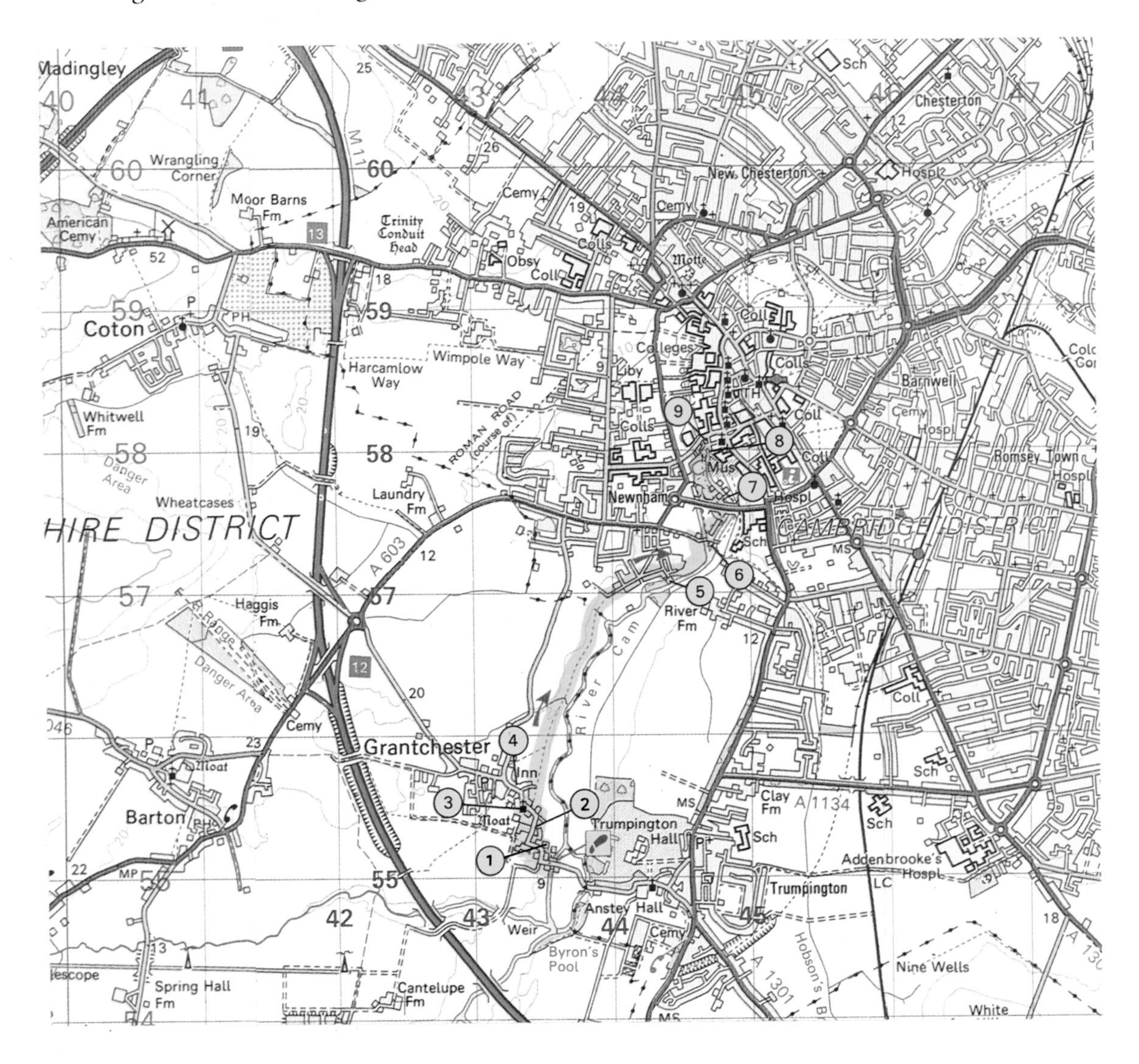

and draught beer) onto the footpath through Grantchester Meadows. The path runs along the top of a bank sloping down to the winding Granta (or Cam – the map says one thing, locals another) which loops through the meadows under the willows. This is a favourite picnic spot for undergraduates and tourists alike. The tourists are identifiable by the smartness of their clothes and the restraint of their chatter; the undergraduates by the empty beer bottles and full scribbling pads littering their strongholds, and the bursts of wild laughter from their friends as they somersault from the bank into the water. Bathing, kissing and cuddling, throwing each other into the river, chasing barefoot through the grass of the meadows, roaring with laughter at private jokes – it's very much a students' preserve where the outsider may either get two fingers stuck up in his camera lens, or be courteously offered help when getting over a stile. On the river the yellow punt poles go rhythmically up and down and the passengers tumble into the water just as they did in Rupert Brooke's day.

The path approaches Cambridge through a street named 'Grantchester Meadows' – turn right at the end into a rough lane (443571) which leads to a stile into Owlstone Croft Nature Reserve. On your right a side-stream of the Granta flows under the nettlebeds and willow suckers along the edge of an islet known as Paradise[5], whose single house (once a pub) was regularly flooded in winter before new locks were built at Sheep's Green just downstream. Undergraduates and townspeople flocked to skate on the meadows near Paradise when the floods froze. Byron's close friend Matthews drowned near here, entangled in weeds at the bottom of the river.

The Granta runs on to divide at the foot of Sheep's Green (447572), the main channel continuing to the right past Hodson's Garden, a patch of ground walled off by John Hodson in 1887. He built himself a little summerhouse here, still standing at the water's edge[6], from which he could keep a prudent eye on his daughter as she bathed in the river. The left-hand channel flows under a footbridge by a playground with swings, slides and a paddling pool – you go over the bridge (447573) and cross Sheep's Green to follow the Granta (beginning to be called the Cam hereabouts) under the Fen Causeway and on over the green spaces where lovers lie and others stroll. Beyond the far bank looms the coppery-green roof of the Fitzwilliam Museum, and further downstream the tall chimneys of Peterhouse. The river goes under the green lattice-work girders of Robinson Crusoe's Bridge[7] (448577), a favourite place for local lads to bombard punting undergraduates with missiles, their prey returning fire enthusiastically with water pistols and squirts of river water from bicycle pumps.

At Scudamore's Boat Station[8] (447580) there is another division of the waterway. Punts have to be dragged out of the river, across the footpath and down a ramp into the mill pool to avoid the race of water in a narrow tunnel which once powered King's and Bishop's Mills here. Crowds of sightseers lean over the weir railings to watch intrepid canoeists charging the rush of water and being swept away into the pool. There are many pubs in the side-streets in this area – they catered for bargemen and workers in granaries, warehouses and mills when this waterfront was a busy industrial area.

Immortal ritual on the Granta. The next move is to fall in, laughing madly.

Beyond Small Bridge[9] are the Backs, green stretches of lawn and garden separating the Cam from the colleges that line the riverbank for the next mile. Queen's, King's, Clare, Trinity, St John's and their connecting bridges – there's only one way to see them from the river, and that is, of course, by punt. Scudamore's will hire

Grantchester Meadows, little changed since Rupert Brooke bathed, ran and boated here.

one out to you, and you can spend the next hour in heaven.

Walking back to Grantchester through those lovely water meadows, you slip once more into Rupert Brooke's beloved rural world. Towards the end of his short life he became a kind of ideal of clean-limbed English youth, especially during the first year of the Great War when the older generation was beginning to realize how quickly those golden boys and all they represented were disappearing. Winston Churchill, in his *Times* obituary three days after Brooke's death, wrote of a young man 'joyous, fearless, versatile, deeply instructed, with classic symmetry of mind and body, all that one would wish England's noblest sons to be.' Life for an undergraduate, then as now, was not lived entirely under cloudless skies, and at certain times in his existence Rupert Brooke might have smiled wryly at that eulogy. But Grantchester Meadows, perhaps even more than that other well-known 'corner of a foreign field', still hold the very best of him:

> *'I only know that you may lie*
> *Day long and watch the Cambridge sky,*
> *And, flower-lulled in sleepy grass,*
> *Hear the cool lapse of hours pass,*
> *Until the centuries blend and blur*
> *In Grantchester, in Grantchester . . .'*

Extracts are taken from The Poetical Works of Rupert Brooke, *edited by Sir Geoffrey Keynes and published by Faber and Faber.*

River Chelmer

OS 1:50,000 Sheet 167/168
13 miles

This is a one-way walk, but there is a good bus service from Maldon to Chelmsford.

The River Chelmer's two distinct aspects meet at Chelmsford. Upstream of the town the Chelmer winds in its natural state from village to village of inland Essex, while downstream it takes a straighter and more formal course between long avenues of willows. This section of the river was canalized in 1797 to allow seagoing vessels passage through eleven locks to and from the coast at Maldon.

From Chelmsford the riverside footpath leaves the A12 road bridge (719063) and runs eastward on the north bank of the Chelmer to the lock at Barnes Farm (726065), where an old weather-boarded mill stands behind trees by its mill-pond. From here the path continues through the pasture fields, taking a short cut under two red-brick bridges to emerge by the Chelmsford bypass which accompanies the walk noisily for the next mile.

Soon the Chelmer enters that rural Essex landscape that drivers on the A12 never see. The flat fields are overlooked to the south by the swell of the Danbury Ridge, crowned with trees where it rises above the silver-green willows that frame the white-painted mill on the river below Little Baddow[1] (760083). Wide views, big skies, narrow lanes and intensely-cultivated fields are the keynotes of this countryside. From the mill you can either enjoy a tranquil ramble on through the Essex Naturalists' Trust's Chelmer Meadows nature reserve, or make a detour along the side road (761083) to visit the church of St Mary the Virgin[2] (764081) with its fourteenth-century oak figures of a man and a woman and its beautifully carved seventeenth-century monument to Henry Mildmay and his two wives. From the church the lane climbs past the intriguingly named Holybreds Farm to the Rodney pub[3] in Little Baddow (778080), then turns downhill to reach the river at Paper Mill Lock[4] (777090). The Chelmer & Blackwater Canal Cruising Company operates river cruises from here in summer – a pleasant way to get back to Chelmsford if you don't want to do the rest of the walk to Maldon.

Downstream of Paper Mill Lock the river gets heavy recreational use – canoeists, motor-boat cruisers and fishermen share the water with the swans, ducks and moorhens. The tiny thirteenth-century All Saints Church at Ulting[5] (801088) makes a charming picture, almost

All Saints Church at Ulting, half hidden among trees on the bank of the Chelmer.

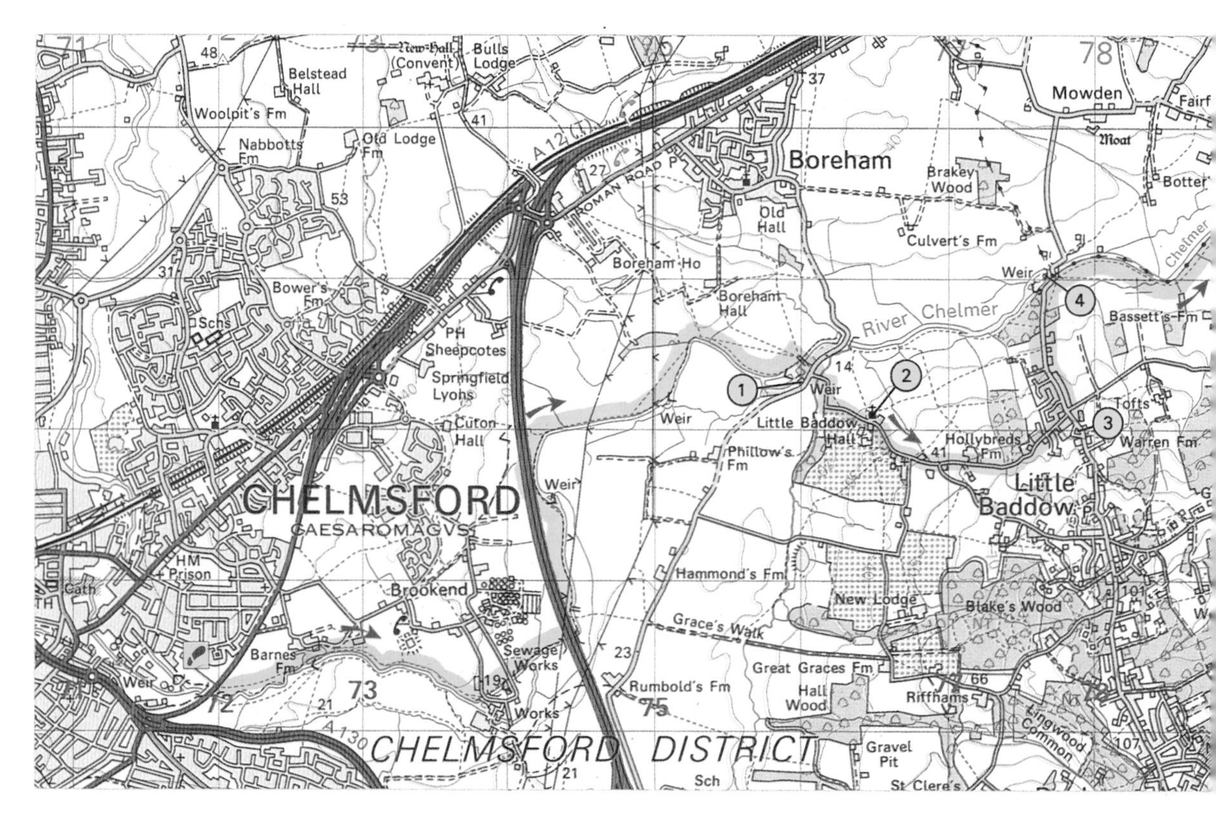

hidden among trees on the far bank with its octagonal wooden spire reflected in the river. Beyond the church the Chelmer makes a horse-shoe bend round a wild, sedgy area of gravel pits before reaching Hoe Mill Lock[6] (808082) where the old lock-keeper's house stands above the lines of moored boats. Cross here by the bridge to the north bank of the river and walk on down the widening valley where herons patrol the banks and the willow avenues give way to more open farmland.

Just south of Langford is a complicated meeting-place of rivers and canal[7] (840084), overlooked by a grand house built on the site of the twelfth-century Beeleigh Abbey. Cross the Chelmer by the lock bridge, and then the long weir by another concrete bridge. Here the River Blackwater flows down from the north and bypasses the Chelmer through the Langford Cut – under the red-brick bridge facing you – to reach the estuary by its own mouth. In times of flood, however, the Blackwater overflows down the weir into the Chelmer, whose wide, muddy banks show the influence of sea tides.

Keep to the right of the red-brick bridge, and just before reaching the shaven greens of Maldon Golf Club bear sharp right through the trees to come to the flood wall on the left bank of the Chelmer. The river snakes towards the broken arches of a viaduct[8] (846076) which was opened in 1889 to carry the New Essex Line of the Great Eastern Railway from Woodham Ferrers into Maldon. It survived until 1959, but for the last twenty years of its life only goods crossed the river.

The path runs under the viaduct arches and on for a final half mile by a silted-up pool to the A414 road bridge, known locally as Fullbridge[9] (851074). Here you can turn right and climb up steep Market Hill into Maldon on its hilltop site. The town contains some fine old pubs – the King's Head and the Blue Boar are two good examples – a fifteenth-century Moot Hall and All Saints Church with its triangular tower.

Alternatively you can carry on beyond Full-bridge to explore the waterside industries which are still carried on here: the flour mills on the quayside, the boat yard and the Maldon Crystal Salt Company works where sea salt is panned in the way it has been for centuries. The church of

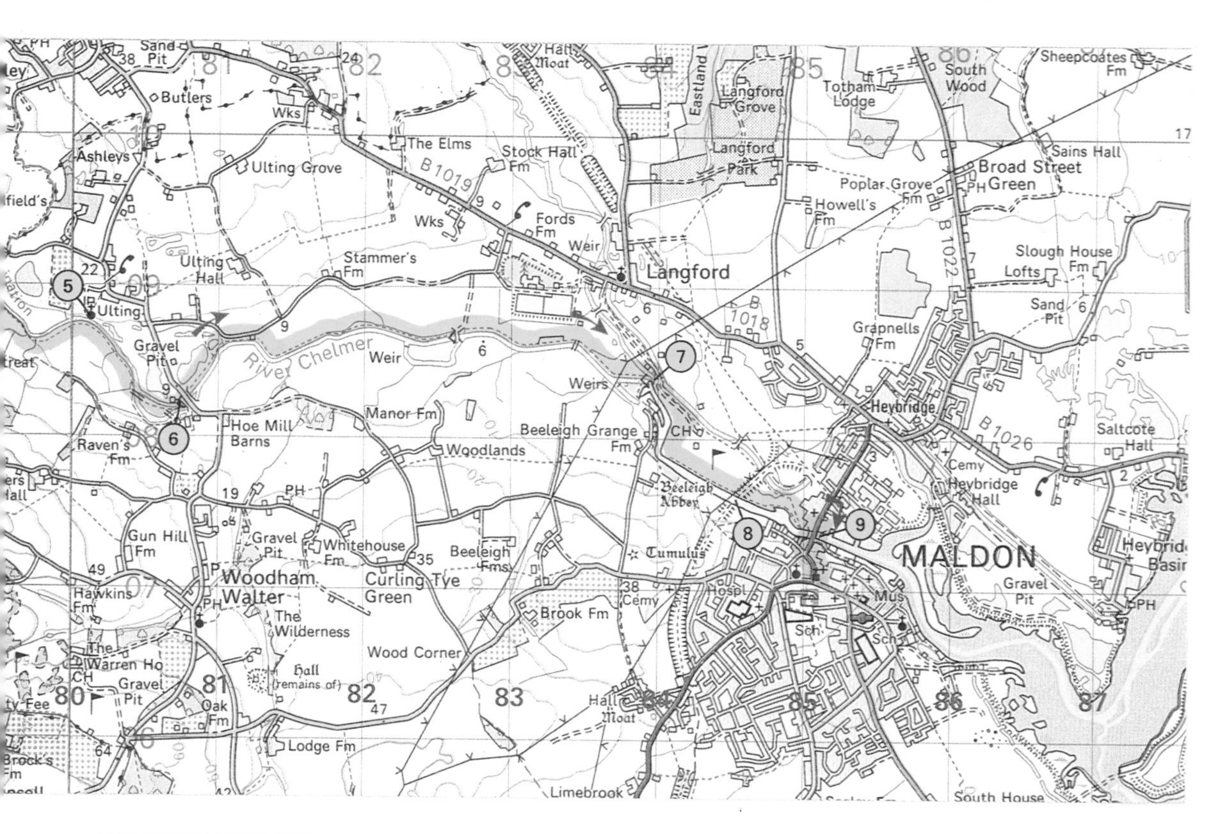

St Mary the Virgin (857068) overlooks the water beside the cosy Jolly Sailor pub, a good place to end the walk on the muddy and windy Blackwater estuary.

Straight willow avenues, big skies and low ridges – the rural Essex of the River Chelmer east of Chelmsford.

River Stour – Constable Country

OS 1:50,000 Sheet 168
$3\frac{1}{2}$ miles

Meandering with the River Stour for a couple of miles through the lush meadows of John Constable's Dedham Vale, this walk presents you with one famous view after another. It is a good idea to take a book containing Constable's best-known landscape scenes (Edward Allhusen's *John Constable*, published in 1976 by the Medici Society, is an excellent companion) so that you can fit paintings and countryside together. Remarkably little has changed here in the century and a half since the painter died.

Constable was born in 1776 at East Bergholt,

two miles north-east of Dedham at whose river bridge[1] the walk begins (057335). For a time he was apprenticed to his father Golding Constable, a well-to-do miller who owned the two watermills at Flatford and here at Dedham. *Dedham Lock and Mill*, painted in 1820, shows the old brick mill (later replaced by the present one), its mill-pond, sluice and the lock which admitted barges to the upper reaches of the Stour. Dedham's late fifteenth-century church and wide, tree-lined High Street of half-timbered medieval houses are well worth a visit.

From the bridge you walk up the B1029 road, turning left past the mill by a red-brick house into a lane to reach a watersplash. Go over the stile on the right (058335) and pass through the grounds of pink-faced Dedham Hall[2] to bear left at the top of the drive onto a footpath dropping diagonally down through cornfields and trees towards the Essex bank of the Stour (065336). The broad stretch of river which you follow from this point down to Flatford is in fact a canal cut when the Stour was being opened up for barge traffic in the early eighteenth century – the

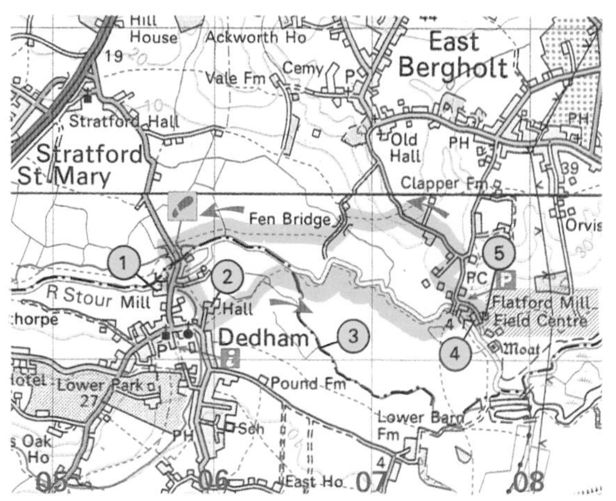

original course of the river is marked by a narrow channel[3] which runs in the fields to your right.

Handsome trees dominate these water meadows where sheep and cows graze. The path winds beside the river among gnarled old willows to reach Flatford by a bridge where you can compare the view with the one John Constable painted in *Flatford Mill* (1817). His impatient lad astride a huge, placid barge horse has his present-day counterpart in the boys waiting with bated breath for a bite on their fishing lines – otherwise it's all much the same tranquil scene of water, trees and mellow buildings. There is a superb and photogenic view of the mill across the water a few yards further down the bank. To reach the mill, cross the bridge and turn right down the lane by the thatched sixteenth-century Bridge Cottage (teas, boat hire, Constable exhibition, shop). Just beyond is the brick-floored dry dock of *Boat-*

Golding Constable's mill at Flatford. Mellow is the only word for this lovely old brick building.

The house that all the visitors come to see – Willy Lott's cottage, looking just as John Constable painted it in *The Haywain*.

building near Flatford Mill (1815), recently rediscovered complete with the skeleton of one of Golding Constable's river barges – perhaps the very one painted by his son.

At the end of the lane is Golding Constable's mill[4], given to the National Trust in 1943 and now a field studies centre. Across the mill-pond stands a feature of the most famous scene of all – Willy Lott's cottage[5], which overlooks the carters, horses, spaniel and wagon in the sun-splashed *Haywain* of 1821.

From Flatford Mill retrace your steps up the lane past Bridge Cottage to the top of the large car-park on the hillside, and turn left into a narrow lane which climbs in half a mile to a right-hand bend (072339). A stile on your left brings you onto a path descending the slope of a field, from which there is a wide view over the whole of Dedham Vale: poplars, willows and oaks standing tall above the corn fields and meadows with the tower of Dedham Church above all, reaching up into those broad Constable skies. Gleams of the Stour's shallow bends complete the scene from *The Valley of the Stour, with Dedham in the distance* (c 1805).

The path turns left at the foot of the slope (068339) to cross a wooden footbridge and bear right (067337) into a tunnel of trees. It runs in the leafy gloom before emerging into the meadows beside the Stour. From here it's a short walk back to the Riverside Tea Gardens at Dedham Bridge, where you can hire a boat and have the pleasure of doing the whole thing over again – by river, this time.

River Blyth

OS 1:50,000 Sheet 156
6 miles

The church of the Holy Trinity at Blythburgh[1] (450753) is a church only in name – its local title of 'Cathedral of the Marshes' fits it better. It stands splendidly above the wide, flat meadows where the River Blyth meanders to the sea, a monument to Blythburgh's great days as a trading port in the Middle Ages. As ships increased in size and the river channel became too narrow to hold them, so the town declined. Nowadays it's a quiet little cluster of houses around the magnificent church whose fourteenth-century tower points up into a great bowl of sky.

The body of Holy Trinity is so full of treasures that you could happily spend an hour exploring them. The eleven carved and painted angels in the wooden roof survived the crashing through of the spire in 1577 – they were luckier than two members of the congregation in the church at the time – and the marksmanship of Cromwell's soldiery in 1644 when they came to Blythburgh under the command of William Dowsing, notorious despoiler of Popish images. Dowsing ripped up the brasses in the tomb slabs, but luckily his zeal did not extend to the fifteenth-century bench ends showing the Seven Deadly Sins, among them a leering Slander with his tongue hanging out, a pot-bellied Gluttony and Avarice putting his money where his brains are. The crooked brick floor and tall arches of the nave are bathed with light from the clerestory windows by day, and by night the outside of the church gleams with floodlight. Neglect during the last century and death-watch beetle during this almost made an end of that lovely roof, but tremendous efforts by local people (and visitors' pennies in the collecting box) keep the curly-haired angels flying.

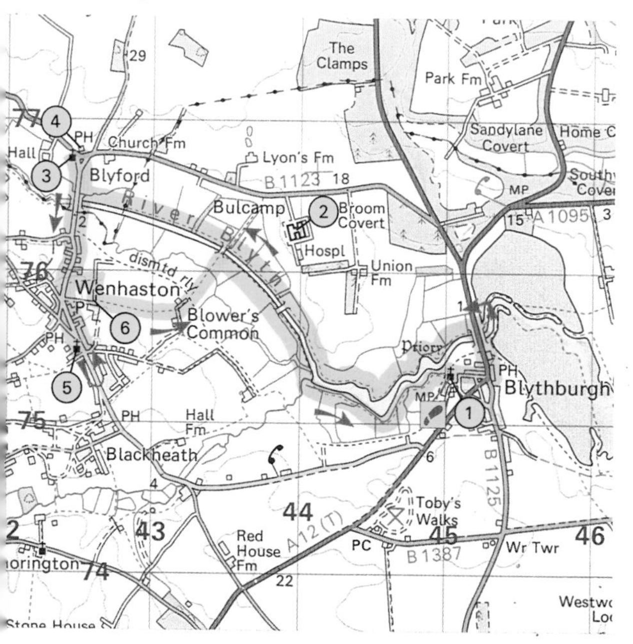

A lane leads from the church past the Priory, a handsome old house in whose garden stand the remains of the twelfth-century Augustinian priory of Blythburgh. The White Hart on the A12 (452755) serves good food and Adnams beers from nearby Southwold. The garden behind the pub, with swings and an aviary, looks out over the islands of muddy saltings in the broadening mouth of the River Blyth.

Walk north up the A12 to cross the river and turn left at a public footpath sign (452757) onto the river bank path, with a fine view to your left of the Cathedral of the Marshes. Sunlight pouring through its windows gives the church a lightness and transparency from this angle at odds with its great size. The salt-brown channel of the river bends through the meadows between acres of feathery reeds under enormous skies. The path leads west under the red-brick sprawl of Bulcamp old people's hospital[2] (440762), which was built in 1765 as a 'House of Industry', a euphemism for a workhouse. Local government laws at the time forced the poor of several parishes in the area to be housed together in the one building, which led to an attack on the new workhouse by an enraged mob. They succeeded in damaging their target, but when the excitement had died down it was repaired and the overcrowding went on.

From the bridge below Blyford (425765) a lane rises to the tiny hamlet – a farm, a pub and a fine pink-faced hall among trees behind All

Saints Church[3]. A round-arched Norman doorway opens into a plain, narrow nave where a battered wooden cross hangs by the pulpit, inscribed 'Capt W E Day RE. Killed in Action 5th June 1916. RIP.' This was not one of the droves of beardless youths slaughtered on the Somme, but an experienced officer in early middle age. He had been in France for just two months when the news of his death arrived at Blyford Hall. Remembrance Day poppies pushed into the framework of the wooden cross show how the memory of this second son of the family is still kept green. Across the road the Queen's Head[4] is a cheerful, low-ceilinged old smugglers' pub serving Adnams ales and bar food.

You recross the river to reach the village of Wenhaston, where the church of St Peter[5] (425755) contains an item that William Dowsing would have given his eye teeth to get his hands

Looking over the reed-fringed River Blyth towards Blythburgh.

on – and what bigotry didn't destroy, ignorance almost did. The story goes that during a restoration of the church in 1892 the old coat of arms board was pulled down from its niche in the chancel arch and thrown out to rot in the churchyard. A heavy shower of rain swept over the village, and as it washed away the surface layer of paint on the board fiendish faces and naked bodies began to show through. Cleaned up, the original decoration stood revealed as a pre-Reformation 'Day of Judgement' scene. The colours still glow from the huge, barbaric picture where it now stands in a place of honour in St Peter's. On the left St Peter himself welcomes pasty-faced kings and bishops, and someone in a smart red hat with ribbons, into the New Jerusalem; in the middle a grinning, warty-nosed devil waits for his share of the souls being weighed in a balance; on the right the damned are in the process of being chained up in Hell like passengers on a crowded ferry – Hell itself is the gaping mouth of a beast that looks like an uneasy cross between a fish and a bear. A harlot is carried off kicking and screaming over the shoulder of a demon, while his colleague blows a blast from a serpentine horn in the ear of another wrongdoer. The middle ground of the

picture holds various lesser souls creeping around aimlessly behind low hedges – perhaps they are doing time in Purgatory. All these sinners and saints are stark naked. Above all a red-robed Christ sits calmly on a rainbow, gazing down at this vivid, savage scene.

From the church you walk back through Wenhaston, turning right at a public footpath sign over a stile just above Hill Farm (424759). The path curves in a dog-leg round the field edges before striking out[6] in a bee-line for the distant tower of Holy Trinity church at Blythburgh. From Blowers Common (432758) – a lonely couple of houses at the end of a lane – you walk down to the Blyth (435761), bearing right here along the river bank. Holy Trinity tower soon reappears over the fringed heads of the reeds, which give good cover to herons, snipe and a variety of ducks. A final half-mile through the meadows brings you back under the shadow of the Cathedral of the Marshes.

The Cathedral of the Marshes: Holy Trinity at Blythburgh, dominating the flat landscape.

River Nar

OS 1:50,000 Sheet 132
7 miles

When the Marriott brothers began to build their maltings in the 1830s near the river at Narborough, the ancient town had been gradually declining for centuries into a roadside village. There was still some bustle around the river, which had been canalized in 1759 and carried cargoes of coal as well as bones for the crushing mill just downstream of Narborough. (This was the legal traffic – tobacco, French brandy and silk came free of excise duty and under cover of dark to be hidden away in the nearby marshes.) The Ship Inn was the centre of social life where the bargemen would down their six free pints, courtesy of the barge owners.

Robert Marriott was a giant of a man, more popular in the village than either squire or parson, a superb wrestler and swimmer who dominated any company he was in. He and his brother virtually ran Narborough, owning maltings, bone mill and the rights to the navigation tolls. The farmers in the neighbourhood grew some of the best barley in the country, and soon the maltings were sending barge-loads of malt downriver to Kings Lynn. Robert Marriott ended up the owner of the handsome red-brick Tudor mansion of Narborough Hall. He would be puzzled to see present-day Narborough split in two by thundering traffic on the A47, its water-mill standing empty and Marriott's Maltings crumbling around the little industrial enterprises that now occupy the buildings.

From the Ship Inn (746133) you turn right up the main road to cross the River Nar at the brick-built mill[1] where fresh trout from the adjacent Narborough Trout Farm are sold to passers-by. A few yards up the road a wooden public footpath fingerpost on the right (747131) points out a detour around the houses that brings you out on the south bank of the river opposite the maltings[2]. The Nar flows fast over a gravel bed where green wigs of weed trail in the current. The path follows the bank westward to the junction of the river and a side-channel to the maltings, where the rotting remains of one of the Marriotts' barges can be seen sunk into the tip of the 'island' between the two streams. The brothers owned forty barges in 1845, the heyday

The River Nar rushes past the great water-wheel of the Marriott brothers' bone mill, now rusted and immobile.

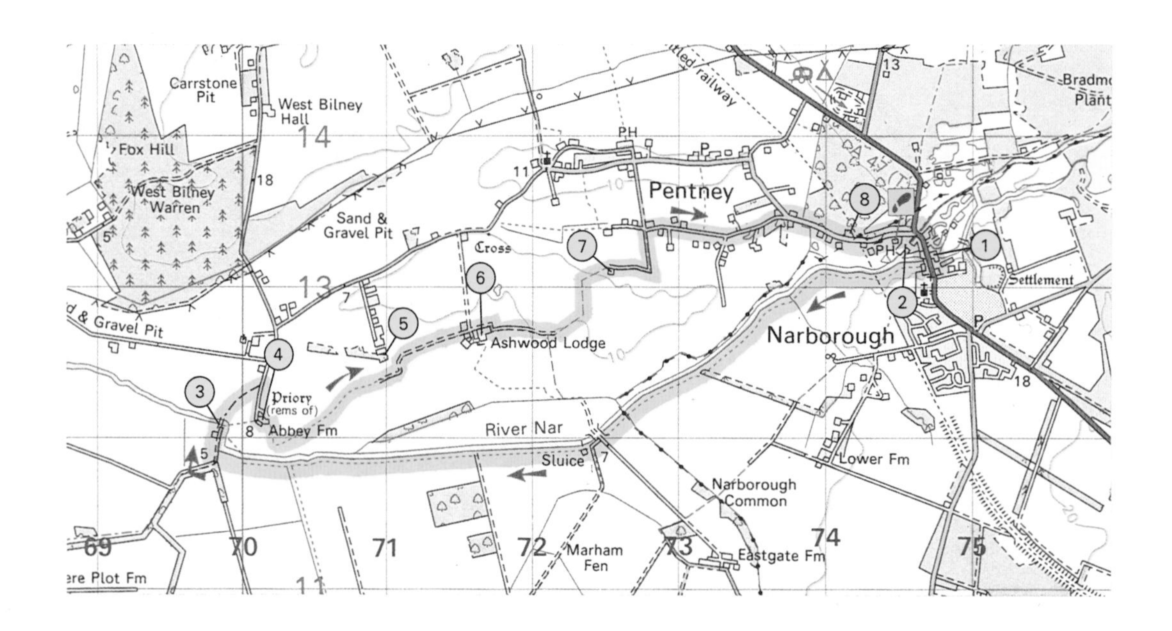

of the maltings, but the railway arrived the following year to kill the Nar navigation by slow starvation – it finally gave up the ghost in 1884, by which time there were fewer than ten barges plying the river. After fiercely opposing the railway the Marriotts swallowed their pride and reached out to the iron road by way of a siding. For more than a century railway and maltings benefited each other, but harsh economic reality put paid to both in 1968.

Turning your back on the grey château-like roofs of the maltings you walk on past the stumpy piers of the bridge that carried the trains across the Nar (744131). The gravel bed of the river is sheathed from here on in a coat of waterproof clay in which can be seen the wooden bars that show where the staunches stood. These were a primitive kind of lock behind whose gates the water was dammed up; on releasing it the waiting barges were swept forward into the next level of the river. This section of the Nar winds gently between lines of willows beyond which the cornfields stretch away, smaller and with more hedges than the Fenland prairies further west. Wigeon and mallard fly up from the water, jays screech among the trees and invisible larks sing overhead.

Where the Marriotts' bone-crushing mill stood there's nothing but a tangle of bushes framing a rare treasure of industrial archaeology – the sixteen-foot diameter water-wheel, rusty and lichen-blotched but still intact and in place above the lock. Bone-crushing seems a ghoulish business, but it provided excellent fertilizer for the heavy local soil. The bones were brought here by barge, crushed and then powdered between stone mill-wheels, three of which still lie half-buried on the far bank. Some of the bones were of exotic origin, stripped from the carcasses of Greenland whales in the blubber sheds at King's Lynn.

From the water-wheel the path runs on to a flow-gauging station (723119), where there's an abrupt change of character in both countryside and river. Suddenly the trees that have lined the Nar all but disappear, the landscape flattens, the fields enlarge to five times their previous size and the Nar ceases its gentle curving and flows in a disciplined straight line for nearly two miles before bending round the impressive ruins of the gatehouse of Pentney Priory. Here you cross the water over a rickety bridge[3] (699121) and enter a green lane to turn right (701123) down a farm track leading to the priory gatehouse[4] (701121).

The Nar valley earned the nickname of 'Holy Land' because of the number of religious houses along its length, and Pentney Priory must have been one of the finest if its entrance is anything to go by. It is a great block of flint and dark red medieval bricks in the Decorated style, nearly fifty feet high, its central double window standing over a wide gateway. A colony of rooks caws and flaps around its tottering battlements, and the interior is choked with grassy rubble fallen from the walls. Behind it, and dwarfed by it, shelters Abbey Farm, the two buildings standing alone in the fields. They make a strange and poignant sight, a lonely remnant of the Norman priory whose church and buildings perched here on a knoll known as the Isle of Eya. They were completely encircled by water,

The impressive buildings of Marriotts' Maltings, once the industrial heart of Narborough.

and could only be reached by boat. Perhaps the legendary liaison between Prior Codde of Pentney and the Abbess of Marham Abbey was conducted afloat – a medieval shipboard romance.

The footpath back to Narborough is obscure and unmarked, and the farmers have sacrificed much of it for the sake of a couple of extra feet of produce. Go over a gate at the far side of the field below the farm and turn left along the hedgerows, keeping them on your left and aiming for the house with a centrally placed chimney seen ahead across the fields. Half-way there you pass below a sinister group of battery sheds[5] crouching low behind a screen of trees with blank windows and immense runs of grey roofing. Here a rutted track (710124) leads between the farm buildings at Ashwood Lodge[6] (715127) to end at a drainage ditch (721127). You work your way around the field edges where the earth clots your boots into heavy lumps to reach a derelict red-brick barn[7] (725131) from which a green lane runs up to the road (728134). Turn right here for the final one and a quarter miles back to the Ship Inn at Narborough. On the outskirts of the village stands the railway station[8] (742133), complete with awning, ornate iron brackets, yellow-brick offices, platforms and a tiny bay-windowed and diamond-paned station master's house beside the road. Shortly before the First World War he and his family were rehoused in the solid building below the station. He must have been glad to leave those cramped little quarters, for all their style.

River Witham

OS 1:50,000 Sheet 121
$4\frac{1}{2}$ miles

This walk along the River Witham draws a line along the history of the city of Lincoln, beginning at the foot of the ridge on which the old town stands. It runs south through the Victorian extension to the city which helped to revive it from centuries of slump and decay, and enters the suburbia of twentieth-century Lincoln. Finally it climbs to the top of the limestone cliff for a panoramic view of both old and new city.

From the railway station entrance, turn left and walk to the corner of the High Street (974710). From here there is a splendid view up to the cathedral[1] standing 200 feet above the river on its bluff, the tops of the towers thrusting up nearly as high again. The Romans, who knew a good defensive site when they found one, built their fortress up there shortly after invading, and the town of Lindum Colonia grew up round it. The Romans' newly-engineered roads helped to develop the settlement – Ermine Street and the Fosse Way met here. The Danes held the town as a local government centre. When the Normans arrived they expressed their power and permanence in building the castle[2] that stands to the west, and made a start on the cathedral. It was finished by 1280, and the city below prospered with it. Wool and cloth – including Lincoln Green for the merrie men of Sherwood Forest – travelled inland and abroad by the navigable waterways. The Witham was crowded with vessels and the narrow streets of the old town were a magnet for trade. However, the country for miles around was a dreary waste of fens, sand heaths and pools, undrained and unworked. Famine and plagues were frequent – half the population died of the Black Death in the summer of 1349 alone. As the great sand bars off the east coast were finally broached and washed away by the sea, the emerging ports began to take Lincoln's trade. New through roads between North and South were built, isolating the city among its heaths and bogs. A population of 6,000 when the Normans were here had shrunk to 2,000 by the mid-fifteenth century. When Daniel Defoe visited Lincoln 300 years later, it was still an 'ancient, ragged, decayed, and still decaying city.'

However, where Bath led, Lincoln could follow. The city took on the role of a fashionable resort, the Witham navigation was improved and things began slowly to get better. During the eighteenth century small industries sprang up along the river – sail and rope manufacturers, boat yards, breweries, maltings. The countryside was properly drained around this time, and a hundred years later the railway brought a lifeline to the outside world. Shortly afterwards iron foundries and heavy engineering works

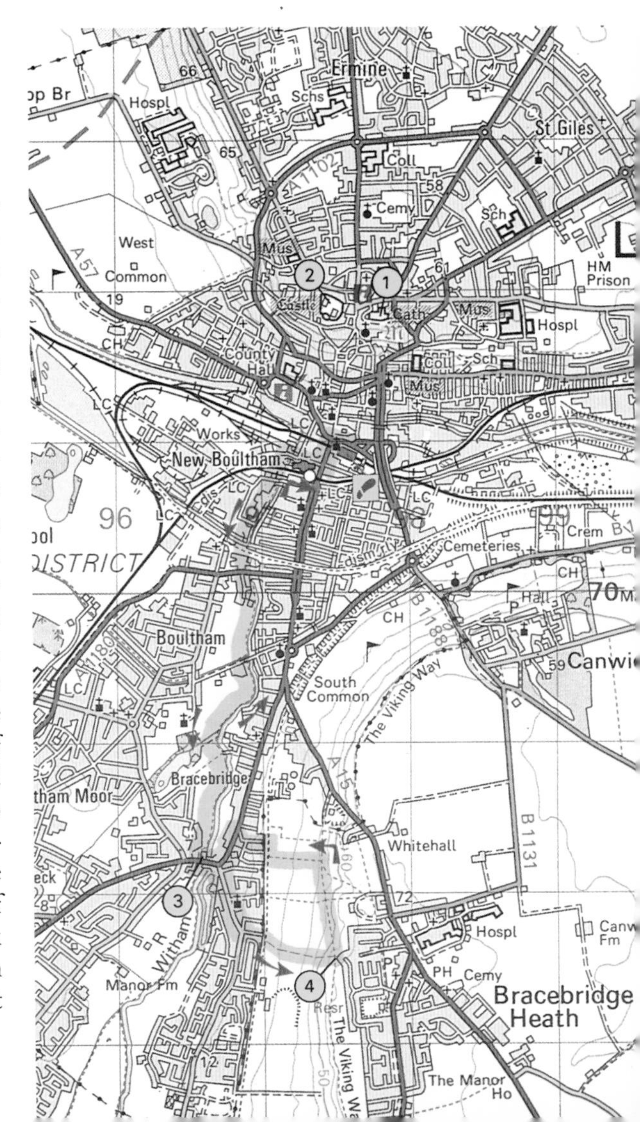

were set up south of the old town, and the revival was complete. Almost all the building along our route is from this later period, when the long terraces of workers' houses were run up to feed the insatiable demand for manpower from the engineering works: Ruston's, who produced steam locomotives, agricultural machines and, during the First World War, planes such as the Sopwith Camel; Foster's, who turned out the tanks that made such a sensational impact in France when they first went into action in September, 1916.

Turn left down the High Street, over the level crossing, and right at the next set of traffic lights into St Mark Street. Pass the bus station and cross the Witham (972709), turning left down steps to the path beside the river. Here the industrial energy of the Victorians is on display – iron bridges, red-brick warehouses, railway offices and signal boxes. Confined by buildings and walls, the scummy waters of the Witham become gradually cleaner as it passes the tall red chimney of Crown Mills and a gas turbine plant. A lift bridge spans the river just beyond; it was raised in its framework on runners to allow laden barges to go underneath.

On the far side of the A1180 there is a handsome variation on the standard brick terraces – a solid villa beside the Witham, ornamented with Edwardian terracotta moulded plaques. From here swans and water-lilies further improve the river scene, and there are varied modern houses on the bank. At a footbridge the path divides – take the left-hand fork to continue along the flood wall. Long ribbons of 1920s and

The Viking Way gives wonderful ridge-top views over Lincoln and the surrounding countryside.

1930s housing away to the left join the city to Bracebridge, a small village in Victorian times which was separated from Lincoln by a mile of open fields.

At Bracebridge a three-arched bridge carries the A46 road across the Witham (966682). You leave the river here and walk up to the Plough Inn[3] next to the bridge. It serves food and has a river terrace and a back garden with swings, slides, a climbing frame and a giant 'old woman's shoe'. The bar is plush and panelled in Edwardian style.

Cross the bridge and go right at the traffic lights (take care!) up Brant Road past the Romanesque All Saints Church (968679). Continue along Brant Road, turning left where the road bends right to go up a track by the side of Brantley Manor (968677). The track ends in a field (970677); bear right and up the field edge to a gate, then on up to meet the Viking Way long-

Looking back towards the city of Lincoln from the southern outskirts.

distance footpath on the top of the ridge[4] (975676). Turn left here and walk along, with Lincoln ancient and modern laid out at your feet like an animated map and a view beyond over twenty miles or more of flat countryside and steaming cooling towers.

At the far side of the second field (974682), turn downhill by a hedge graced with tall ash trees to the bottom of the hill. Bear right into Poplar Street, then left around the towering Gothic of Grosvenor Hall onto the A46 (968684). From here any bus that passes will take you back to the railway station, or you can return to the river bank to walk north towards the cathedral, castle and old city.

River Humber

OS 1:50,000 Sheet 112
7 miles

'At Whitton's town end, brave boys, brave boys,
At Whitton's town end, brave boys,
At every door
There sits a whore
At Whitton's town end, brave boys'

Times have changed. Today Whitton is a quiet little village looking out across the broad River Humber from its position at the end of a ruler-straight road. It has a combined shop and post office off the main village street, where you should park your car – there is no room by the river itself, where the road comes to a stop. St John's Church, which you pass on your way down to the Humber, has a Norman tower and is heavily Victorianized inside.

A waymarked stile leads to the grass-smothered path on top of the flood wall (904246). From here there is a wide view over the mud banks of the Humber, more than a mile across at this point, to the hills behind the northern shore. Away to the east a tall chimney sends out a plume of smoke, and to its right rise the great supporting piers of the Humber Bridge, its suspension cables standing out in spidery lines against the sky. The only route across the river from Roman times was by ferry between South and North Ferriby, often a rough and sickening trip. In 1981 the opening of the Humber Bridge saved travellers a round journey of many miles and conquered one of the last great natural barriers in the country. It is the longest single-span suspension bridge in the world, 4,626 feet between the piers.

The mud banks in the Humber are marked by bright-red lightships – this is a dangerous section for navigation, and skippers skirting round Whitton Sand take their mark from St John's tower. Between the flood wall and the river is a strip of rough grazing and marsh where lapwings and oystercatchers feed. The black and white shelduck prefer the fields inland, behind which the tower of All Saints, Winteringham, stands under its hill.

Just before a warning beacon – like a red wicker wastepaper basket upside down on a pole – the rough path along the overgrown flood wall descends to a stony road on the landward side. Small brown reed buntings cling to the

reeds in the drainage ditch on the right of the road. The view over the river is blocked by the wall, but you can spring up onto the top from time to time to see the boats going to and from the docks at Goole, and the sunshine lighting up the great white blocks of the cement works at South Ferriby. Where a farm road leaves the track and runs straight across the fields to Marsh Farm, you rejoin the path on the top of the flood wall (924243)[1]. The mud banks in the river are piled up in thin ledges like the layers of a French pastry.

The path on the wall meets a road at the Humber Yawl Club (934228). A short lane to the left leads to Winteringham Haven[2], a narrow channel of sloppy, slimy mud where club members moor their boats. Ermine Street, the

Smoking chimneys are the only upstanding feature of the inland River Humber landscape.

great north road of the Romans, broke off here to continue by ferry over the Humber. At very low tides in times of drought the rotting remains of a jetty, which may have been built by the legionaries, can still be seen low down in the mud. The Haven continued to bring goods – coal, timber, malt and corn – to and from Winteringham until well into this century, but now the only bustle here is made by the yachtsmen.

Turn right from the river to walk down the road into Winteringham village. The Haven made it a 'great and populous town', with a market, fine buildings, a superb church and riverside activity which included wharves, shipbuilding and a ferry. But Ermine Street had been half-buried under sandstorms by the time of the Conquest, and was no longer the main South–North route. Gradually trade moved away to other sites along the Humber. During the nineteenth century Winteringham dipped a toe in the murky waters of the drug market, growing opium poppies for conversion to laudanum, that insidious addictive of so many unsuspecting ladies and gentlemen. Nowadays Winteringham is a pleasant, placid place where people still greet walkers with 'Where you been?', and have time to enjoy a chat about their village.

The muddy creek of Winteringham Haven where Romans crossed the Humber.

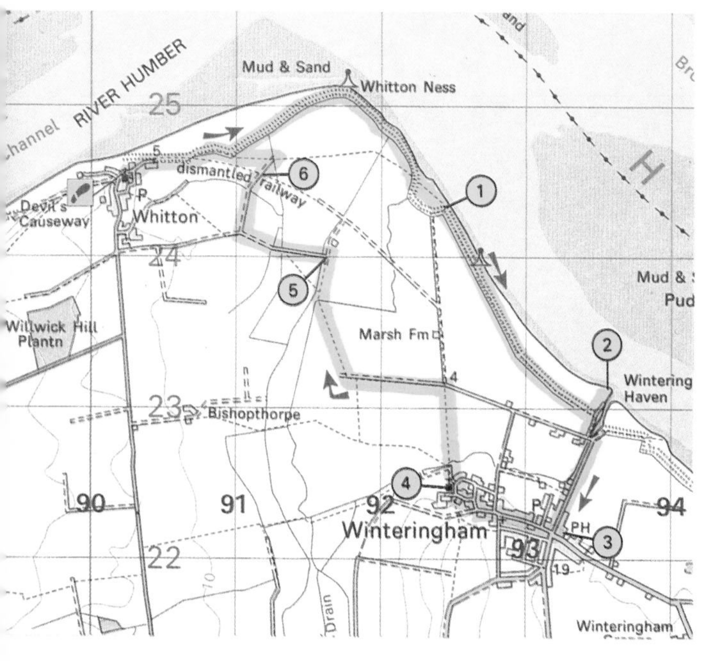

At the crossroads[3] (932222), turn right down West End past the Bay Horse pub – the post office opposite sells various goodies, including ice cream. You pass the decayed hulk of the red and white brick Wesleyan Chapel of 1891, which sports two six-pointed stars above its doors. All Saints Church[4], at the end of the winding road, has rounded Norman arcades on the north side, and a wonderful effigy of a thirteenth-century knight, probably a member of the Marmion family, who seems to have been both to and in the wars. Angels round his pillow guard his long sleep.

Walk down Meggitt Lane by the side of the church, and take the footpath (925226) which runs straight ahead below All Saints' towards Marsh Farm. The Humber Bridge rears above the fields to your right. Three hundred yards before the farm a wooden public footpath sign points you to the left (924232) along a farm road towards the tower of Whitton church. Where the road ends, turn right (917232) around two sides of a field, making for a group of red-painted silos ahead among trees. Turn left again before you reach them[5] (916240), and in a few hundred yards right again up a lane opposite a large old willow (910242). The path crosses the track of the disused light railway to Whitton[6] (917243), which was opened in 1910 but did not survive long. At the flood wall climb up onto the path and turn your back on the Humber Bridge for the last half mile into Whitton.

SECTION FOUR

The Midlands

River Avon (Stratford-upon-Avon)

River Windrush/River Eye

River Thames

River Nene

River Lugg

River Severn

River Dove

River Avon – (Stratford-upon-Avon)

OS 1:50,000 Sheet 151
10 miles

Tourists who are tired of Stratford-upon-Avon probably are not tired of life – just surfeited with Shakespeare. Here is a walk to revive those jaded palates. It only contains a couple of Shakespearian connections, but it does introduce you to the pretty, quiet villages along the banks of the Bard's river, and it ends where he ended – in Holy Trinity Church, where he lies beside the Avon.

> *'Daft Dorsington, lousy Luddington,*
> *Welford for witches,*
> *Binton for bitches,*
> *An' Weston at th' end of th' 'orld.'*

runs an old rhyme, and we pass through or very near to all except 'daft Dorsington.'

William Shakespeare lies buried in Holy Trinity Church beside the Avon at Stratford.

Just downstream from the fourteen stumpy, grey stone arches of the fifteenth-century Clopton Bridge (206548) is the red-brick bridge of 1826 that carried the long-defunct Stratford to Moreton-in-Marsh horse-drawn tramway across the Avon. From here the riverside path, fringed by weeping willows, follows the left bank of the river opposite the Royal Shakespeare Company's square brick theatre[1], opened in 1932, which has established Stratford as one of the world's major theatrical centres. Holy Trinity Church[2], where Shakespeare's remains lie buried, stands a little further downstream, its eighty-five-foot spire and golden-grey stone tower and walls reflected in the river.

Now the path passes Lucy's Mill[3] (200540), valued in the Domesday Book at ten shillings and 1,000 eels, but nowadays converted into luxury flats and valued at rather more. Behind it stands the monstrous block of another mill, itself now derelict. You go past a footbridge which crosses the river, and under the disused Stratford–Broome Junction line of the grandly-named Evesham, Redditch and Stratford-upon-Avon Junction Railway, at seven miles not much longer than its name, which opened in 1879 and closed for good in 1960. The path runs easily by the river to Weir Brake or 'Anonymous Lock'[4] (199536) – named thus in honour of the anonymous donors who supported the reconstruction carried out on the Upper Avon Navigation in the early 1970s by a mixture of volunteers and boys from the Hewell Grange Borstal. The river had been navigable since 1637, but the locks and other works had gradually fallen into disrepair. On the island by the lock gates a plaque carries the names of the crane driver and welder who worked on rebuilding the lock – a nice touch.

Here the footpath leaves the river and climbs the steep bank by zigzag wooden steps to run along the top among the trees (nightingales can be heard here on summer nights), with occasional glimpses of the river valley and ridge of hills to the north, once clothed with the Forest of Arden. Soon the path emerges into fields, dotted with masses of speedwell, and descends to Stannell's Bridge[5] (187533), a girder construction that carried yet another railway over the river – this time the line from Cheltenham. Keep the railway embankment on your right and go over a stile and through the embankment, guided by one of the helpful waymarks along the walk – a white arrow on an olive-green circle. Cross the River Stour by a footbridge[6] and walk on along the right side of the embankment through the flat watermeadows. The cottage of Ann Hathaway, Shakespeare's wife, stands on Shottery Hill to the north (184547). At a gate in the first hedge you come to, turn right and walk down to the river, which you follow below Milcote Manor (172523)[7] among enormous willow trees, each trunk a mass of knots, bumps, crevices and cracks. Milcote Manor's thick chimney stack is dated 1564, and the house is reputed to have been burned by Cromwell's troops in 1644; some local historians think it was the big house at Upper Milcote[8] (192528), a little behind you and to the east.

This spot was the scene of a gruesome episode in Elizabethan days. Ludovic Grevill had started to build a great house, Mount Grevill, and began to covet the money of one of his tenants. He murdered the man, and persuaded an accomplice to impersonate the victim and leave all his money to Ludovic in a sick-bed bequest. However, another member of the plot blurted out the story during a drinking bout. Ludovic soon shut this conspirator's mouth permanently and had his body thrown into a pond. The body was discovered there shortly afterwards and Ludovic Grevill sentenced to a horrible fate, that of being pressed to death; but as he had steadfastly refused to plead or say anything at all about the crime, his estates escaped the customary forfeiture to the Crown and passed safely to his son.

The spire of Luddington church overlooks the river on the opposite bank, and by the lock below the church the path turns up to the left over the ridge to join a grassy track[9] to Weston-on-Avon. The tiny fifteenth-century church of All Saints[10] (159519), built of butter-coloured

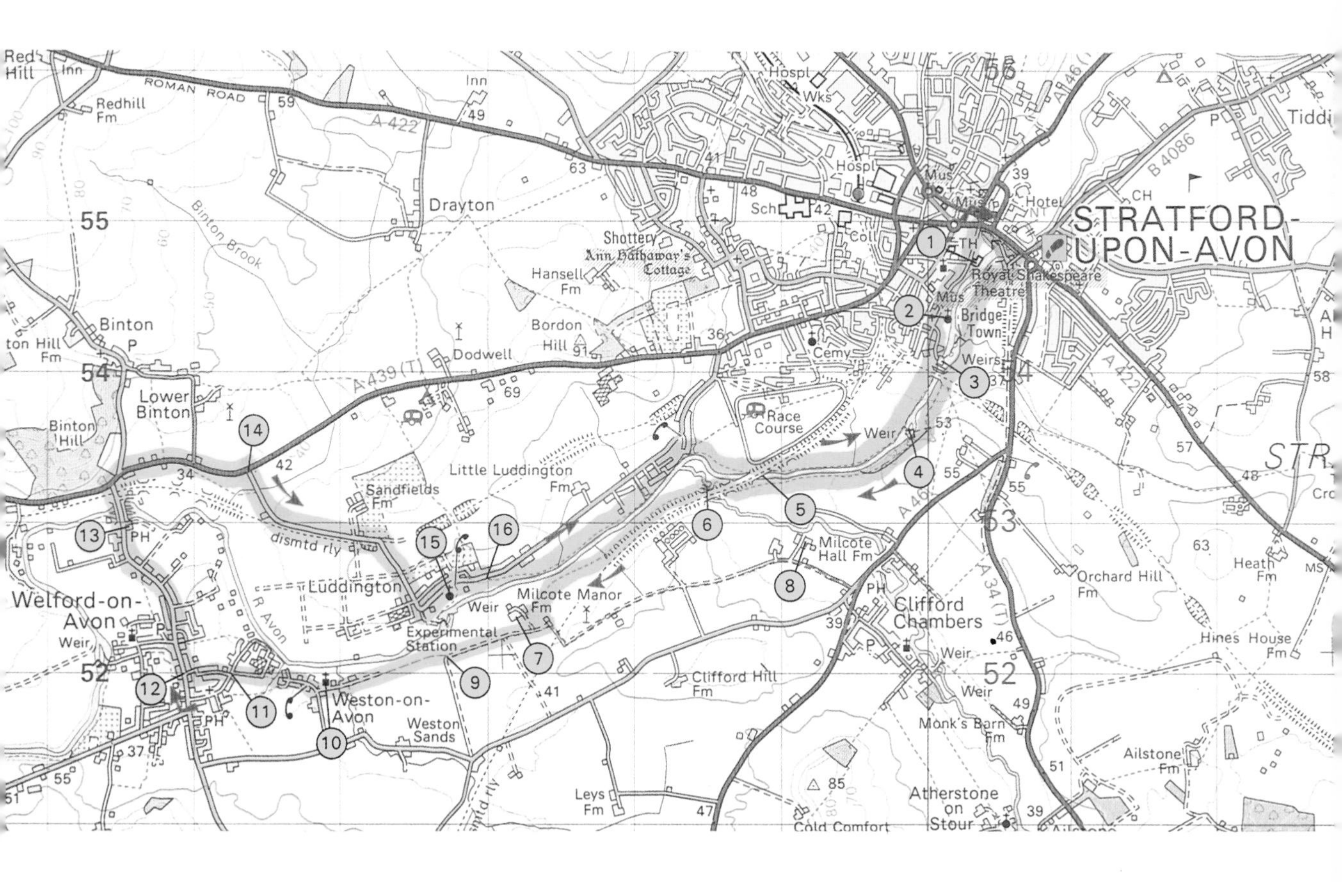

stone, contains some fine sixteenth-century brasses to the family of Ludovic Grevill, and the stumpy tower is adorned with four leering gargoyles – three crested devils and what looks like a nun playing the flute, all holding lead water pipes in their wide-open mouths. You follow the road through the little thatched village, curving left and round the top of the hamlet to go in front of glasshouses (154520) and reach a T-junction[11]. Turn left here, and immediately right down Millers Close to come to the road through Welford-on-Avon. Just up the road to the left is the village green with its seventy-five-foot maypole, topped by a weathercock.

Retracing your steps to the road junction with Millers Close[12], continue northwards through the village to Binton Bridges, where the Four Alls pub by the river[13] (145530) serves food and beer from the hand pump. The pub's name, graphically depicted on the sign outside, is taken from an ancient rhyme in the 'pity-the-poor-farmer' tradition:

'The King who rules over all
The Parson who prays for all
The Soldier who fights for all
The Farmer who pays for all.'

The public bar has a stained-glass window carrying the theme a stage further. The soldier is busy fighting the war from his easy chair, and hasn't noticed that his pint of ale is about to spill all over his knees. The farmer slumps in despair at his counting desk, obviously struggling with his EEC quotas. Only the red-robed king looks as if he's in control.

Apparently many customers feel the need to placate the river gods by offering them beer glasses – this is a constant problem for pubs with riverside gardens. The Four Alls charges a small deposit on glasses taken outside, but they still make a hefty loss this way in the summer. Fishing permits can be bought over the bar.

Now comes a stretch of road walking – up to the A439 Stratford to Evesham road, then turning right for half a mile of grass verge before going right again[14] (153533) for a long mile into the village of Luddington. WH Hutton, that sad Roman Catholic travel writer, said in 1914 of the village: 'There is no need to visit Luddington as there is nothing there.' Lucky Luddington! It has escaped most of the development suffered by villages in the area, and the black and white cottages stand peacefully by the road. An avenue of pollarded willows leads to the church[15] (167524), built in 1872 after a gap of nearly one hundred years during which the villagers of Luddington waited in vain for the old church, which had been burned down, to be replaced. They were eventually provided with a ferry across the Avon to take them to worship at Welford.

The dark interior – every window is filled with stained glass – holds an ancient Bishop's Bible, printed in 1595 and rescued from the flames. If legend were proven fact, this old bible would just have missed the glory of taking part in the marriage of William Shakespeare and Ann Hathaway in 1582 – for Luddington church is claimed as the scene of their wedding, though no records survived the fire to bear out the story.

From the church you continue along the road for a few hundred yards, ignoring the first wooden public footpath fingerpost and taking the second one[16] (170526) to drop down the bank to the river. Soon the path passes through the river frontages of the neat bungalow gardens that line the north bank of the Avon. Here is a perfect mallard's eye view of the British gardener at work – shaven lawns, immaculate flower-beds and little flights of steps adorned with helpful arrows taking the walker through the twisting obstacle course, over the tiny footbridges and round the compost heaps. Where the gardens end, the path goes on along the river bank, under Stannell's Bridge again and back to Lucy's Mill.

A lane at the back of the mill leads up to Holy Trinity Church (201543), our final stopping place. Glorious roof, wonderful windows, superb organ-loft, intricately-embroidered hassocks – all play second fiddle here to the row of well-worn stone slabs that lie side by side just inside the altar rail. At the extreme left lies Ann, beloved wife – and next to her the Swan of Avon himself. The celebrated lines on his memorial slab, supposedly self-composed, do not exactly reflect the richness of his genius, though they are direct enough:

A narrow boat chugs down the Avon at Luddington, where Shakespeare and Ann Hathaway are reputed to have been married.

'Good Frend for Iesus sake forbeare
To Digg the Dvst encloased heare
Blese be ye man y^{t} spares thes stones
And cvrst be he y^{t} moves my bones.'

Above the tomb is a bust of 1623 of the poet, reputed to have been taken from his death mask, with cheerful colour in the cheeks and a dapper waxed moustache.

Before leaving the church and returning through the RSC's garden to Clopton Bridge, do not miss the fifteenth-century misericordes carved in the dark wood of the choir seats. They include lively devils in various grotesque poses, a mermaid and merman, a lady with a distaff rising from a whelk shell, an ape in the act of providing a urine specimen in a flask, a woman eating a sausage – or is it a scold's bridle? – and a squabbling man and wife, he pulling her hair and trying to ward off her scratching fingernails aimed at his eyes, she pulling his beard and kicking him the while in a very tender spot. These unique carvings highlight the preoccupations, the fears and the sense of humour of the generations that produced William Shakespeare.

Rivers Windrush and Eye

OS 1:50,000 Sheet 163
6 miles

Bourton-on-the-Water is referred to in tourist brochures as the 'Venice of the Cotswolds'. It certainly shows signs of sinking under the weight of visitors in the summer months who come to be photographed on the eighteenth-century miniature stone bridges that span the shallow River Windrush as it runs beside the village's main street. This walk along the valley of the Windrush starts at the bridge on the western edge of the village (160210) that carries the A429 Cirencester to Stow-on-the-Wold road; and turns its back on Bourton's ice-cream and souvenir shops, the motor museum, the model railway and even the famous model village – though they lie in wait for you at the end of the walk.

The bridge[1], which stands on the site of the paved ford constructed by the Romans for their Fosse Way, carries a plaque on the Bourton side showing a figure of Capricorn, a goat with a salmon's tail – the badge of the Second Legion which was quartered at Salmonsbury Camp a quarter of a mile to the east of the village. The arches of the bridge are remarkable for their shallowness – three or four feet above the river, which is only three feet deep hereabouts. The path crosses the field on the right bank of the Windrush, making for a gate half-way between the river and the embankment of the disused Kingham Junction to Cheltenham railway[2]. This was opened in 1862 and closed for passenger traffic, much to local regret, in 1962. From the gate the path runs on a terrace overlooking the gently winding Windrush in the valley bottom, where swans contemplate their reflections as they sail serenely along. This is stone wall country, prosperous by virtue of the sheep that brought wealth to the Cotswolds in the Middle Ages, and the long runs of wall emphasize the

Tiny stone bridges span the River Windrush as it flows through Bourton-on-the-Water, the 'Venice of the Cotswolds'.

length of the valley. The stone wall below the railway comes gradually nearer, and the path climbs onto the railway track (152212), which it follows for a hundred yards before leaving it to run on the right and drop downhill to Little Aston Mill[3] (150213). The stone-built mill, whose race can be heard rushing from the interior of the garage, is sited prettily at the bottom of the valley beside the Windrush, which chuckles quietly over its shallow, weedy bed.

Cross the bridge and climb uphill to a T-junction, turning right to pass to the left of Aston Farm house. The track beyond heads for the woods, in which it switchbacks up and down—a muddy stretch, which drops gradually to meet the river. A series of stiles by red-painted gates leads to a road[4] (129225), where you turn right to cross the river on a raised footway by the cobbled ford and come to Lower Harford Farm. The path behind the house turns right through a waymarked gate and climbs the steep slope diagonally to the Naunton–Bourton road[5] (132227), up which you trudge for a mile with views widening out over the Windrush valley. At the T-junction at Wagborough Bush[6] keep straight on down a track and through a gate down the right-hand side of a copse (151229). Take the left of three gates and follow the field edge down to Upper Slaughter. The village and its twin, Lower Slaughter, look as pretty as a picture in the valley bottom, Upper Slaughter Manor and the spire of Lower Slaughter church dominating their respective stone clusters of houses.

Upper Slaughter Manor[7] (156230) was built in the year of the Dissolution of the Monasteries, 1539, and is a fine example of a Cotswold great house with its tall chimneys and rows of mullioned windows. Until recently open to the public, it is now strictly private. Follow the road through the village and round a left-hand bend by an old iron water pump. Turn right here at a green public footpath sign down a track which crosses the crystal-clear River Eye[8] (157232). Go diagonally right up the bank on the far side and make for a wooden kissing-gate half-way along the fence, from where the footpath runs in the fields just above the river. Upper Slaughter Manor shows to good advantage among the trees behind you on the right. Hug the river bank past the railed-off enclosures of the Cotswold Stud, with the red-brick chimney of Lower Slaughter mill ahead contrasting with the

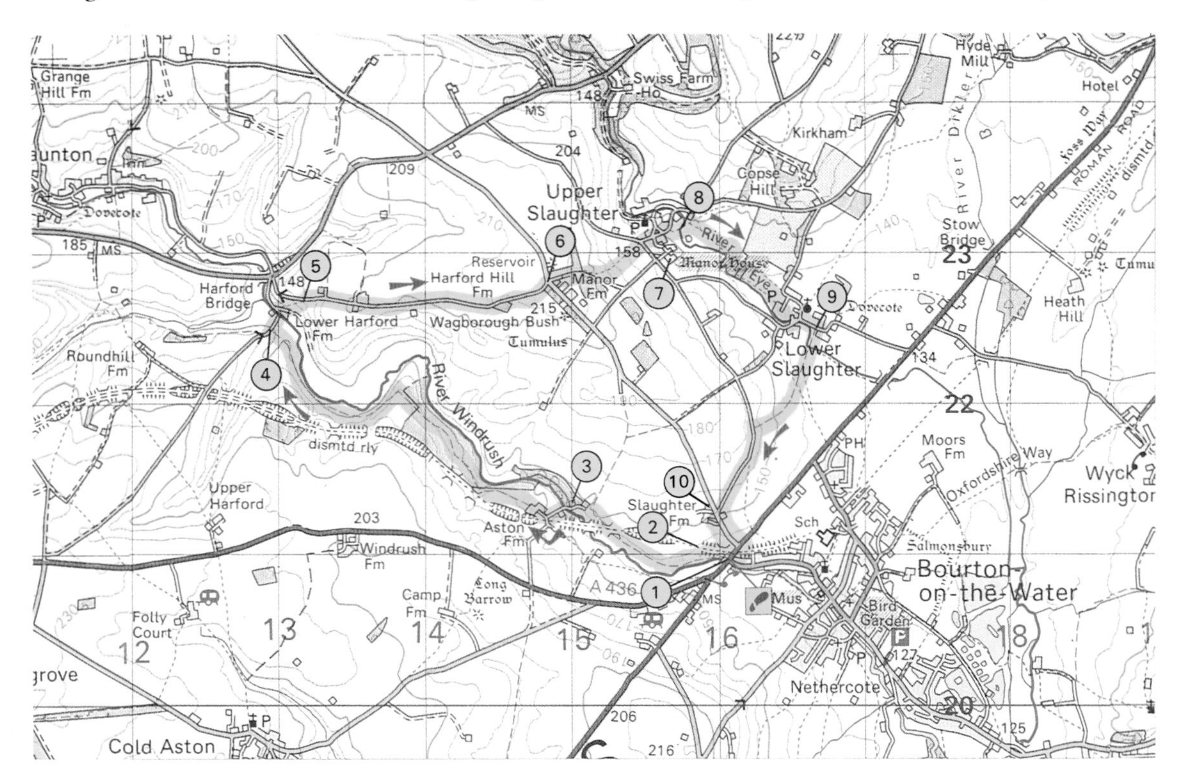

creamy Cotswold stone houses on each side of it.

The old mill (163226), a bakery since 1956, last ground flour in 1948, but the rusty and moss-grown wheel is still there. There has been a mill on this site since Domesday time. Lower Slaughter is another wonderfully pretty village, its river crossed by tiny stone bridges and its houses stone-walled and stone-tiled. St Mary's Church, built in 1867 to replace the previous one which was pulled down after it had fallen into ruin, contains brass plaques to members of the Whitmore family, who held the manor from the time of James I until they sold it in 1964 – after which the village awoke from the sleep of ages and began to allow some private building. Like Bourton it is thronged with visitors in the summer, but jealously clings to its lack of tourist facilities and unviolated charm.

Intrusive brick amid the classic Cotswold stone. The mill at Lower Slaughter stands with its wheel over the River Eye.

The Manor House next to the church is now a hotel and restaurant. Opposite the main gates (166225), turn right[9] down the riverside path which runs uphill past a public footpath sign on the left, and soon swings left (165222) as a tarmac track making for a line of modern houses on the main road. You keep straight ahead, however, mounting the slope with a hedge on your right to reach the lane at the top by a beech spinney (162219). Turn left here to Slaughter Farm[10], which has a line of ancient mill-wheels built into its boundary wall and a gate made of old horseshoes. Turn left again to reach the Fosse Way and Bourton Bridge.

River Thames

OS 1:50,000 Sheet 164
14 miles

Time this long walk properly (six–seven hours) and you can wind up at the Trout Inn[1] at opening time – a pub for all moods (485093). If you like laughter and liveliness between black beams and stone flags, the Trout rings with it; or you can sit outside and dream away a couple of hours to the sound and sight of the Thames seething through seventeenth-century Godstow Bridge. A tall, rickety wooden footbridge, green with age, crosses just below the weir onto the island opposite the pub known as Pixey Mead, complete with rockery, shaded seats and stone lion grinning like a Cheshire Cat among the trees.

The Trout had its origins as the hospice for Godstow Nunnery, founded in 1133, whose ruins stand in the meadow on the far side of the bridge (484091). You start the walk by crossing Godstow Bridge and its younger brother of 1780, which spans the cut leading from the main river to the lock just downstream. On your left are the pale walls of Godstow Nunnery[2], where fair Rosamund came to break her heart at leisure after her love affair with King Henry II. The lovers had been discovered in their Woodstock bower by Henry's wife, Queen Eleanor of Aquitaine. Rosamund returned to Woodstock to die, allegedly poisoned by the jealous queen, and her body was brought back to Godstow to be buried at the nunnery. King Henry in his grief marked every place where the bier-carriers stopped to rest between Woodstock and Godstow, and had a cross put up at each. Colonel

The River Thames at Godstow – Trout Inn on the left and the lock-cut bridge on the right, with little Godstow Bridge squeezed in between.

Fairfax destroyed the nunnery buildings during the Civil War, and the graveyard was dug up in 1790 when the lock was being built. The poet Thomas Love Peacock wrote of the nunnery ruins in *The Genius of the Thames*:

'The wind-flower waves, in lonely bloom,
On Godstow's desolated wall:
There thin shades flit through twilight gloom,
And murmured accents feebly fall.
The aged hazel nurtures there
Its hollow fruit, so seeming fair,
And lightly throws its humble shade,
Where Rosamonda's form is laid.'

This is very much an Oxford poet's walk; young Matthew Arnold, and later Laurence Binyon, based poems on the punt trips they took, like generations of Oxford undergraduates before and after them, along our route from Godstow Bridge to Bablockhythe.

At the far side of the bridge you drop down to the towpath at a public footpath sign marked 'Eynsham 4'. From the path there is a fine view back to the Trout Inn, the two small arches of the old bridge and the two wider ones of the newer. The riverside route goes under the new bypass and becomes a tarmac path along the gravelly banks of the Thames through flat, wide watermeadows. Wytham Great Wood rises on the left, and to the right the tall chimney at Wolvercote Mill sticks up above the trees. At King's Weir[3] (478103) the path passes the cranes and barges of the British Waterways Board and the grey-painted lock gates. In the lock wall is a notice 'Flood Mark March 1947', showing how the melt water from the great snowfall of that year rose to a foot below the rim of the lock. At each of these locks the channel was cut for the navigation through a loop of the river, leaving an island in mid-stream. These are curious places – some neatly gardened and tamed by the lock-keepers, others left to grow jungly.

The river-bank path runs on over the grass, the spire of Cassington Church away to the right and the white buildings of the University Field Station on the left below Wytham Great Wood. Coots and moorhens skitter over the water, getting up steam for their short, agitated flight from the intruding walkers. Swans congregate in the enormous empty meadows – I counted fifty-one in one gathering. The River Evenlode is neatly signposted as it comes down from Charlbury to join the Thames, and shortly afterwards the path meets the corner of Wytham Great Wood[4] (454092). Laurence Binyon, gliding upstream, noticed how the herons, disturbed at their fishing, made for the shelter of the trees:

'High woods, heron-haunted,
Rose, changed, as we rounded
Old hills greenly mounded,
To meadows enchanted.'

The path through the outskirts of the wood is churned up, not by the usual horses' hooves, but by bicycle tyres – typical Oxbridge! Swinford Toll Bridge[5] (443087), just below the lock, was built in 1777 by the Earl of Abingdon to carry the main road from Oxford to the West. There is a list of charges in the Toll House at the Eynsham end of the bridge. The original tolls were 1d per horse; ½d for a pedestrian; 5d a score of pigs; 4d a 4-wheel carriage; 2d for a carriage with less than 4 wheels; 1d for every horse, gelding, mare, mule or ass; ½d for an ox, bull, cow, steer or heifer; ¼d every calf, pig, sheep or lamb.

The walk continues through sedgy meadows to the premises of Oxford Cruisers[6] (443076) where a diversion is necessary up the drive to the road, turning right for 200 yards and then right again past Thames House down a signposted path to the river. Pinkhill Lock[7] (441072), built in 1791, was famous for the beauty of its garden, which gained the 'best-kept lock on the Thames' challenge cup in 1910 for its keeper. However, according to the present incumbent (who still keeps an immaculate garden), this was not an unmitigated blessing:

'Old Frank used to take it a bit far. He'd spend a couple of hundred pounds to get £50. One year when he didn't get the prize he chucked all his gardening tools into the lock. And if the general public stepped on his grass – he'd just about annihilate them. That garden inspection caused a lot of hard feeling among the lock-keepers. It was a good day when we did away with it.'

Half a mile upstream was Skinner's Weir

A gleam of spring sunshine on the Earl of Abingdon's toll bridge at Swinford.

(440065), where '... On a small island, planted with fruit trees, a thatched cottage offers repose and refreshment.' The thatched cottage was the Fish Inn, a profitable sideline for the keeper here. Nowadays the island[8] is completely overgrown, and from the bank there are no signs of the house or the fruit trees. A curiosity – the island appears to be moored to the far bank on its southern end. See if you can work out from the map how customers could get to the Fish Inn both by water and by land!

Farmoor Reservoir, hidden by its embankment on the left, is now left behind as the path approaches Bablockhythe. A solid mile of mobile homes stand shoulder to shoulder on the opposite bank. A line of tall poplars leads to the Ferry Inn on the west bank[9] (434042) – shuttered and closed when I was last here. The ferry, too – named in 1279 as the 'ferry of Babbelak', and in continuous operation for well over 1,000 years – was suspended, with no prospect of resumption. If you find it resuscitated, ring for it and cross the Thames to the pub for a well-earned drink. Matthew Arnold knew this spot well, and had his *Scholar Gipsy* lazing here on a summer's night:

'Thee, at the ferry, Oxford riders blithe,
Returning home on summer nights, have met
Crossing the stripling Thames at Bablock-hithe,
Trailing in the cool stream thy fingers wet,
As the slow punt swings round:
And leaning backwards in a pensive dream,
And fostering in thy lap a heap of flowers
Pluck'd in shy fields and distant wychwood bowers,
And thine eyes resting on the moonlit stream ...'

From the ferry, turn left and in twenty yards left again at the fork in the road (435042), up a track which dwindles to a horse-trodden path in the trees. It's a quaggy uphill stretch, but a footway of sorts runs among the bushes on the right. At the top of the hill you pass the isolated Long Leys Farm and turn left at the road[10] (452044) to Upper Whitley Farm with an extensive view ahead towards the Midland hills. Keep on a track to the left of the farm buildings, and bear right over a stile down the right-hand side of the copse below the farm to reach a pylon in the valley bottom (450050). Turn right here over a stile and follow the hedge down to the road at the foot of Farmoor Reservoir. Cross the road and turn right along the fence round the reservoir. This path leads to a stile[11] (451057), a track between bungalows and the B4017 road, up which you turn to the left to reach the gates of the reservoir. At the gatehouse you can buy a cheap permit, enabling you to walk around the two sheets of water separated by a causeway and join the Thames tow-path between Skinner's Weir and Pinkhill Lock – otherwise it's a mile of road walking to Oxford Cruisers.

From here you retrace your steps to Swinford Toll Bridge (the Talbot Inn, a quarter of a mile up the road towards Eynsham, has swings in the garden and serves good food and beer), and to the corner of Wytham Great Wood. Keep by the edge of the wood from the tow-path gate with a view opening up ahead of the dreaming spires and tower-blocks of Oxford. A little short of its north-eastern corner the path leaves the wood edge to cross a plank footbridge[12] (467093) and two waymarked stiles above the University Field Station[13]. Turn left down the hill, keeping to the right of the buildings and aiming for the farmhouse below[14] (476094. From here it is a short walk over stiles to the river bank, the bypass and the Trout Inn.

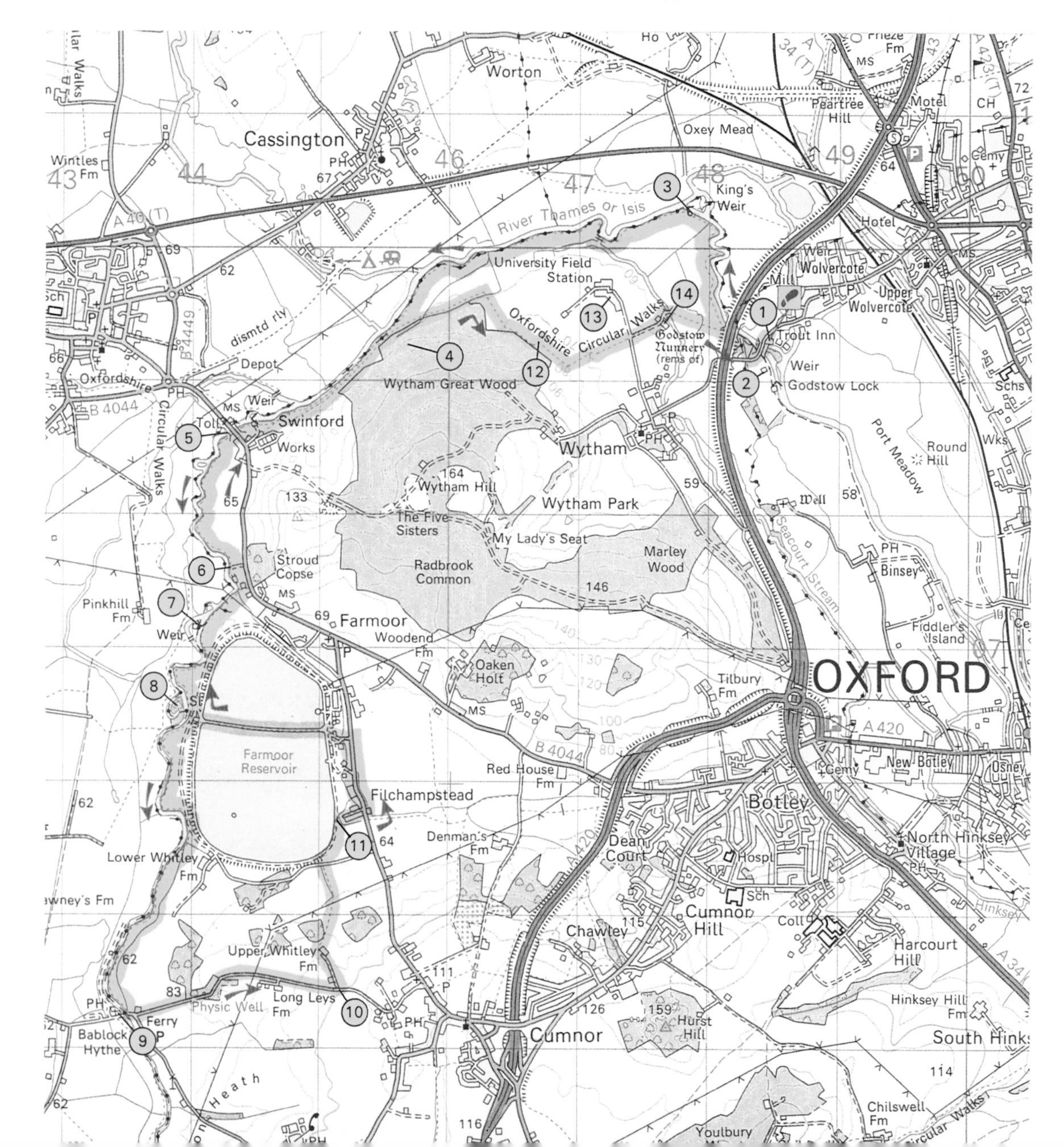

River Nene

OS 1:50,000   Sheets 141/142
3½ miles

When BB, that sharp-eyed writer of country books, came in the 1960s to spend a summer cruising on the River Nene he had a bit of bother with the local lads at Upper Barnwell Mill, just below Oundle. BB did not have much time for long-haired yobboes:

> *'A bunch of hoodlums with girlish flowing locks gibbered and hooted at us like a troop of baboons. These weedy youths seem to me to be a disquieting aspect of England today.'*

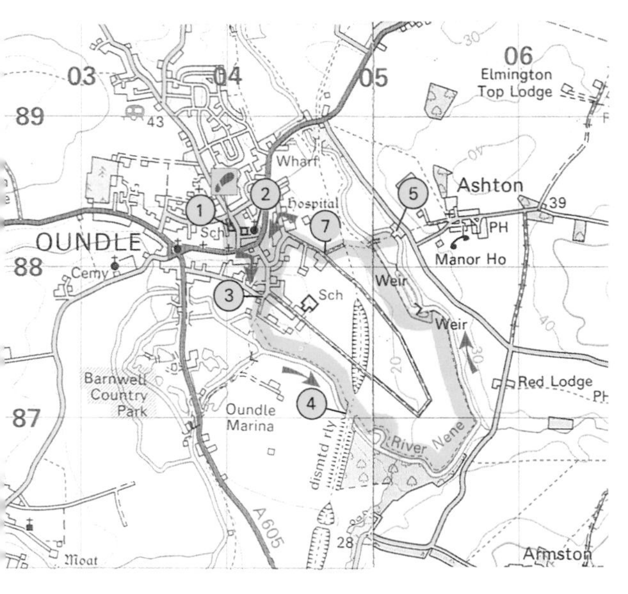

What would BB have thought of the multi-coloured punks of Oundle in the '80s? Not much else has changed since his visit to the little stone-built town on the eastern border of Northamptonshire. Oundle occupies a gentle rise of ground above the Nene, its houses and shops blending pleasantly with each other and with the softly rolling riverside landscape. Its life is still that of a small country town, focused around the public school whose yellow stone buildings stand among old hotels and houses. The heavy through traffic that used to shake the long central market street has been siphoned off by a bypass, bringing peace and quiet back to Oundle and making it a perfect place to spend a strolling morning.

The school[1] was founded in 1556 by an Oundle grocer, William Laxton, who in due time rose to become Lord Mayor of London. Most of the original school has been replaced by late Victorian and Edwardian buildings which stand each side of New Street. Beside the school, Church Street leads down to the church of St Peter[2] (042882), its gracefully tapering 210-foot spire the hub around which this walk revolves, visible in its raised position for miles in each direction. The angles of the spire are decorated with crockets, semicircular stone projections one above another and about three feet apart. In 1880 an Oundle schoolboy, one Bailey, managed to climb up the crockets of the spire to touch 'Peter', the weathercock at the tip. The reception committee waiting for Bailey as he came to earth again included the headmaster, who in the best public school tradition first gave him a good thrashing for insubordination, and then presented him with a sovereign for his daring.

The church, mostly thirteenth century, contains a beautiful brass lectern 500 years old – the eagle whose outstretched wings carry the Bible looks rather more like a roc. Near him is a pulpit of about the same age, adorned with stars and repainted brightly in its original colours, standing on one slender wooden leg. In the porch is a seventeenth-century wall memorial to Eleanor Raymond and her '6 Children who Died in their Infancy', with a sad and forbidding footnote:

> *'Reader Consider that Thou alfo art but Duft'.*

Walk down from the church to the market place and carry on down the street by the side of Bramston House, passing the Angel pub to turn right into South Road (043880). Where the road bends sharply to the right[3] keep straight ahead down Bassett Ford Road (042876) and go over a waymarked stile to reach the river bank. The Nene here is wide and slow, running not far

The jungly bank of the River Nene near Oundle.

below the level of the meadows each side. Cows graze among the pollarded willows, and behind you tall oak trees mask all of Oundle but the grey stone needle of its spire.

From the water meadows the path enters a long thicket of head-high reeds, among which lean grotesquely twisted and swollen trunks of ancient willows. You go under the bypass (049871), carried over the Nene on the purple brick arches of the disused Wellingborough–Peterborough railway line[4], and emerge into a classic English river scene. The Nene bends in a great curve from south to north under a hanging wood, its sluggish waters fringed with thick beds of reeds, rising farmland rolling away to a low skyline straddled by a red-brick farm. The cattle chomp contentedly at the lush grass of the meadows, and in the dips and scoops of the river bank sit fishermen, hoping for a bite from roach, chub or the bream that can grow to seven pounds in this stretch of river. I walked here one morning when the final of a competition run by the local paper was being fished, and passed at least 200 intent contestants in a single mile of river bank. It was a pleasure to watch experts at work, threading line, fixing swing tips, sorting through floats and weights, ruminatively running their hands over their batteries of different kinds of rods, considering and weighing up water, wind and light conditions – and never a word spoken.

The spire of St Peter's rises above the fields to your left as you walk on past two weirs which enclose an island of willows, a favourite picnic place for Oundle families. The Nene flooded copiously, and disastrously for local farmers, until 1930 when a series of locks and weirs was built. Beyond the weirs a tubular footbridge crosses the river and leads to Ashton Mill[5] (052882), in BB's day a peaceful backwater and now a remarkable museum and testimony to the energies of the banking family of Rothschild.

There have been mills at Ashton since Domesday times – four of them in 1600, three for grinding corn and one for fulling. In 1900 Nathan, 1st Baron Rothschild, decided to use the power of the mill-race in a different way. He fitted up Ashton Mill with a set of turbines to provide electric power for Ashton Wold, the mansion he had built above the Nene valley for his son Charles. Around the same time Charles

had rebuilt Ashton village, just up the ridge from the mill, and the turbines brought electricity to the houses there as well. Lord Rothschild was a keen innovator in farming techniques, and a number of machines at his estate farm ran on Ashton Mill power. Water pumps were also installed at the mill to bring a constant supply of water to the house and village. These modern wonders attracted many visitors to the new village, which on Charles's insistence had been constructed of local materials and had a bathroom in every house – something rare at the turn of this century.

The red-brick mill above its pond is open to the public every day except Tuesday and Wednesday. Inside stand the original machines, their great toothed cog-wheels and flywheels with curved spokes connected by driving bands to the spindle under the ceiling which drove the whole concern via its connection with the mill's water-wheel. Impressive as they are, the turbines, pumps and generators are not the only attractions of Ashton Mill – there is a museum of fishing and a collection of historic farming tools and machines. The mill also houses a conservation exhibition, for the Rothschilds have been notable champions of the countryside and its disappearing wildlife. Charles was one of the founders of the conservation movement, an expert botanist and entomologist; and his descendant Dr Miriam Rothschild, who still lives at Ashton Wold, carries on the good work. She started a project in 1979 to collect seed from the wild flowers threatened by pesticides and disturbance – primrose, cowslip, sweet violet, lady's smock, toadflax, yellow rattle – and to grow them in the walled garden at Ashton Wold for seed harvesting. The seeds are distributed and sown in such lifeless places as motorway embankments and highway roundabouts, and anywhere else that wild flowers are disappearing. Oundle's new bypass is one potential wild flower desert that has bloomed thanks to her initiative. At Ashton Mill the mill-race has been stocked with yellow water-lilies and arrowhead, and the waters left undisturbed to attract kingfishers and dragonflies. The woodlands around Ashton Wold have also been carefully conserved, and now harbour many kinds of birds including nightjars, long-eared owls and nightingales.

From Ashton Mill you return to the footbridge to cross the Nene and follow the footpath up to the bypass. Take care crossing – traffic comes very fast from both directions. On the far side the track leads to a lane[6] (047881), where you turn right and make for the spire of St Peter's, seen ahead through the trees. The seventeenth-century Talbot Hotel in New Street is a relaxed and comfortable place to eat and drink – children are welcome, and there is a good choice of bar food. The hotel's staircase is said to have been brought here from Fotheringhay Castle a few miles downriver, and to be the one down which Mary, Queen of Scots, took her last walk to the scaffold. There is a painting of the scene in the lounge bar – Mary, pale and apprehensive, clutching a crucifix, descends the stone stairs on the arm of a courteous warden in long brown boots. Behind her a gentleman is whispering a commentary in the ear of his companion, while one of her few remaining friends weeps uncontrollably into a handkerchief.

Ashton Mill peers over its greenery into the mill-pond.

River Lugg

OS 1:50,000 Sheet 148
6 miles

Hands up all those who have heard of the Battle of Mortimer's Cross, 1461! If you come from this part of the Welsh Marches, you will have – local people are very proud of, and knowledgeable about, their moment of glory during the Wars of the Roses, even though more than 500 years have passed since that bloody day by the River Lugg. We pass the site of the battle during this walk in the Anglo-Welsh border country of woods, green hills and purple earth.

The village of Aymestry is strung out along the Romans' Watling Street, known today more functionally as the A4110. Weaving was the industry that maintained Aymestry in times gone by, and limestone from the nearby quarry built its houses. The church[1] is dedicated to St John the Baptist and to an obscure saint, Alkmund, a Christian soldier against the Danes in the eighth century. It contains one special treasure – a sixteenth-century rood screen with beautifully carved linenfold panelling and foliage. A hole in the north-east corner of the bell-ringers' chamber once carried a rope which rang a bell every evening to guide benighted travellers. The ringer was paid through a legacy left by a man who had spent a miserable night in a nearby wood being led astray and bamboozled by a mischievous fairy. The bridge over the Lugg[2] (425655) carries a plaque dating it 1931–2; it 'replaced a narrow structure of similar design which was erected after the Great Flood of 1795'. Cross the bridge and after 200 yards turn right[3] up the far side of the lodge at the entrance to Yatton Court. A grassy track leads towards the dark spruce and glowing green beech trees in School Wood on the hill ahead. Old parkland lies each side of the path, with some fine oak, ash, sycamore and horse chestnut trees. Two gates cross the path – take the left one, through which our route runs by a tattered, tall Wellingtonia to curve right and enter the wood by a stile[4] (429652). Silvery gleams from the fast-flowing Lugg on your right are seen between the trees – the river is known to local children as the Slugg, more for the sake of rhyme than anything else!

A bend of the Lugg glints beneath a skeletal tree in the fields between Mortimer's Cross and Lugg Green.

Bracken grows thickly beside the path which passes the thin grey stratified bowls of old limestone quarries and climbs gently to leave the tail of the wood (427641). Here you turn your back on the river and walk east to meet the B4362[5] road at a house named Beech Croft. Turn right for a few hundred yards, enjoying a view over fifteen miles to the hills behind Hay-on-Wye, to reach the bridge at Mortimer's Cross[6] (427637). Upstream of the bridge is Mortimer's Cross Mill[7], which was built in about 1750 as a paper mill. Business waned, but in the 1820s the mill had a new lease of life grinding flour. In the 1940s it finally ceased work, but has recently been restored, and now turns out animal feed – a genuine survivor. A knock on the door of the cottage above the mill building will (subject to time of day and availa-

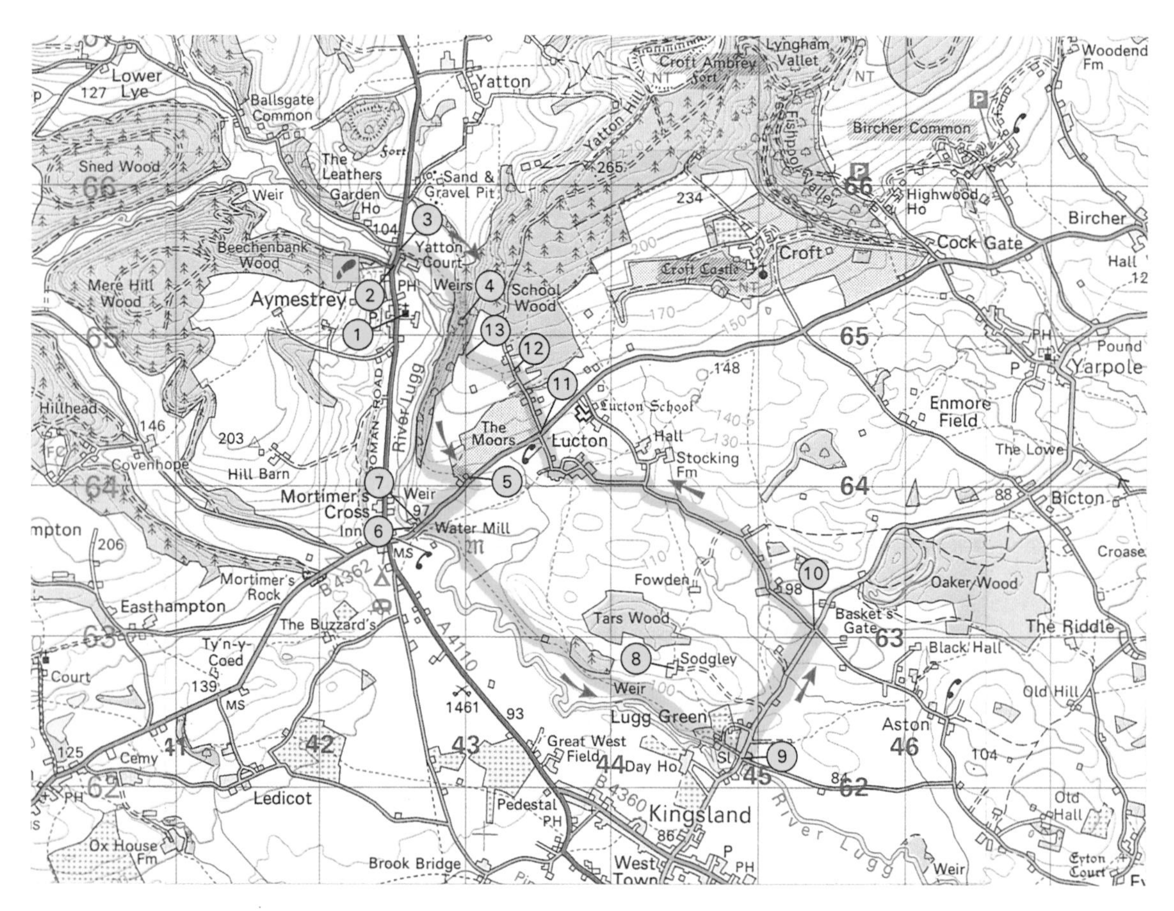

bility of owner) gain you access to the old mill in exchange for a few pence.

On the feast of Candlemas, 2nd February, 1461, the white rose of York confronted the red rose of Lancaster at Mortimer's Cross, just down the road (425636). Edward, Duke of York, and Jasper, Earl of Pembroke, brought 40,000 men to grapple for mastery over the crown of England; and by the end of the day 4,000 of them lay dead. Gentlemen on the defeated Lancaster side were beheaded and local peasantry slaughtered less delicately in the aftermath of the battle. A triple sun had been seen in the sky before fighting started, and Edward, taking it as an omen of his victory, subsequently adopted the sun as his personal device. The sign at Mortimer's Cross Inn shows that sun, the white rose of York and a cross to signify the 'crowning glory' of the victory.

Go over a gate beside the bridge onto the riverside path on the east bank of the Lugg. Purple and white comfrey, campion and strong-smelling wild garlic dot the banks with bright

Opposite above: Wild flowers brighten the waterside where the River Lugg slides under the bridge at Mortimer's Cross.

Opposite below: The old mill at Mortimer's Cross, still going strong in the animal feeds trade.

View across the river towards Day House at Lugg Green.

patches of colour; and horsetails, those descendants of the plants of the early world, grow in the wet margins of the fields. On the semi-islands formed by the meanders of the river, sallow and willow luxuriate in isolation with rogue crops of barley from the surrounding fields at the water's edge. The path follows the rim of the old bank of the river, cut when the Lugg flowed more broadly than today, and now high and dry. Keep well to the left under the hills, or you may find yourself stranded by side channels.

Under the yellow cottage of Sodgeley[8] (444628) the official path disappears under the oil seed rape and among barbed wire fences, and it is best to follow the river's edge to Lugg Green, where you pass between a house and a heavily-buttressed old barn to reach the road (449622)[9].

Turn left here, and in three-quarters of a mile left again[10] (454630) into the long lane to Lucton. It gets narrower and more flowery the further you walk – a typical Welsh borders lane, so quiet that bird song and the lowing of cows in the green fields seem magnified. Lucton has no pub, no post office, no pottery – the school up the hill has closed and the village shop has been converted into a private dwelling, a fate that has also visited St Peter's Church. There is just a handful of houses – some ancient black and white, some modern – and two or three farms with huge, ramshackle wooden or stone barns; all sheltered under the hills in their upland setting.

The lane goes through the village to meet the B4362 road[11] (435643) by Lucton war memorial, sited on a grassy knoll at the crossroads. Lucton, tiny and remote, lost no fewer than twelve of its young men in the slaughter of the Great War.

Go across the road and climb up the No Through Road lane, passing between the buttresses of an old bridge whose arch has vanished. Opposite Hill Croft[12] (433648) go over the stile at the top of the bank and cross the field to a gate. From here the path runs diagonally across the next field to a gate half-way down the hedge, and thence to a stile[13] at the top of the wood (430648). A very steep path drops down between the trees, faint and hard to decipher. Deer can be seen standing stock still in surprise at the intruder before bounding away into safety.

After scrambling and sliding down the contours you meet the path along the bottom of the wood, where you turn right to the stile from which you return below Yatton Court to the bridge over the Lugg at Aymestry. The Crown Inn by the bridge does bed and breakfast, serves meals and has a garden.

River Severn

OS 1:50,000 Sheet 138
14 miles

River and railway – the out-and-back routes of this walk – held the key to the prosperity of the towns that grew up along the Severn valley. The railway breathed new life into the area when the once-bustling river trade was in decline in the nineteenth century, but it, too, declined and fell under the axe in 1963. Now superbly restored by volunteers, its steam engines and coaches in Great Western Railway livery shuttle backwards and forwards in the summer months between Bewdley and Bridgnorth, the starting and finishing points of this walk. You can reach Bewdley by rail from British Rail's Kidderminster main line station. Returning from Bridgnorth by the Severn Valley Railway, you can appreciate in reverse the wonderful scenery of the valley from the series of embankments that carry the trains above the river.

Bewdley traded in many exotic goods – cotton, sugar, tea and even slaves as well as more prosaic coal, timber and corn – thanks to the connection with Bristol via the Severn. Its bargemen were famed for their toughness and skill in handling their flat-bottomed 'trowes' or barges. They had to be tough to fight off pirates based in the Wyre Forest who swooped down to plunder their cargoes, and press-gangs from Bristol, who frequently came up to Bewdley to take men for the Napoleonic wars. Leland, visiting the town in the sixteenth century, said that 'att rising of the sunne frome the este the hole towne glittereth, being all of nuy buyldings, as it were of gold.' Bewdley means 'beau lieu' or beautiful place, and it well deserves the name, with its fine old half-timbered houses sloping gently up from Telford's three-arch bridge over the Severn. The wharves were lively places until the eighteenth century, when the building of the Staffs and Worcs Canal stole the river trade. The town ran gently down into retirement as a pleasant riverside haven.

The walk to Bridgnorth begins at the west end of the bridge (787754), where steps lead down onto Coles Quay, past black and white houses and two old pubs, the Cock and Magpie and the Mug House. Worn flights of stone steps drop to river level where the trowes once made fast. The path leads north, passing the tall piers of the long disused branch railway to Tenbury Wells[1] (780764) – buttressed and faced with blue brick and ornate corner stones – monuments to Victorian optimism and modern pragmatism. The river runs north in a narrow, shallow valley, along whose sides white-painted cottages face the river in their neat little gardens. There are many waterside bungalows and mobile homes, too, each staking out its owner's patch of bank and muddy foreshore.

Just before Folly Point a line of low brick arches comes down the bank in a series of ever-widening leaps until they take off and soar over the river in the single graceful curve of a lattice-girder bridge[2] (775782). The path continues past a gnarled and twisted ancient oak, at least twenty feet round its squat trunk, alternating between long fields and groves of ash and beech. Green woodpeckers haunt these quiet glades above the fast-flowing river. Some of the fields are of East Anglian hedgelessness and length, though the warm red earth and wooded hillocks each side of the valley make up for their lack of features.

The path goes under the Severn Valley Railway's carefully restored Victoria Bridge[3] (767792), stamped '1861 John Fowler Engineer. Messrs. Bradley & Co. Contractors, cast and erected by the Coalbrookdale company.' This is a favourite spot for railway photographers waiting to catch a train crossing the bridge in full steam and reflected in the river underneath. Each side of the bridge are round-topped Great Western Railway boundary markers of 1897.

The Harbour Inn at Arley[4] (765799), on the left bank, is a gem. Here I was handed a cool pint through the kitchen window, which I drank on a bench under the trees in the garden, looking across the river to the red-brick houses of the village. Understandably, it gets very crowded on summer weekends, so enjoy it on a weekday in spring if you can!

The road ends arbitrarily in the river where

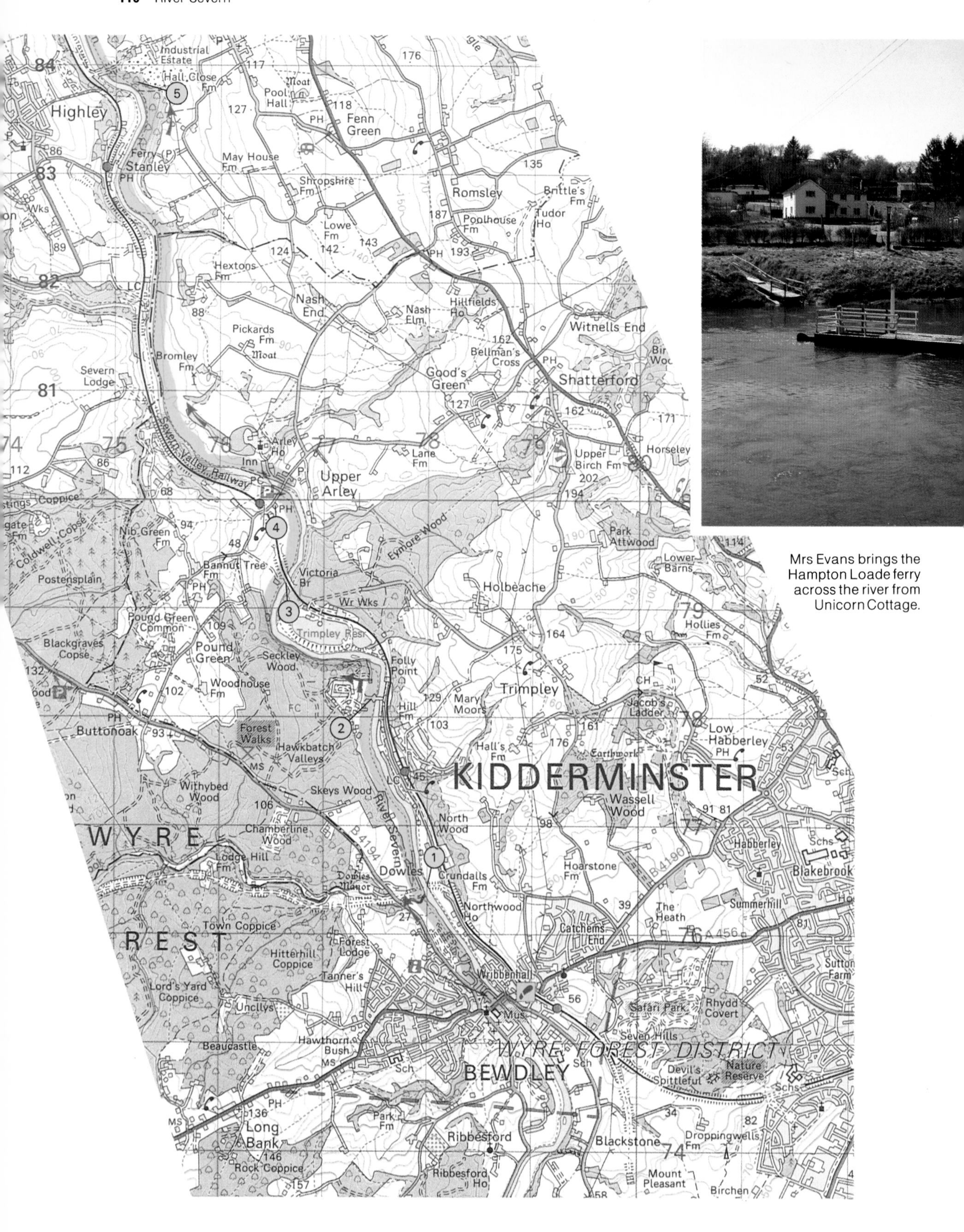

Mrs Evans brings the Hampton Loade ferry across the river from Unicorn Cottage.

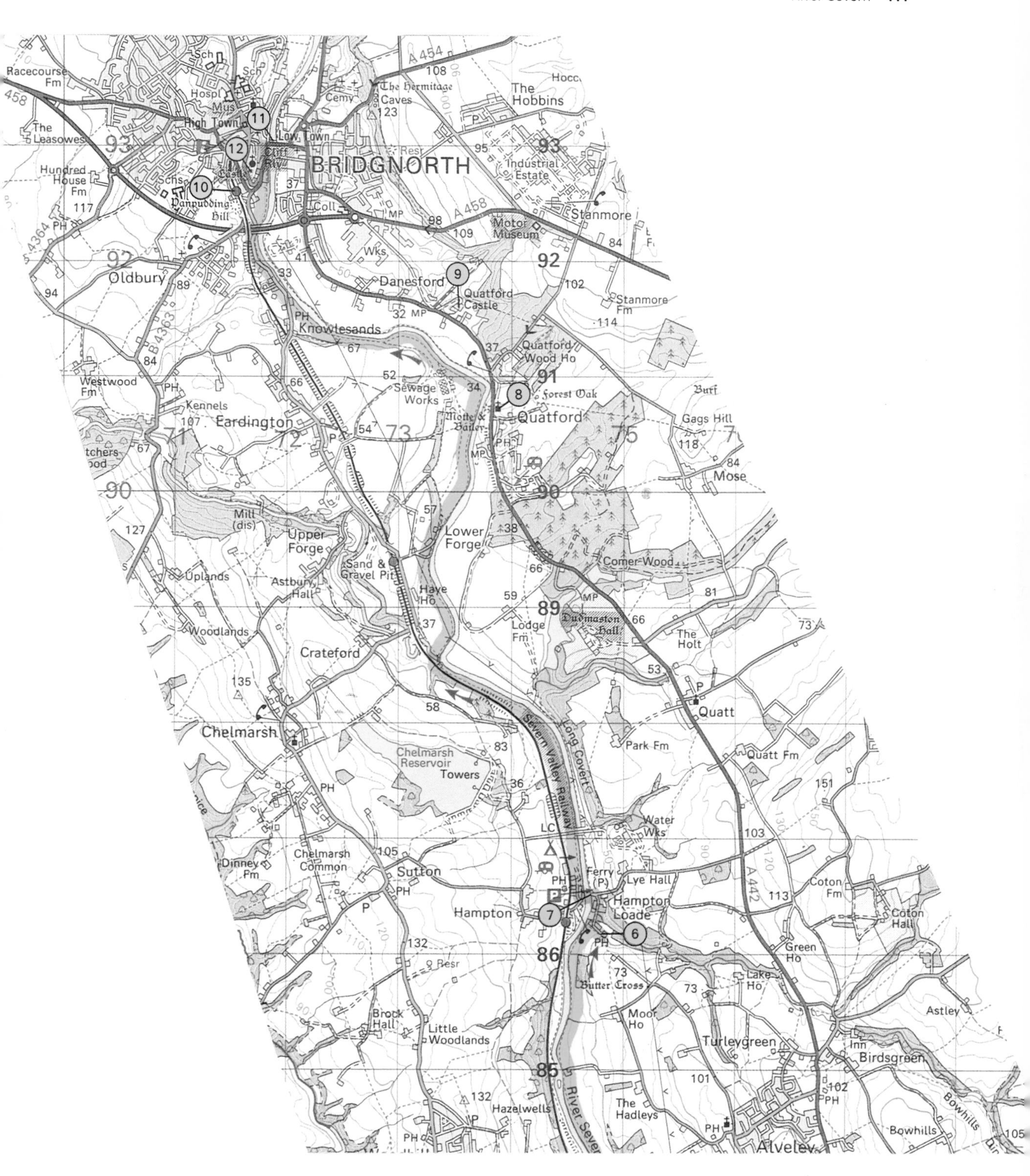
BRIDGNORTH
High Town
Low Town
Castle
Cliff Rly
Pan Pudding Hill
Racecourse Fm
The Leasowes
Hundred House Fm
Oldbury
The Hermitage Caves
The Hobbins
Industrial Estate
Stanmore
Motor Museum
Danesford
Quatford Castle
Stanmore Fm
Knowlesands
Quatford Wood Ho
Sewage Works
Forest Oak
Motte & Bailey
Quatford
Westwood Fm
Kennels
Eardington
Gags Hill
Mose
Mill (dis)
Upper Forge
Lower Forge
Sand & Gravel Pit
Comer Wood
Uplands
Astbury Hall
Haye Ho
Woodlands
Dudmaston Hall
Lodge Fm
The Holt
Crateford
Quatt
Chelmarsh
Park Fm
Quatt Fm
Chelmarsh Reservoir
Towers
Severn Valley Railway
Long Covert
Water Wks
Dinney Fm
Chelmarsh Common
Sutton
Ferry
Lye Hall
Hampton
Hampton Loade
Coton Fm
Coton Hall
Green Ho
Butter Cross
Lake Ho
Moor Ho
Astley
Brock Hall
Little Woodlands
Turleygreen
Inn
Birdsgreen
Hazelwells
River Severn
The Hadleys
Bowhills
Alveley
A 454
A 458
A 442
B 4363
B 4364

the ferry used to be, so cross the Severn by the footbridge and go in front of the Valentia Arms to continue the walk in the wide sheep-grazing meadows on the river bank. Huge red sandstone blocks lie jumbled in one of the fields, the relics of some river enterprise that came to nothing. Suddenly the landscape changes, first to a wood clinging to the rock face of the river bank where trees have worked their roots between the boulders of stone and then swelled into fantastic shapes; then into a desolate wilderness under an abandoned coal-mine[5] (752838) opposite the waterside settlement of Stanley. Here even the brooks run black, and chips of coal surface the path. After half a mile the alien surroundings vanish, hidden by the trees, and the peaceful meadows wind on by the river to Hampton Loade.

The Lion[6] (748862), just up from the path on the edge of the village, serves an ambitious range of food and has a garden where you can eat and cool your thirst. Then follow the road down to the ferry[7] (747865), which you summon by ringing an electric bell set into a post on the bank. The ferry is run by two sisters, Mrs Jones and Mrs Evans, one of whom will emerge from the white-painted Unicorn Cottage above the ferry and bring the square floating cattle-pen across the river. The only motive power is water pressure on the rudder. The sisters have been doing this job in rain and shine for thirty years, making a little in the tourist season and drawing in their horns in the winter, when floods can raise the level of the river not far below their house. Mrs Evans was born in the Unicorn pub, just behind the cottage, and hopes that the family tradition of working the ferry – the last one of its kind in the country – will pass on down the generations. Her collection of old photographs includes one of a team of horses hauling logs through the shallows along a man-made ridge in the river bed just downstream of the ferry.

On the left bank again you continue under the startling blue bow-girder bridge at the waterworks and resume the path through more long hedgeless, tree-lined fields. Under Quatford the river snakes in a sharp bend, continuing year by year to grind away the sandstone crag where the eleventh-century church of St Mary Magdalene[8] stands proudly overlooking the Severn (739907). A castle was built on this point shortly before the church, but was demolished when a better site was found nearby. Now the crag is left to a colony of jackdaws who bicker up and down its cracks and ledges.

Further along the right bank the crenellations of Quatford Castle[9] (735917) rear up above their surrounding trees – not the successor of the one on the crag, but a nineteenth-century folly designed by a local builder, John Smalman, who lived there in magnificence.

On our side of the river, the path runs for the last two miles close under the road and railway, and enters Bridgnorth along the backs of gardens, from which narrow old alleys run up to the road. The Severn Valley Railway station[10] is just up the slope on the left as you enter the town (715926), but it would be a pity not to go the extra half-mile up to Telford's massive bridge (718930)[11] and the town itself, divided into Low Town and High Town, and connected by a cliff railway, the steepest in Britain at a forty-five-degree incline. Like Bewdley, Bridgnorth waxed fat on the river trade, and was a manufacturing centre for clothing and hat-making before turning its hand to engineering when the Industrial Revolution came along – its steam pumps and engines were much sought after. Teams of men were harnessed together to draw the coal barges into the wharves by the river. The mooring rings can still be seen in the bridge and river walls, as can the flights of loading steps and the warehouses and pubs that crowded the river frontage. Above them the town's varied collection of old brick and timbered houses seem to balance one on top of the other.

At the south end of the town the verdigrized dome of Telford's St Mary Magdalene Church, built in 1792, stands by the castle on its hill (717928)[12]. The castle was built at the end of the eleventh century, and its keep (sixty-five feet high) and famous leaning tower are still there. During the Civil War Bridgnorth was besieged by the Roundheads and much of the medieval town was burned by the Royalist defenders as they retreated up the hill to the castle. Cromwell's men set up their guns on Panpudding Hill, an ancient tump which conveniently overlooks the town, and poured shot at their leisure into the castle. However, the Royalists only surrendered when it became apparent that the attackers were tunnelling into the hill with

Wharfside buildings beside Telford's graceful bridge over the River Severn at Bewdley.

the intention of setting off charges that would blow the castle sky-high – the church nearby was being used by the defenders as a powder magazine.

The entrance to the tunnel – known as 'Lavington's Hole' – can still be seen behind Underhill Street. There are a number of interesting houses too; notably Bishop Percy's of 1580 between Cartway and the old stairway known as Stoneway Steps that runs down from High Town to the river, just downstream of the bridge on the west bank. Another treasure is the house built near the bridge by a local bargemaster, Richard Forester, who had it inscribed in the good broad Midland tongue: 'Except the Lord Build the Owse the labours thereof avail nothing.'

River Dove

OS 1:50,000 Sheet 119
14 miles

This is a straightforward, if long, walk in fine weather. During or after rain it becomes quite a challenge: water- and mud-proof trousers and boots are essential. I speak as one who knows.

One name dominates Dovedale – that of the canny old ironmonger from London who loved to fish the Dove 300 years ago with a six-yard rod of hazel or willow and a fixed line of horsehair, dyed with a pint of strong ale and half a pound of soot. Izaak Walton's *The Compleat Angler* must be the best-known unread book in existence – it's a wonderfully astute mixture of practical advice, humour and comment. His fishing friend Charles Cotton lived at Beresford Hall at the head of the dale – thirty-seven years junior to Walton, he was a spendthrift gambler who was driven to hide out in a cave from his creditors. These two unlikely partners were as one when it came to the gentle art, however; and Cotton, an amateur poet, passionately expressed their devotion to their favourite river:

'Oh my beloved nymph! fair Dove.'

The Dove issues from a spectacular cleft in the limestone, between its two guardian outposts of Thorpe Cloud and Bunster Hill. They are the last remnants of a coral reef built up when this part of the world was under the sea 300 million years ago. Ice Age glaciers wore away the reef, and the river gradually ate itself out a deep gorge, leaving pinnacles of harder rock standing free of their cliffs. Victorian ramblers gave these outcrops suitably romantic names; vegetation had not yet smothered the gorge in the way it does today, and the pinnacles stood out dramatically against the sides of the cleft. Nowadays the National Trust, which owns Dovedale, works hard to keep the trees and scrub manageable, and also has to cope with the erosion of paths caused by millions of visitors every year.

From the car-park at the foot of Dovedale (146509) you can walk up the west bank for half a mile to cross over by the stepping stones under Lin Dale[1] (152513), or use the footbridge just above the car-park to walk along the east bank. From the National Trust board by the stepping stones – an excellent notice with a coloured map and brief explanation of the formation of Dovedale – you walk up the dale on a well-surfaced path under ash woods which cling to the rocky cliffs enclosing the river. The Twelve Apostles[2] stand on the far bank, all overgrown and some more upstanding than others! Stone steps lead up to Lover's Leap[3] (145518), a knob of bare, boot-worn stone where Victorian romantics loved to dice deliciously with the thought of death. In 1761 Dean Langton of Clougher took things a step further by falling to his death off Lover's Leap accompanied by his horse. His lady

Pickering Tor and Ilam Rock tower like knife blades over the River Dove.

companion followed suit, but was allegedly saved by her long hair, which caught in the branches below and left her swinging until rescuers could reach her, much alarmed but not seriously hurt.

From Lover's Leap the path descends by more steps to the river, which flows below Tissington Spires[4] over a series of weirs, built to create deep pools where trout would lie. Dippers and wagtails use the ledges of the weirs as lookouts, waiting there for the right moment to pounce on their prey. Tissington Spires (147521) are wedge-shaped slices of rock, hundreds of tons each in weight, that knife up out of the right-hand cliff and hang over the heads of walkers below. Opposite them is Jacob's Ladder, another great shark's tooth of limestone. In another quarter of a mile the gorge opens out for a brief stretch, and you pass below Reynard's Cave[5] (146524). The pitch-black entrance to the cave, high above the path, is guarded by a natural arch, forty feet high and eighteen feet wide, created by the river's swirling action millions of years ago when it flowed as a wide torrent half-way up the present-day gorge. A steep scrambling path leads from the river bank up to the cave entrance. Arrow-heads and pottery found inside the cave prove its value as a stronghold to less secure generations than ours.

The gorge narrows again, and the river runs between buttresses of rock no more than fifteen yards apart. Now there are the first glimpses ahead of the outside world – the grassy head of Hall Dale. Before reaching it the river passes Ilam Rock[6] on the left and Pickering Tor[7] on the right, two seventy-foot towers (142531); Ilam Rock is the more finely cut, a smooth blade inclined backwards which climbers find irresistible. At the base of the rock a footbridge crosses the river, but our walk sticks to the right bank round the craggy face of Hall Dale and under the black mouths of Dove Holes[8] (142535) – one even has a uvula of rock dividing the two channels of its throat. These are not true caves, as they run only about twenty feet back into the hill. They were carved out by swirling river water in much the same way as the arch at Reynard's Cave.

From this point the most dramatic glories of Dovedale are behind you, but the upper section of the gorge has its own special attractions. The

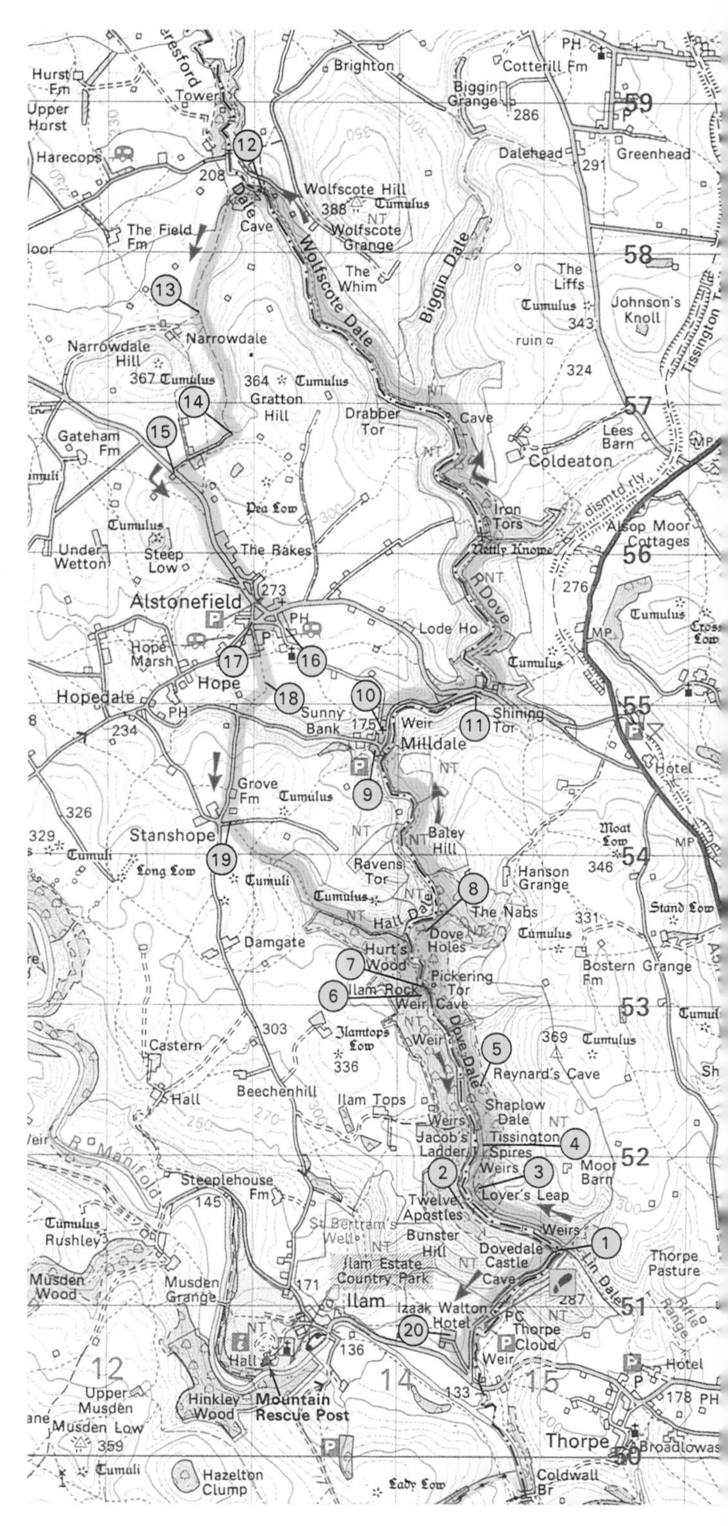

Thorpe Cloud and Bunster Hill flank the narrow outlet of Dovedale's spectacular limestone gorge.

narrow dale sides open out a little and become lower, and the views ahead widen to include stone walls and sheep nibbling at the steep hillsides. Cows graze on the flat ledge of grass by the river, which runs under the stony brow of Ravens Tor to Milldale[9] (139548). The little group of houses crouches at the valley bottom by the three-foot wide pack-horse bridge – however did the heavily-laden horses squeeze themselves over it on their journey between Alstonefield and Tissington? A mill by the bridge converted locally-mined iron ore into the ochre used for dyeing before the advent of modern synthetic colours, and the gentle Dove ran orange. One arch of the bridge spans the river; the other crosses the mill-race.

Go over the bridge to the west bank and turn right past a shop, dated 1896, which sells maps and ice-cream, and has tables outside where you can study the former and lick the latter. The signposted 'Chapel in the Valley'[10], a tiny box of a building a few yards up a side road, is plain and peaceful.

The road runs on the west bank up to Shining (formerly Shinning) Tor, where another mill stands by the bridge[11] (146551). It was the centre of a busy community where lead, mined in the hills above the Dove, was brought to be smelted. You cross the bridge and turn left to walk up the east bank again on a slippy, sloppy track in wet weather, rather like walking on buttered glass – two steps forward and one step back. Here you have passed from Dovedale into Wolfscote Dale, where many plant species grow, including rock rose, wild violet, mossy saxifrage and wild thyme. The river winds under Iron Tors (147561), where the iron for Milldale was won; a stony clitter tumbles down the side of the dale from top to bottom. Biggin Dale comes down to the right to join Wolfscote Dale, its prow-like promontory standing high above the path.

Under Wolfscote Hill you cross the river by a footbridge of stone slabs carried on timber beams[12] (131584). Just upstream is Charles Cotton's home, Beresford Hall; in the grounds stands the small, square 'fishing temple' built by Cotton and Izaak Walton, whose initials are entwined over the door.

Turn right from the footbridge on a narrow path through bushes round the corner of a wood, and make southwards for the left-side of Narrowdale Hill[13] (126575). Narrowdale, aptly named, rises to open out; the path climbs uphill over stiles and through gaps in stone walls, then bears left over a curlicued iron gate[14] (128568) that looks as if it might once have been part of some farmer's bed. A stone-walled lane leads to a road (124566)[15], where you turn left to reach Alstonefield, a pretty hilltop village very popular with visitors in summer. Turn left at the centre of the village for the 'George'[16], a welcoming pub with horse-brasses and old paper money on its beams, food and beer from the hand-pump. I spent a pleasant hour in front

of the roaring fire here watching my clothes steam dry over the backs of the landlord's chairs.

Follow the road through the village past the telephone box to a road sign 'Welton, Ilam and Dovedale'. Walk down the lane opposite Yew Tree Farm[17] (130555), going straight ahead through a narrow stile where the lane bends right. The path goes downhill with a stone wall on the right, and swings right[18] (131551) to drop down a very sharp descent to the road in the valley bottom. A stony, walled lane opposite climbs equally steeply up to the road at Stanshope.

A green footpath sign, 'Milldale 1', points you left up another walled lane, which you follow for one hundred yards to another sign, 'Dovedale 1'. Go through a stone stile[19] (129542) and walk down into the deep cleft of Hall Dale, where in spring there are banks of cowslips on the sides of the dale, with one or two small clusters of purple orchids among them. The footpath descends to meet the Dove opposite Dove Holes, and turns right through the bottom of a wood to the footbridge under Ilam Rock. From here you can enjoy the splendours of Dovedale in reverse, all the way back to the car-park. Just up the hill is the comfortable but expensive Izaak Walton Hotel[20] (143508), which in Walton's and Cotton's day was a farmhouse where the two friends often went for a meal after a day with rod and line on their beloved Dove.

SECTION FIVE

Wales

Ebbw River

Afon Teifi

Afon Tywi

Afon Trannon

Afon Dysynni

Afon Glaslyn

Ebbw River

OS 1:50,000 Sheet 171/161
7 miles

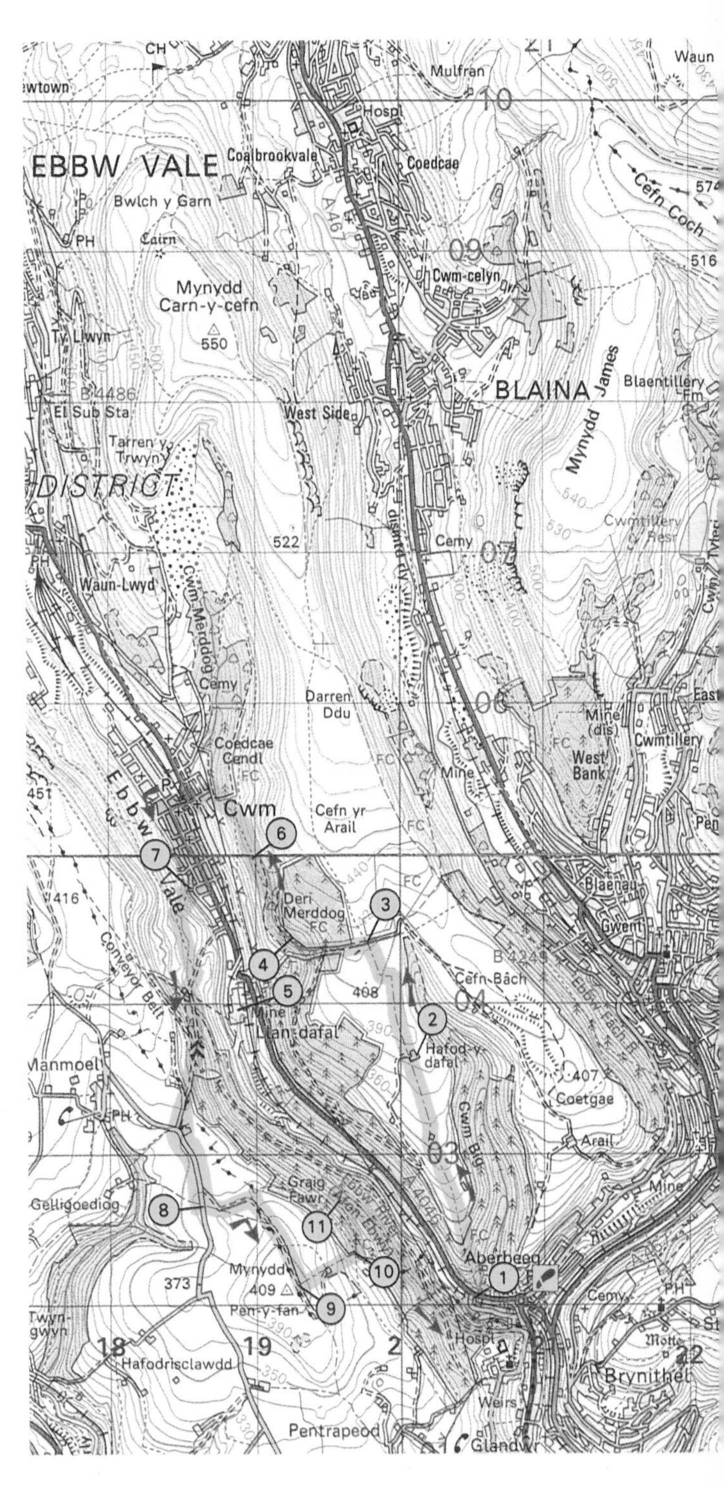

The Ebbw River is a dirty old thing. For the best part of 300 years man has poured a variety of poisons into it – coal, iron ore, industrial chemicals, rubbish, sewage and excrement. Somehow or other it still survives; culverted, piped, bridged and diverted, condemned officially as 'grossly polluted', sparkling cheerfully down its steep narrow valley past the collieries, the steel-works, roads, railways and long, long lines of nineteenth-century workers' houses. To be properly appreciated, the Ebbw valley has to be seen from two levels: high up on the hillside, looking down from the untouched heights on the industrial sprawl along the floor of the valley; and down among the grimy old houses, pubs, chapels and reading rooms of the villages that sprang up at a colliery owner's or an ironmaster's bidding.

Aberbeeg is the starting point for this walk, a small community whose colliery did not survive the economic effects of the Depression. Park your car under the A467 flyover (209020), and look at the grimy Ebbw, stained dark with coal dust, a grey and brown algal scum on the stones of its bed. One day soon it may run clear again, when the last industry is axed from this valley. Now you cross over the railway which still brings coal south from the Marine Colliery near Cwm. At the A4046 road turn right, and in a few yards left (205021) up a path[1] which climbs steeply up the hillside past a wooden Forestry Commission signboard. The path enters the ranks of spruce and pine, snaking to gain height until it emerges to cross an old forestry road (204024) and continue upwards between gnarled, twisted old beech trees. They were planted to shelter drovers and their beasts, for this stony old track was an important route, keeping well above the marshy, overgrown valley bottom, before coal and iron began to drum on the doors of history.

To the left, the steepness of the Ebbw valley is apparent – farms and fields on the skyline, conifers at low level. What lies below them can't yet be seen. Soon the first hints appear – the black and green tiers of the huge, sphinx-like slag heap above Cwm on the left, and on the right the purple cliffs of spoil above Cefn-Bâch. The hooting of a train and the rumble of the Marine Colliery come faintly up to these windy heights, where the path reaches the crumbling, blank-eyed old farmstead of Hafod-y-dafal[2] (201037). It's a wilderness of rusty machinery, drifts of mud and dung in the recesses of the abandoned farmhouse and hanks of sheep's wool on bushes and fences – only a mile away from the floor of the Ebbw valley, but at least three centuries away as well.

Beyond the farm the path makes a dog-leg (sheep-shank would be more appropriate) before coming to a T-junction of old roads[3] (198044). It is thirty yards wide here, testament to the amount of room a herd of cattle or sheep needs to round a corner. Turn left and follow a stone wall down to cross a forestry road and continue on down, bearing right[4] onto a green grassy track below.

Marine Colliery is the sole surviving coal-mine in the Ebbw valley.

The whole valley from top to bottom is now in view; down below the twin winding wheels of Marine Colliery[5] (189040) stand starkly over the sheds, buildings and rows of miners' cars. A line of conveyor-belts zigzags up the hillside opposite, carrying the spoil up to be tipped beside the ever-expanding slag-heap on the skyline. The path runs above a wood of dwarf oaks, the lichen on their branches showing the purity of the air up here. A hundred years ago, when the whole valley was a thundering night-and-day industrial hive, they were probably struggling for survival.

At the end of the wood (190050) the valley floor is again in full view – road, railway and river, and the village of Cwm, five streets wide and more than a mile long. Here is a good place[6] to stare down and reflect on the story of the Ebbw valley and its neighbours. Until the eighteenth century the valleys were a sheep-farming area, sparsely populated and rarely visited by outsiders. Then the iron industry began – mining, smelting and working – at first at their northern ends, then gradually moving down. Ebbw Vale ironworks were founded in 1789 and covered everything nearby in a film of brown dust which persisted for the next two centuries. The iron industry declined, but coal – until the mid-nineteenth century mostly used to feed the ironworks – began to boom as the steam-powered machines, steamships and railways gobbled up all they could get. The drift mines that ran into the hillsides gave way to the deep shaft pits in the valley floors. In 1843 there were twenty-four collieries, four ironworks, two iron foundries, two tin works and a copper works in the Ebbw valley. Crowded, cramped, insanitary villages like Cwm sprawled along the valley floors, covered all year round with a pall of smoke and dust. The main colliery was sunk in the 1890s, and by 1911 2,500 men from Cwm worked there. Spoil from the Ebbw Vale ironworks formed a huge, rusty red heap at the head of the town. The miners, many of whom had come into the valley from other parts of the country in search of work and wages, were strong Union, strong Chapel and strong drinkers.

Then the rot set in. Worked-out seams meant

deeper and deeper pits, more expensive machinery, longer hours of work to be paid for by the management, and eventually redundancies and closures. In the 1950s 13,000 men worked at eighteen pits in the area; by 1984 only four mines still operated, employing 3,000 men. Today the Marine is the only pit still open in Ebbw Vale; and Cwm men, unlike most of their neighbours, can still find work. The great steel works at Ebbw Vale, three miles up the valley, is a shadow of its former self, and men are leaving the place where their fathers and grandfathers worked. You can buy a bedroom suite for a few pounds in the local fourth-hand shops, and a terrace house for a few thousand. The pit heaps are being levelled, the industrial workings replaced by industrial estates. Soon the valleys will be as they were three centuries ago – quiet and nearly deserted.

The path drops downhill into Cwm and passes the Victoria Arms Hotel, where you can sit and chat with elderly ex-miners, whose hands and faces are scarred and seamed with blue coal-dust. Turn left down the main street of the village, and right by the Central Garage to the bottom of the cul-de-sac. Cross the playground and go over the Ebbw River by an iron girder bridge[7] (185048), from which a track climbs up to the left to a path running south-east under an outcrop of rock by an old iron ventilation chimney. The path, whose surface is made of a mixture of limestone, industrial slag and chippings of coal, meets a road which goes under the Marine Colliery's conveyor-belt (186041) and climbs steeply into the trees above the mine. The buildings dwindle to toy-size far below as the road rises to a view ahead of hills which might be in deepest rural Radnorshire.

You turn left at a T-junction (185032) and walk up the road; the houses of Markham Colliery are over to the right, scene of desperate strife in the disastrous miners' strike of 1984/5. In half a mile go over a waymarked stile on the left[8] (186027), from which a track leads to Pen-y-fan. From the summit trig point (192021), a few yards to the right of the path, there is a splendid view up the Ebbw valley to the enormous cluster of buildings around the steel works; the Brecon Beacons stand out in jagged line to the north.

Opposite the trig point, go over the fence on your left[9] (no stile) and drop downhill, passing to the left of an abandoned farmhouse (195022) down a sunken lane. This crosses a rugged road above the trees, and goes straight on down to a stile a hundred yards below[10] (197023) which leads into the Forestry Commission wood. Ignore the tempting path which runs on the level to the left, and plunge down between the trees to a track a few yards lower down – don't lose heart; it *is* there! Turn left down this path, walking on a soft carpet of pine needles, until it meets another track under green power lines[11] (196027). From here turn sharply right downhill with glimpses through the trees of the Ebbw River far below. The track descends, crossing a logging road, to a gate from which you go down to the flyover at Aberbeeg.

Cwm village, a long ribbon of terraces jammed down into the floor of the steep-sided Ebbw valley.

Afon Teifi

OS 1:50,000   Sheet 145
4 miles

The day of the coracle is not yet quite over. These tiny oval fishing boats, small and light enough to be carried on a man's back to and from the water, were once to be seen on many rivers in Wales, but the advent of less bobbish craft and modern man's distaste for cold, wet labour has almost put an end to them. In times past they were square-made and about four feet long, which was the length to which a coracle-builder could stretch an animal skin to cover the hull of split hazel or willow twigs. Today the Teifi coracles are oval, but they still remain the same strong, light little boats. You may be lucky enough to see coracles at work on the Teifi if you do this walk in the salmon season, the occupants netting or spinning for the fish that enter the river at its mouth in Cardigan Bay.

The bridge at Llechryd, our starting point[1] (218437) spans the river with five arches, but more are hidden inside the extension on the southern bank of the Teifi. The bridge was built in 1656, and replaced a ford downstream around which the original village grew up and from which it took its name – Llechryd means 'ford of the rock.' Local lads, too young to go coracle-fishing, trail their lines off the narrow bridge at whose ends drivers exchange courteous 'come-on' flashes of lights, often coming on at the same moment to shuffle for supremacy above the water. On the south bank a footpath sign points downriver beside the gatehouse of Castell Malgwyn[2], these days a hotel (213435) but in former times the residence of Sir Benjamin Hammett, a draper's assistant from Taunton who made good. When he came to Llechryd he was already an Alderman of the City of London and a rich banker. Settling here and building his fine country house, he had soon opened a tin works which employed several local people; other poor and disadvantaged men he put to work on his estate. Alas, his son frittered it all away.

The open throats of Himalayan balsam flowers make drifts of purple under the green shade of alder and oak as the path passes the tall archway and pepper-pot tower of Castell Malgwyn's slate-built stable block. The fast-moving Teifi curves in a series of generous bends towards the sea, its speed of flow slowing all the way and its colour changing from brown to slate-green as it nears the tidal influence of the salt water. The gently rolling farmland through which the Teifi goes is hidden by the splendid

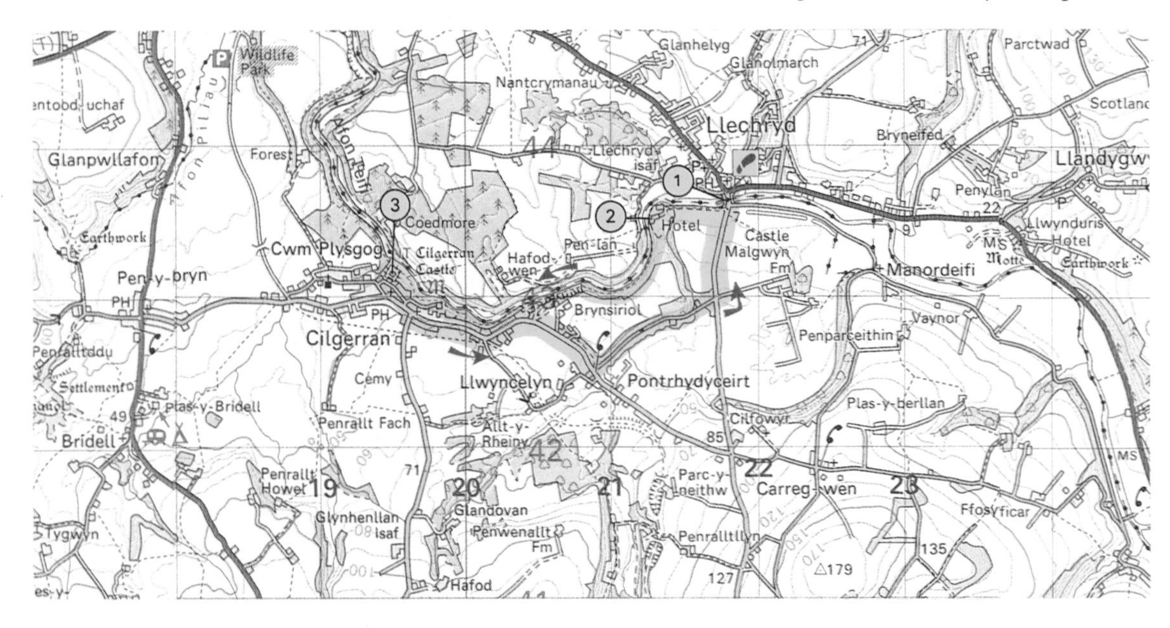

Pink and white patches of Himalayan balsam beside the Afon Teifi at Llechryd Bridge.

beech trees which enclose the river in a deep, leafy avenue.

Under the green fields and woods lie bands of slate, and the remains of disused quarries stand behind the bushes and undergrowth that cover the southern slope above the path. Half-way between Llechryd and Cilgerran a flight of wide, rough slate steps rises to pass the mossy ruins of quarrymen's huts huddled under the light-grey slabs and niches of one of these workings. The quarry face, bare of any plant growth, is cut into squares and sharp corners like a cubist painting, all sloping downwards at the same angle. Seen through the screen of leaves and branches, it looks as if a giant tin shed has subsided at one end and is lying canted against the bank.

From here on the glinting downflows of quarry spoil follow the path in almost continuous line. The Teifi flows gently westward in its open-topped tunnel of trees until the foliage parts and there in front of you stands Cilgerran Castle[3] (195432), high on its rock above a bend of the river. There are benches here from which you can enjoy this impressive view up to the yellow-stone towers above the tree tops, their cylindrical walls pierced with narrow, cross-shaped arrow slits. The present Cilgerran Castle was built from 1223 onwards, replacing one which had passed back and forth between Welsh and Norman occupants as a pawn in their long and bloody tussle for Wales. During one of these adventures Owain ap Cadwgan made a daring raid on Cilgerran, not for blood but for love. He carried off his prize, the beautiful Nest, wife of the Norman incumbent, Gerald de Windsor, and set fire to the castle as a parting gesture. Gerald only escaped the flames by having himself lowered into the Teifi on a rope's end by way of the garderobe.

By 1387 those stirring times were over and Cilgerran had declined far enough to be described as a 'ruinous fortress', which may explain why it was one of the few Welsh castles to escape a siege by the rebel leader Owain Glyndwr during his campaigns against the old enemy at the turn of the fifteenth century. The protective bluff above the river turned out to be the castle's undoing in its old age. It was founded on slate, and was quarried to such effect that in 1863 a great chunk of the north-east wall, twenty feet high and fifty-six feet long, tumbled into the river.

Parts of the castle wall still lie mingled with the quarry spoil on the north side, which you reach by continuing along the river for a few hundred yards. Above you a tall archway and jagged remnant of a tower show where the fall tore the face of the castle away. From here a narrow path winds up to run back around the wall of the castle to the entrance. Cilgerran now belongs to the National Trust and is open to the public; from the top of its towers a panorama of the tree-lined Teifi valley stretches away.

After refreshing yourself in one of the three good pubs in Cilgerran village, you can return to Llechryd Bridge either along the riverside path or by the little roads to the south; from these there are fine views over the hedges to the low hills and long ridges of this part of rural Wales.

Wide bend of the Teifi curves under the massive towers and walls of Cilgerran Castle.

Afon Tywi

OS 1:50,000 Sheet 146
2 miles

If Merlin is to be believed, the citizens of Carmarthen had better pack their bags and get ready to run. The famous oak tree that stood for centuries in the main street succumbed to disease and old age a few years ago, and according to the wizard's prophecy the death of his favourite tree will one day bring a catastrophic flood of the Afon Tywi, and the destruction of the town.

The few people who live in the remote valley where the Tywi starts its seaward journey can sleep easy – those couple of farms under the hills stand well out of reach of the river. It flows tamely enough out of the dam that walls in Llyn Brianne, a dragon-shaped sheet of water curving deep in its valley under mountains that bristle with conifers as far as the eye can see. This is high, wild Wales, where the narrow roads have to squeeze and wriggle around the steep-sided hills as best they can. Our path alongside the sturdy infant Tywi runs through a reserve of the Royal Society for the Protection of Birds, which they have established up here well out of the way of disturbance from large numbers of intruders. Not many people come to the little Information Centre (788471) near Ystradffin to learn about the variety of birds they may see in the woods here: hunters such as buzzards, peregrines, kestrels and that hard-pressed fugitive symbol of rural Wales, the red kite; summer visitors like pied and spotted flycatchers, redstart, blackcap, tree pipit and the wood, willow and garden warblers. Fewer still set off from the car-park along the line of duckboards that takes them among the alders, oaks and silver birches towards the river.

The duckboard trail is an excellent idea, allowing you to tread dry-shod over marshy areas that would normally be impassable. It comes to an end at a T-junction of paths under the trees (785469), where you turn right to walk down to the rocky channel of the Tywi. To the north the hills plunge down, forming the narrow gully through which the river comes noisily down from Llyn Brianne around the boulders in its bed. As the river loses height and forges between the slopes these obstacles in its path grow larger, some reaching the size of a small truck, and the strongly-flowing water rushes more and more noisily. On the right across the river exposed bluffs of rock stand out from the hillside, while on the left the oak trees mask the crags of Dinas Hill, around which the nature reserve path runs. It's a stony route, climbing up to skirt outcrops of rock forming the defile in which the river flows, then dropping by wooden steps or muddy slides to water level. In this lonely valley one is conscious all the time of the size and weight of those great over-hanging rock faces, some 300 feet above the path and appearing to lean over it.

Richard Fenton, riding this way in the early nineteenth century to inspect the mine at

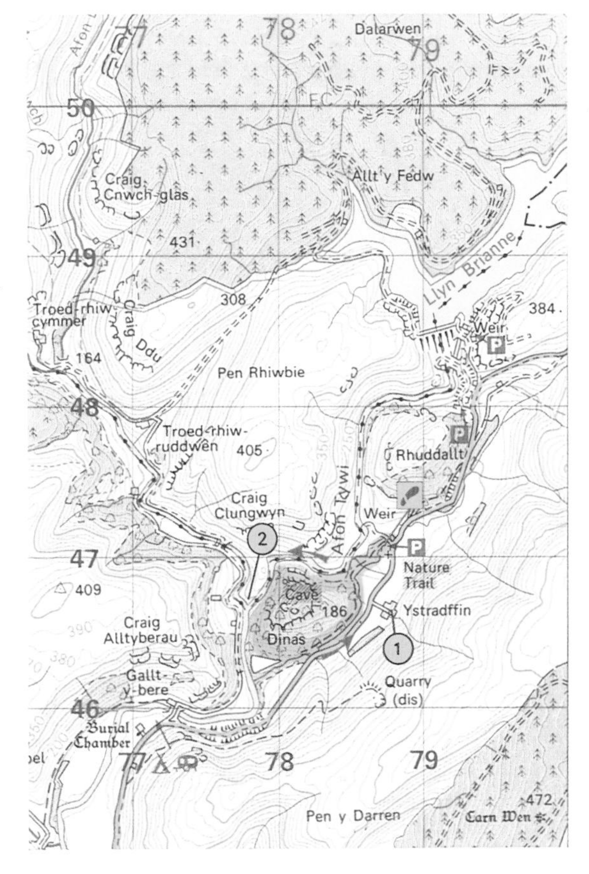

The Afon Doethie flows in on the left to join the Tywi in a rocky valley.

Ystradffin, was impressed by 'the curious and romantick conical hill' of Dinas. The name means 'hill fortress', and many an outlaw used its jagged, encircling crown of rocks as a hideout. Looking up to the left from the path, you can see how impregnable a stronghold in one of the caves on top of the hill would be to all but heavy artillery. No one could arrive at the summit in any condition to do battle with desperate occupants. Thomas Jones, a notorious local robber and bandit, appreciated the defensive qualities of the hill, and made himself a refuge in a cave in the rocks above the confluence of Tywi and Doethie which still carries his name – Twm Shôn Cati, or 'Tom Jones, son of Kate.' He was a well-educated man, turned outlaw after being accused of stealing a bullock. A contemporary writer tells of Thomas's infatuation with a girl who lived at Ystradffin[1] (788466) on the other side of the hill. She was to inherit the property, in those days more of a mansion than a farmhouse, which brought with it 2,000 head of sheep.

Whether the outlaw was attracted by her beauty or her future possessions is not known, but somehow he made her aware of his passion. She very properly gave him the brush-off, whereupon Thomas left his cave by night and made his way to Ystradffin. There he appeared at his lady-love's window and tried to talk her round:

> *'While her fuitor was pleading at her window, by fome accident fhe put her hand through, when he feized it, and fwore he would cut it off unlefs fhe vowed folemnly on the fpot to become his wife.'*

The girl refused to listen, whereupon Thomas suited deed to word. The blood that spurted forth from the girl's severed wrist was to be seen by credulous visitors many years later, still staining the ceiling. One doubts whether this rough wooing had the desired effect, but at least the importunate Thomas had enough sense not to try climbing down the chimney to get further to grips with the heiress of Ystradffin. The householders in the district had the pleasant

custom of fixing two scythes across the fireplace, sharp side up, to cut off the prospects of intruders. Thomas reformed in later years and died a magistrate in the odour of legality.

Ystradffln Farm, whose heiress gave her hand – literally – to the impetuous robber Twm Shôn.

The waters of the Tywi meet those of the Afon Doethie at the foot of a grey rock shaped like the prow of an upturned boat[2] (778467). A side path runs down to the slowly-revolving pool where they mingle before continuing their winding route down the valley. With the high, rounded hills pressing down on the meeting place of the two rivers, and the gushing noise of the waters constricted into twisting strings of foam by the rocks in their beds, this is a good place to sit and stare. In 1950 it was the scene of an angry meeting called by Plaid Cymru to protest against Forestry Commission plans which would have deprived local farmers of their livelihood by filling every valley and hill with trees. Politicians, conservationists and farmers made hot-blooded speeches from the back of a lorry parked above the meeting pool, some of them threatening a campaign of tree-burning and civil disobedience. They won their case later in the cooler atmosphere of Parliament and the hills were left unblanketed.

The path continues around the trees before turning away from the river to round the flank of Dinas Hill. The noise of the water dies away, and you may be able to hear some of the birds that prefer to stay hidden among the bracken. From here it is a straightforward woodland walk back to the car-park, looking out between the trees to the farm where Tom Jones once amputated the hand of his darling.

Afon Trannon

OS 1:50,000 Sheet 136
6 miles

A famous Montgomeryshire owner of fighting cocks once lived in Trefeglwys. It was noticed by local followers of the sport that he was very choosy indeed about which birds he would bring to fight. If the sun happened to be shining brightly, the owner would set out a black-red cock; on a day of sun and cloud it would be big blues; pied birds were his choice if it was overcast or raining. Probably the canny fancier had worked out that his birds' opponents would be more easily put off their stroke if their antagonists blended in with the general background colours dictated by the weather. But as he seldom lost a contest and was making a good thing in side bets, his success was put down to witchcraft and his battles were half-way to being won even before the spurs had been fitted.

In this remote part of rural Wales, belief in witches and the supernatural had a far greater influence than the church on the daily lives of people until well into the last century. If the butter wouldn't churn and the cheese refused to come, shoulders were shrugged in the dairy – it was the work of a spirit or goblin, and nothing could be done about it. The curse had probably been laid on the farm by a beggarwoman who had been sent away empty-handed. Next time one came to the door, the dairymaid would be a bit more careful.

Ironically, Trefeglwys means 'home of the church', and this walk along the steep valley of the Afon Trannon begins at St Michael's (970906), a plain building inside and out with no stained glass, frills or fripperies. On the other side of the road through the village stands the Red Lion, a friendly pub – and welcome after the stiff climbing during your return journey to Trefeglwys.

Turn left down the road from the pub past the village shop and garage to cross the two-arch brick bridge over the Trannon. In a hundred yards go right down a tarmac lane[1] (968902), signposted 'Trannon Caravan Park' and rich in foxgloves and honeysuckle. It runs on the left bank of the shallow little river below those small, rounded hills so characteristic of the Welsh border country, dotted with sheep and striped with hedges. In one third of a mile you reach Talgarth[2] (962902), a fine half-timbered old house set in a fork of the lane. Most of the

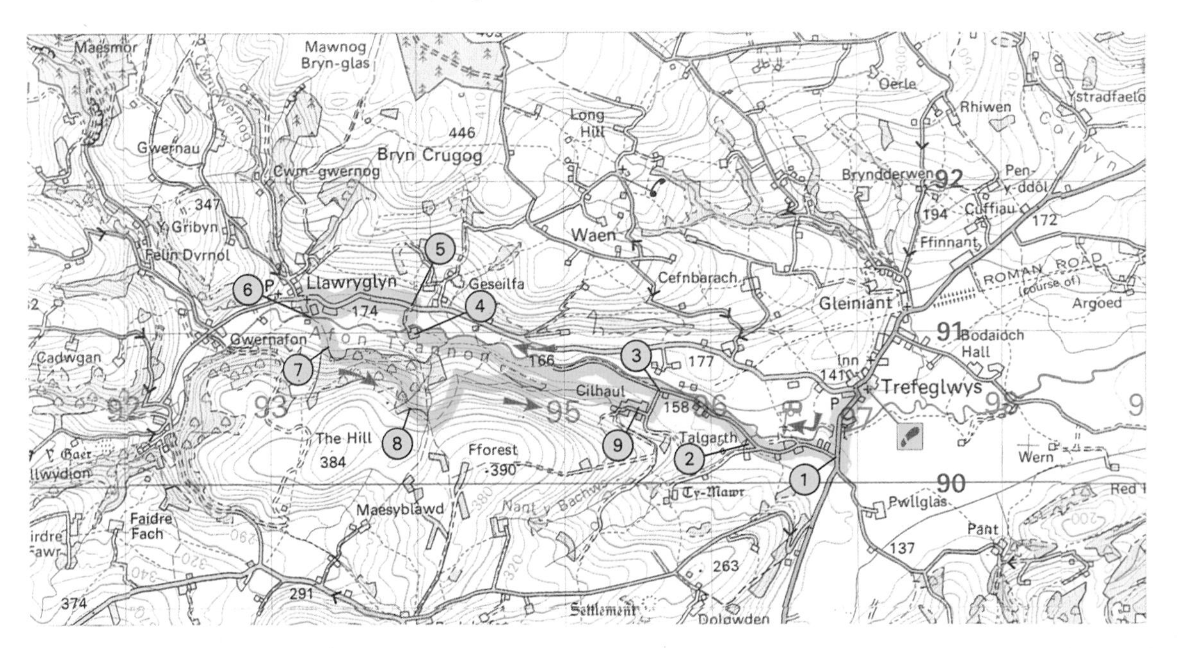

building dates from the end of the sixteenth century; in 1660 it was the home of Roger Lloyd, a Royalist so loyal that King Charles II rewarded him for his devotion through the long years of the Commonwealth by making him a Knight of the Royal Oak. Some of the oldest parts of Talgarth are medieval, and may have stood when Hywel ab Ieuaf lived here. He was a great Welsh war chief, Lord of Arwystli and mighty in battle, who once made the poet Cynddelw a present of a bull, 'a sleek and monstrous beast that tears the ground.'

Pass to the right of Talgarth and walk on above Rhydcarw Mill (959906), a low building lying crossways by the river in the narrow valley bottom. Just beyond the mill the road swings left to climb up to Cil-haul Farm under the bony brow of the moorland hill called Fforest. Keep straight ahead here[3] over a cattle grid (956906), rising gently under oak trees with the Trannon rustling over its bleached stones far below, then descending to a gate beyond which the path runs beside the river to join a farm road. Go through a farmyard of old stone barns[4] and cross the river on a wooden footbridge (939910). The drive beyond leads to the road, where you turn left[5] to reach Llawryglyn.

View from the edge of the woodland above Llawryglyn.

'Bottom of the valley' says the name, quite rightly. The steep slopes sweep away up to the skyline in all directions. Llawryglyn was judged 'a large, straggling and beautifully situated hamlet' in 1879, and hasn't changed since then. Beside the retired chapel on the eastern edge of Llawryglyn turn left down to the old ford[6] (933911), where you cross the river on a wooden bridge and bear left to walk up a grassy track into the woods. Here the track forks left[7] and climbs and climbs through the well-spread oaks and mountain ash, crossing side paths and passing old stone workings to wind steadily up to a gate, crusted with lichen[8] (939905). Beyond this you keep on up to ford a stream and find yourself 400 feet above the floor of the valley, a good place to rest your calf muscles and enjoy the rewarding view to the east, north and west.

'Fforest' means not trees but moorland. Peat cutting was an important activity up here before canals and railways brought coal within the reach and the price range of ordinary people. Looking back at isolated Llawryglyn from this height it's easy to imagine how superstition grew and fed on itself at lonely farmsteads like Craig Wen. The mischievous spirit which plagued that farm, however, eventually got its come-uppance when the farmer applied a bit of common sense. For some time the most extraordinary things had been happening – the mistress's best silk dresses and shawls were mysteriously cut to pieces, the cream was found to be mixed with dust, the cheese was pushed off the shelf into the milk pan, the crockery smashed all by itself. They called in the Wesleyan minister to lay the ghost, but while he was praying the sprite was rattling the windows and even, some said, came inside and carried the Bible around the room.

Then the farmer and his wife began to ask themselves why the servant-girl was never there with them when the smashes, crashes and rattlings were going on. They put two and two together, sent her away – and the goblin immediately decamped as well.

A green track (941904) leads diagonally down the hillside opposite the farm of Geseilfa ('place of the mountain recess'), where lived Valentine

Looking down into the valley of the Afon Trannon. This memorable view is your reward for a long, sweaty climb.

Ashton. His memorial tablet in the church at Trefeglwys records that he died in 1816, aged 92, and that 'He lived in Wedlock with Mary his Wife, 70 years.' The path runs down to a fence and gate (947907), through which you go to walk along the top edge of a narrow wood, then drop further down to the rough road to Cil-haul Farm[9] (955905). Here one morning in 1835 Farmer Bennett was keeping his horse waiting at the mounting block. The impatient steed pawed the ground with its hooves, and the astonished farm workers and domestic servants saw a flash of silver in the soil. The horse had broken the side of a pottery jar which had lain under the ground for nearly 2,000 years, and inside was a hoard of more than 200 Roman silver coins. The farmer, alerted by the noise, came out to find his workers making off with whatever they could grab. Those coins that remained were hung up in the farm kitchen in a glass jar by Mrs Bennett, whose pleasant custom was to show the treasure to visitors and invite them to take any coin they liked the look of.

Unfortunately you can't turn the clock back – instead, walk past the farm and down the lane back to Trefeglwys, where you can console yourself with a pint or two in the Red Lion.

Afon Dysynni

OS 1:50,000 Sheet 124
$4\frac{1}{2}$ miles

Until the 1860s Abergynolwyn, tucked away in its crevice of valley among the southern spurs of Cader Idris, was just a hamlet of a few houses. It lies at the junction of the Afon Dysynni and the Nant Gwernol, where after heavy rain a whirlpool formed which gave the place its name: 'meeting of two waters in a white wheel.' Slate, that useful building and roofing commodity demanded by the growing industrial towns, had been quarried from the hillside to the south-east of Abergynolwyn for a few decades, but the mountainous terrain that necessitated transport by pack-horse had kept the industry small scale.

Then in 1864 the Manchester cotton baron TH McConnel, fearing a blockade of supplies that might be brought about by the American Civil War, formed the Aberdovey Slate Company as an alternative investment. The Bryneglwys quarry was expanded, and strangers came in over the hills to lodge in the village and nearby farmhouses. Three hundred men were employed in the quarry in its heyday, prising out the blocks of raw slate in the candle-lit workings with crowbars and gunpowder, or splitting them by hand into individual wafers of slate – a skilled worker could produce six from a slab one inch thick. Abergynolwyn village expanded as well; slate-built terraces were put up, three chapels were built and shops and pubs opened. Up on the bare hillside the quarry buildings multiplied – workshops, offices, canteens and dormitories for those who lived near the workings all year round. The quarry frequently got into financial difficulties, closed, and then re-opened when matters improved. Finally no one could be found who would put up with the primitive conditions, dangerous work and lonely lifestyle: allied to a lack of investors and the emergence of cheaper, more easily produced materials such as clay and asbestos tiles, this decline had killed off Bryneglwys Quarry by 1947. During its lifetime it had produced 300,000 tons of slate.

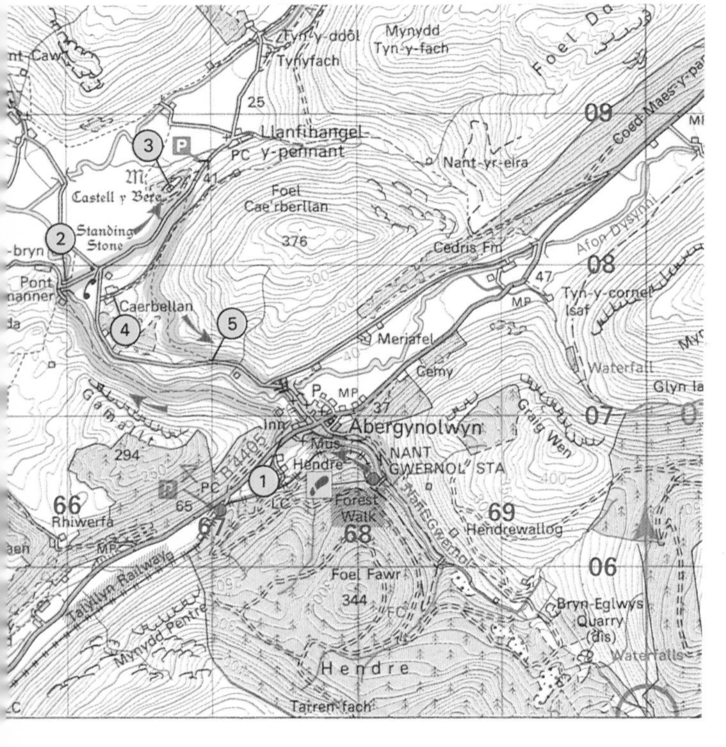

The Talyllyn Railway was opened in 1866 to transport the slate from Bryneglwys to Tywyn on the coast, where it was transferred to the main-line railway system. Passengers could travel on the little trains, bucketing along on their 2ft 3in gauge track, as far as Abergynolwyn – thereafter the line got down in earnest to the stern business of slate-moving. A mile of fairly gently climbing track led to Nant Gwernol station, from which an incline rose sharply up through the trees to the quarry high above the village. Here the slates were loaded into wagons and winched down to Nant Gwernol, their weight pulling up the empties in the opposite direction. If you were a victim of one of the frequent accidents at the quarry, it was best not to sever your leg with a circular saw or crush your head under a fifty-ton block of slate if there happened to be a strong north-easterly blowing at the time; for then the truck bringing the doctor up from Tywyn would be pinned back by the wind and unable to come to your assistance.

When the quarry closed the little railway was expected to follow suit, but train-smoke has always been a powerful promoter of unlikely dreams. A band of enthusiasts decided they would have a go at running the line themselves, and by 1950 had got enough money and willing hands together to form the Talyllyn Railway Preservation Society. Today these pioneers – the first of their kind in the world – are still hard at it, bringing the tourists and steam buffs up into the mountains aboard the Talyllyn's diminutive carriages, hauled by one of their tiny, gleaming locomotives. The Welsh Tourist Board got in on the act, sensing a good thing; it promotes the 'Great Little Trains of Wales' for all they are worth and rubs its hands over the tourists' spending. But it is still enthusiasm and affection, coupled with expert practice, that keeps the Talyllyn Railway on the tracks.

Our walk starts at Nant Gwernol station, used only by the quarrymen until the Preservation Society revived the railway. As *Irish Pete*, *Dolgoch*, *Sir Haydn* or another of the hard-working engines pulls your train away on the return journey to Tywyn, head for the southern end of the platform to cross the Nant Gwernol by a footbridge (682066). The stream runs in a narrow bed of darkly-glinting rocks, beside which you turn left onto a path under oaks and pines. It mounts to a stile and crosses a field to a steep lane, where you bear left to walk down into Abergynolwyn. Pass the end of a double terrace of quarrymen's slate-built houses and arrive at the B4405 road (677070) opposite the Railway Inn (bar food, and children welcome). Turn left here to walk out of the village past the old police station on your left, its door studded with big nail-heads against the kicks of drunken quarry workers.

In a couple of hundred yards go right at a public footpath sign over a stile[1] (674069) onto a grassy path under the elbow of Gamallt hill. Slate is the dominant theme here – footbridges, houses, roofs, memorials and even field boundaries are all made of the stuff. The path curves round the back of Gamallt and enters a wild, lonely valley where it runs on a narrow ridge in the hillside high above the loudly-rushing Afon Dysynni. This is a walker's paradise – a clearly marked path going somewhere purposefully, a strongly-flowing mountain river below and steeply-sloping mountain sides rising above – and hardly a sound outside nature to be heard.

The path skirts a landslip and drops down to Rhiwlas House, whose short drive leads to the single low arch of the bridge over the Afon Dysynni at Pont Ystumanner[2] (660679). Looking north from the bridge, the valley is closed by the sweeping peak of Cader Idris, 2,900 feet tall. Dwarfed in its shadow stands a little hummock of rock which you reach a mile up the road. Glued to the top of the outcrop, and seeming to run together and blend with the rock, is the ruined fortress of Castell y Bere, the 'Castle of the Bird of Prey'[3] (667085). None of your Norman fancifications here – this was a purely Welsh affair, built from around 1221 by Llewellyn the Great and needing neither portcullis nor drawbridge in its impregnable position – so Llewellyn imagined, but he reckoned without the implacable determination of Eng-

The slate-grey Afon Dysynni slips under Pont Ystumanner's low stone arch.

A green skin hides the bones of slate in the hills that dwarf Abergynolwyn.

lish kings. His grandson, Llewellyn, refused to swear allegiance to King Edward I and was beheaded for his trouble. Llewellyn's brother, David, proclaimed himself King of Wales and brought the English down in fury to capture Castell y Bere in 1283. David escaped to a hideout in Snowdonia, but was betrayed, taken, dragged ignominiously through the streets of Shrewsbury, hanged, drawn and quartered. So much for him! The castle was still a desirable property, however, the Welsh and English forces went on taking and retaking it until someone finally put an end to the game by destroying it.

Opposite the castle a footpath leaves the road (668084) and climbs up to a track that skirts the shoulder of Foel Cae'rbellan, running above the closely grouped buildings of Caerbellan Farm[4] (663077). The handsome old grey house behind its massive garden wall was built in 1590, and has been twice restored since then. A low stone building beside it may be the original house built here for the court jester of Castell y Bere – maybe he was just too funny to live with.

Keep a stone wall on your right and the trees beyond Caerbellan below you, and carry on around the side of the hill, looking down on the river and the thread-like track up which you were walking an hour ago. After rain this hillside is drenched with the deliciously fruity smells of wet bracken, gorse and earth. Suddenly the view ahead opens up over Abergynolwyn and the forested slopes above the village, where buzzards circle over the trees.

The track is faintly marked on the hill, but a green footpath sign beckons you down to a stile and the road[5] (670074), along which you walk to enter Abergynolwyn past the Riverside Cafe, two great slate chapels and a long terrace of nineteenth-century quarrymen's single-storey slate cottages. These curve in a crescent up to the B4405 road beside the Railway Inn. Here you cross over and climb up the steep lane to walk across the field and through the trees to Nant Gwernol station and your train.

Afon Glaslyn

OS 1:50,000 Sheet 115
4 miles

Squeezed upwards, buckled, contorted and folded by huge volcanic pressures 400 million years ago, Snowdon must have been a staggering sight as it towered – perhaps as high as Everest – over its great chain of mountains. Even today, worn down by rain, rivers, rock falls and frosts, it dominates the landscape for miles in each direction. Cheeky little man has topped it with a puffing mountain railway, but he has only managed the lightest of touches on its surrounding theme of crags, hollows, and ridges. Under the trimmings of stone walls, fields, farmhouses, roads and railways those tremendous prehistoric upheavals, bitten into sharpness by Ice Age glaciers, stand out and claim attention.

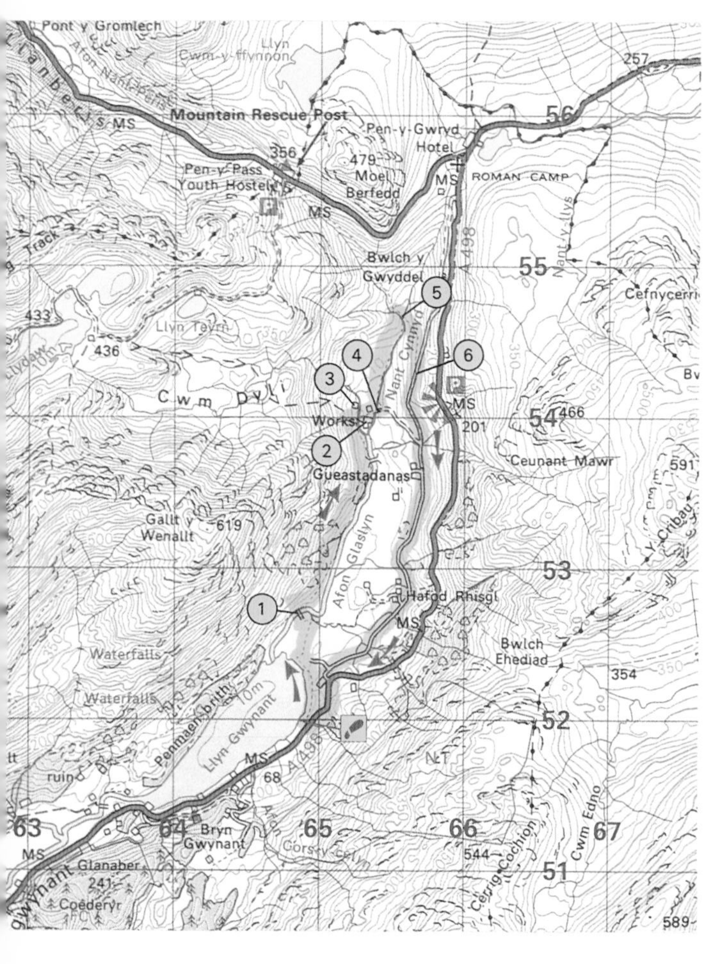

Along the eastern edge of Snowdon flows the Afon Glaslyn, running down from a high pass into Llyn Gwynant (llyn means lake) which lies below the tall crags of Snowdon's flank. These great mountains at the heart of northern Wales attract the rain-clouds blown unimpeded across the Atlantic on the prevailing westerly winds, which release most of their contents over Snowdonia. Your walk is therefore more likely than not to be in the wet – either falling on you or squelching underfoot – the rocks trickling, the turf sodden and the mountain tops wearing a hat of mist. The views are spectacular in sunshine or rain, but you do need a good pair of boots and set of waterproofs to enjoy them properly.

There are several car-parking bays along the A498 road as it skirts the eastern shore of Llyn Gwynant. From the one at the northern end (649520), go down the boggy track and climb a ladder stile to walk among sheep and black-headed gulls around the marshy top of the lake. To your right is a ridge of rock, to your left across the lake the steep crags, ground into sharp spires by the glaciers, which rise up and up to the peak of Gallt y Wenallt ('the high hill'). A skirt of rock just above the water leads to a meadow, across which you walk diagonally between tents and caravans to cross the Afon Glaslyn on a stone footbridge[1] (648527).

On the far side turn right on a narrow, wet and stony track that runs along the bottom edge of a thin wood of ash trees which somehow manage to cling to the steep slopes and survive the winter snows and winds. The landscape seems fixed in solid, rocky permanence, but it is undergoing change all the time, nibbled away by rain and frost which are gradually softening the harsh jaggedness produced by those glaciers.

A waymarked stile over a fence leads down to the shallow, fast-flowing river, whose green water is clear enough to show every stone and pebble in its bed. Beside the path lie lumps of rock, loosened from the slopes above by frosts and washed out by rain to tumble down to their resting places in the valley bottom. The white-

Cwm-dyli power station lies beneath the flanks of the mountains, with the steely waters of Llyn Gwynant beyond.

washed farmhouses in South Wales stand out against their green grassy fields; but the grey and purple farmsteads in this valley blend in with the screes and crags that stand behind them. They are built on ledges of rock to keep them well above river level; but the winds are too strong for shelter trees to stay upright, and they whip the houses unchecked. These meadows are often under water in winter when the swollen Glaslyn bursts its banks, and the river has been hemmed in by the farmers with piles of large boulders against the floods. Farming here is no sinecure – hence the seasonal cash-crop of campers to offset the grim winter months.

The path enters the fringe of the trees again – emerging from them, keep a tumbledown stone wall on your right to cross a ladder stile just below the strongly built block of Cwm-dyli power station[2] (653540). With its Alpine roof and tall ecclesiastical windows it looks curiously at home in this wild valley. The stream coming down from Cwm Dyli, the hollow far above which was gouged out by the glaciers, is channelled by snaking twin pipes down the mountainside to the turbines at the power station. From Cwm Dyli also came the glacier which hollowed out Nant Gwynant valley as it inched its way southward a million or so years ago.

Don't carry on to the left of the power station in front of the old farm above it[3], or you will find yourself – as I did! – climbing up into Cwm Dyli. Instead, turn right to cross the stone footbridge and go through a gate above the station, then along the drive and through the main gate before turning left through a gap in a stone wall[4] onto the right bank of the Nant Cynnyd. This stream used to meet its now piped and confined brother here to form the Afon Glaslyn. Ford the stream a few yards up – note the rusty old motor car, its chrome still brightly gleaming, which some ingenious vandal has dumped here behind a wall. Carry on up the marshy left bank of the Nant Cynnyd until it joins up with two other streams half-way up the Bwlch y Gwyddel, or 'Pass of the Irishman'. Contingents of invaders from the Emerald Isle came over and settled in Wales before the Romans arrived to subdue both them and their hosts.

Ford the Nant Cynnyd where the three streams converge[5] (656547), and turn back on your tracks to climb the steep hillside to a rough farm road[6] (657543). From here there is a splendid view westwards up over Cwm Dyli to the spires and clefts of Snowdon's sides, and southwards over the power station to Llyn Gwynant and its backing ridges.

The farm road slopes down by Gueastadanas and Hafod Rhisgl ('summer pasture at the place of the tree-bark') to meet the A498 road, which you follow back to the car-parking bay beside the lake.

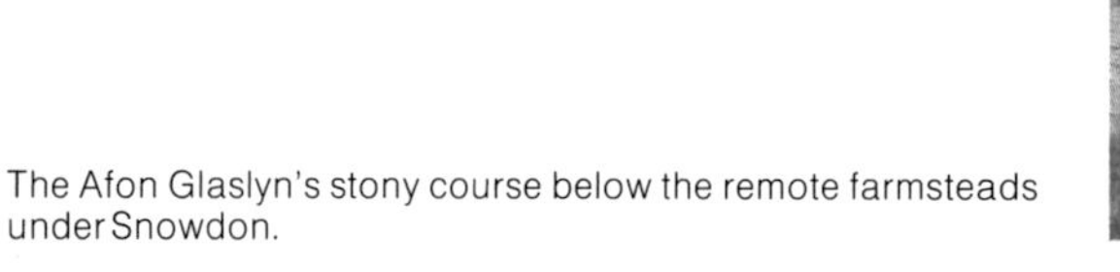

The Afon Glaslyn's stony course below the remote farmsteads under Snowdon.

SECTION SIX

Northern England

River Don

Hebden Water

River Wharfe

River Murk Esk and West Beck

River Esk

River Eden

River Wear

Coldgate Water

River Don

OS 1:50,000 Sheet 111
$6\frac{1}{2}$ miles

A river walk in the South Yorkshire coalfield near a town built on heavy engineering and railway works might sound rather grim – but not when you are lucky enough to have Maurice Hanson as your companion. Maurice, forty-four years a railway craftsman and now the President of the Doncaster Naturalists' Trust, has forgotten more about what goes on by water, wood and field than most amateur naturalists ever get to know – and he carves a superb walking stick, too. Thanks to his humorous, knowledgeable guidance, this walk progressed steadily upwards from the grime to the sublime.

Doncaster is all engineering, railways and coal. The South Yorkshire miners have their base here, the British Rail engineering workshops cover acres of land behind the station, and pylons, power stations and factories fill most aspects of the skyline. Nature does more than cling on by its fingernails, however; it thrives on the derelict sites, along the banks of the River Don and in the woods and ponds that take over from the industrial landscape as you walk south-west out of the town.

On leaving the railway station (571032), turn

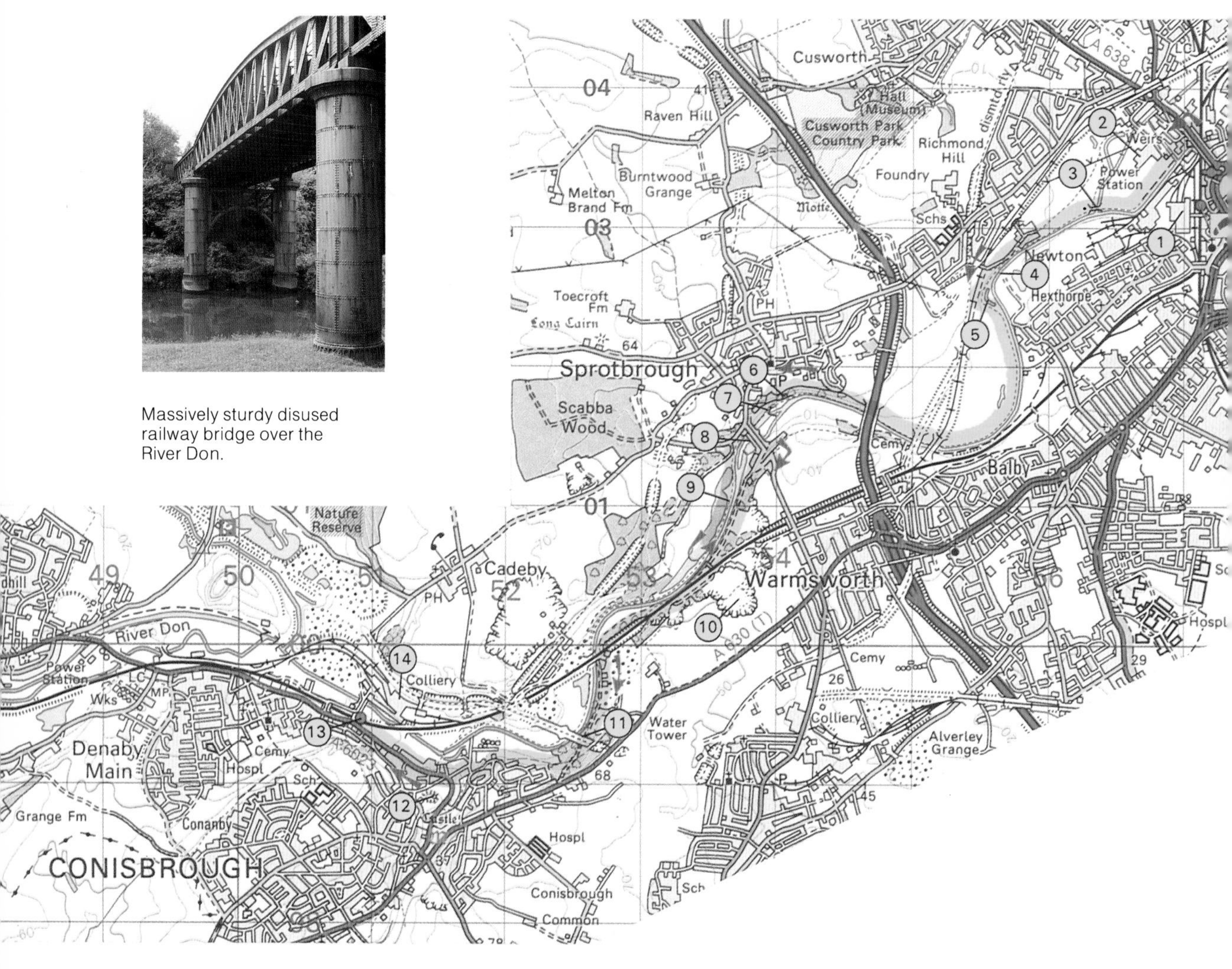

Massively sturdy disused railway bridge over the River Don.

left and walk behind and to the left of Gresley House. Over the river are the long red-brick sheds of the railway works[1], which were established in Doncaster in 1853. *Mallard* and *Flying Scotsman* were among the famous steam locomotives that were built here. Beyond the works rise the two tall chimneys of Crimpsall Power Station[2]. Its design was already obsolete when it was built in the early 1950s on a marsh site. It spent years going in and out of service, and is already closed down and derelict.

Go through the railway arch in front of you and turn left, with the large pile of St George's Church on your right. Walk down a concrete slipway to the canal, which you cross by way of the lock gates, and go up a paved path and over a low wall. Turn left to pass under another railway arch, which leads to the path on the right bank of

the canal. An ornate water tower is reflected in the canal from its place along the chimneys, pipes, tanks, sheds and wagons of the railway works. On your right are the grimy glass walls of the power station (567036) in a sea of greasy mud and water, heavily guarded by barbed wire. This is industrial Doncaster pressed down and running over; but as the River Don flows in from the left to absorb the canal (563031)[3], things begin to be both greener and quieter. The pale stone frontage and many windows of Cusworth Hall stand among trees away to the right, and open country lies ahead as you leave the last outposts of the railway works behind.

Keep to the left of a white farmhouse (559029) on a narrow ledge between wall and river, and walk on among the trees that overhang the water. Bright-yellow charlock grows in the banks of the river and what they call 'fools' parsley' in this part of the world and 'gypsy lace' in the West Country – alias cow parsley. Just opposite a warning notice in the river ('Caution. Keep right for channel'), was the site of a ferry (557027)[4] which Maurice Hanson and his friends in the RAF used to reach the pub. It cost them three ha' pence on the outward journey, and a 'skinful of booze' to the ferryman on the way back. Beyond is a thick bank of black ooze, dumped when the river was widened to take huge barges that never got off the planners' drawing-board. The Don was canalized in the mid-eighteenth century to provide an outlet for goods from the town. It takes a great sweep under the houses of Balby, isolating an ox-bow of water on the right bank, known as Ball Pond[5] (557018). Water violets grow there nowadays, but it has a sad history – a young lady drowned herself in the pond when she heard of the death of her sailor-boy.

The path goes under two railway bridges, the first bypassing main-line Doncaster with coal and steel trains, the second a defunct line which is being converted into a cycleway. This second bridge has solid cylindrical piers with the rivets standing out from the plates like a battleship, and delicate lattice arches between them in contrast. The A1 motorway bridge stands beyond, after which you go into the skirts of a wood where wrens and blackcaps sing, and where early purple orchids grow in the shade. Here the river banks are a jungle of pinky-purple Himalayan balsam. On your right is a derelict pumping house[6], abandoned in 1935, which still contains its iron wheels – it lifted water from the Don up to the fountains at Sprotbrough Hall above the woods.

From Sprotbrough Lock[7] (540017) a pleasure boat takes parties up the river. Beyond the lock stands the old stone house[8] (538016) where Sir Walter Scott stayed while he was writing *Ivanhoe*; he set some of the scenes in Conisbrough Castle, which we visit at the end of this walk. The house is now a pub and restaurant.

Behind it is a courtyard walled in by splendid medieval stone barns – the one nearest to the path is cut at an acute angle like a wedge of cheese.

The coal-mining that still sustains this part of South Yorkshire has resulted in large areas of subsidence, and one of these flooded depressions forms Sprotbrough Flash[9] (531003–537013), a nature reserve maintained by the Yorkshire Naturalists' Trust. Young people on training schemes have built wooden hides where you can sit and look out through observation slits on the wildlife of the long, rush-encircled lake. Nearly 150 species of birds have been recorded here, including great crested and little grebes. On the far side of the flash is Potridings Wood, where marsh orchids grow.

Having gazed your fill, return to the road bridge at Sprotbrough (538014) and cross over to the east bank of the Don. The path runs below the magnesium limestone quarry[10] – first the abandoned eastern end, where there were 500 pairs of jackdaws when Maurice Hanson came here as a boy (seven birds at his last count) – next the active section, clattering away and sending clouds of dust over the nearby trees and fields. The path leaves the quarry area to go under the twenty-one-arch Conisbrough Viaduct[11] (527993) – 1,525 feet long and standing 113 feet above the water. It was brought into service in 1905, but is now disused. Some daring sparks have covered the central girders with graffiti – they must have had cool heads and a sound circus training to get out there!

From the viaduct it is a short step into Conisbrough, whose ruined castle stands up proudly above the village[12] (515989). Its great keep, ninety feet tall, has been held up by its thick radiating buttresses for 800 years, but there is not much else left of the stronghold built in the twelfth century by King Henry II's half-brother Hameline Plantagenet. In fact it was abandoned by the middle of the fifteenth century, and was so far decayed by the time of the Civil War that no one thought it worth either defending or attacking. It owes its good state of preservation to that, and to its construction in magnesium limestone, which is so hard that neither wind nor rain can grind it down.

Conisbrough's church of St Peter is the oldest building still standing in South Yorkshire – its nave, though covered up by Norman work, is Saxon in origin. The village was a busy place when its glass-bottle factory, tanneries, breweries and brick works were operating. Its sickle factory employed thirty-five men, turning out half a million grass cutting tools. The canalizing of the Don nurtured these enterprises, but they all declined as the river did. Opposite the station[13] (509994), however, the large Cadeby Colliery[14] still goes on cutting coal, which accounts for the railway's continued existence. Doncaster trains call every half-hour, and one of these will take you back up the valley of the River Don to your starting point.

A warrior from another age defends the tall ruins of Conisbrough Castle.

Hebden Water

OS 1:50,000 Sheet 103
8 miles

If you just want the icing of this walk, begin it at the car-park under Hardcastle Crags – but the old wool and weaving town of Hebden Bridge makes a better starting point if you want to enjoy the whole cake.

The West Yorkshire countryside around Hebden Bridge is like an animated display of the effects of the Industrial Revolution. Here in a couple of square miles are the bare moor tops, the farmsteads that first made inroads into them, the early weaving cottages, the small, primitive water-powered mills high up on their hillside streams and the conglomeration of terraced housing, huge mills and factories attracted to the valley bottoms by improved roads, canals and railways. Hebden Bridge is packed down and crammed into its narrow valley, mill upon mill and house upon house. Now that steam is no longer king and the overhanging pall of smoke and soot has gone from the Calder Valley, Hebden Bridge is cleaning up its old buildings. The oxidized black overcoat on their millstone grit is disappearing, leaving them as fresh and honey coloured as the day the stone was quarried. 'Tha'll not get a whiff o' wool in Hebden,' John Hillaby was told when he passed through on his journey across Britain in 1965 – not only the smell, but the whirring and clattering of the mills is gone. City-quitters are settling here for the clean air and wholesome surroundings! The Hampstead of the North is the nickname the town has earned, though any true native over forty can tell you about Hebden Bridge when it was muck and brass from top to bottom. Yet a glance forwards from Old Bridge[1] (992273), the ancient pack-horse bridge in the town centre where we begin our walk, travels straight up over mill chimney and clinging terrace to the high sheep pastures from which the shepherds looked down on nearly deserted valley-bottoms of trees, marsh and water only 300 years ago.

The Old Bridge was built in 1510, to carry goods safely across the river at one of the points where men and beasts had to descend to valley level from the safety of the moorland track from Halifax to Burnley. Looking upriver from the bridge, the proud 1898 buildings in classical mode of the UDC stand on the left of St George's Bridge (opened 1893); on the right, the late eighteenth-century Bridge Mill, now split into boutiques and a restaurant. Waterside mills predate their chimneys – Bridge Mill's tall funnel was added in 1820 when steam shouldered water-power aside.

Walk off Old Bridge to the right, and turn left up Bridge Gate past the Shoulder of Mutton pub and the White Lion, dated 1657. Go left up the Keighley road, looking down over the blackened gritstone wall onto Bridge Mill's weir and the squashed-together rows of chimneys, serrated factory roofs and terraces. Opposite the

Old pack-horse bridge leading to steps up the steep hillside and out of Hebden Bridge.

Nutclough House Hotel turn left[2] (994275) down a lane towards the Hebden Water, and peer over the wall on your left into the yard of Nutclough Works. The mill was run by the Hebden Bridge Fustian Manufacturing Society, a co-operative concern, from 1873 until the end of the First World War. It turned out enough fustian (a heavy-duty cotton that outlasted any other material) to make the town 'the fustian centre of the world'. On your right are houses built against a bank so steep that the family living in the top two storeys entered their portion of the house round the back, three floors up. Further down there are some older hand-loom weavers' cottages, their upper storeys full of windows as close together as possible to let in the light.

At the bottom of the lane you pass the blackened stump of a mill chimney and go over the river by a narrow bridge[3] (992278), beyond which a twisty, walled and cobbled lane – half slope and half steps – rises up the hillside. Half-way up, turn right along a path whose central stones have been deeply grooved by the feet of workers going between their houses on the hill and their workplaces down below.

Packed terraces of Hebden Bridge rise from the mills jostling by the Hebden Water in the valley bottom.

In the trees beyond a group of old cottages[4] the path forks – walk straight ahead, then turn down to your right in a hundred yards between oak, birch and mountain ash. There is a long, sheer drop to the river on your right, so do take care. The path crosses a stream whose boulders, scoured of their oxidized black by the water, shine a dark honey colour, and descends to meet a lane above a weir[5] (992282). Here turn left, and left again up a path which is soon enclosed by walls. Just before a farm turn sharp left round a hairpin bend[6], then immediately right up a flight of narrow stone steps – those workers must have had calf muscles of iron. At the top (990285), go right along a wall below the trees, and right again at a 'Calderdale Way' sign and yellow arrow waymark, down the slope on a rough lane. Cold, extinguished chimneys from dead mills poke up into the sky on the hilltop ahead, while down below there is a smoking one at the still operating dye works by the river. Pass the tiny Midgehole Working Men's Club and cross the river by New Bridge[7]. Walk up to the road and turn left to the car-park[8] (988292) at the entrance to the Hardcastle Crags woods.

Once among the trees, you are walking in one of those storehouses of nature which seem to survive no matter how many thousands of people pass through. Red squirrels, long-tailed tits, dippers, woodpeckers; Scots pines, cedar of Lebanon, Indian cedar, Weymouth and Douglas pines among a total of twenty-nine tree species; 158 types of moss; thirty-two sorts of liverwort; butterflies, moths, dragonflies, frogs, toads ... on and on go the lists compiled by the local naturalists. At the bottom of it all runs the clear, sparkling Hebden Water, crossed by dams and siphoned by water races whose mills have vanished, marked only by a few mossy stones on the banks. The path runs beside the river at water level or climbs above it through the trees and banks of bracken, with a feeling all the time of high moorland ahead.

Gibson Mill[9] (973298), standing half-way up the valley and reflected in its grass-choked mill pond, had half a century of water-powered operation before a steam engine was installed and the chimney run up in 1852. Poor communications and competition from further down the valley had killed it off by the turn of the century. Recently it has undergone a series of rather bizarre reincarnations as a restaurant, roller-skating rink and dance hall; but the problem for customers is getting here, and then getting away again. Now it stands boarded up and empty.

From the sluice wheel above the mill dam the path rises to meet a forest road, along which you turn left to pass the Crags[10] (972304), a jumbled group of blocks and boulders fallen from the hillside in a landslip. The path veers left off the road between two National Trust boundary stones, and crosses a beck (972310) that leaps down its steep bed from Wadsworth Moor. Turn up to the right[11] through a stone wall and climb the path on the left bank of the beck. At the top, turn left to go through a swing gate in the angle of a wall on the edge of a stand of pines. The grim black brow of Lord Savile's one-time shooting lodge at Walshaw[12] (973313) peers over the top of the ridge. A tall white pole, topped with a weather-vane, stands in front of the lodge, and a gate beside it leads to stone steps over a wall and a rough track behind the cluster of green-grey, weather-beaten buildings in their remote, high setting.

Turn right down the track, a walled lane which you follow for two miles along the flank of the moor, looking down into the wooded cleft of the Hebden Water valley. The farms along the lane are stark, windy places, some of their houses semi-derelict. Windows are mullioned and latticed, barn doors are arched and their walls pierced with thin slits to admit as much light and as little wind as possible. These isolated farmsteads were tinder for the spark of Methodism in the eighteenth century, and their buildings saw many a farm labourer and weaver transfixed by strong preaching and salvation. That spark grew into holy flames that licked all over the moors and valleys of West Yorkshire – hence the great, plain chapels on the hilltops and in the townships where the itinerant hell-fire preachers would pull their congregations, worked half to death in the grinding labour of the early Industrial Revolution, wholesale into the paths of righteousness.

The views up here to the south, west and east are enormous. The Old Town above Hebden Bridge comes slowly into sight, running down its ridge towards the valley below; and the monument on Stoodley Pike sticks up into the clouds away to the south. The track passes Lady

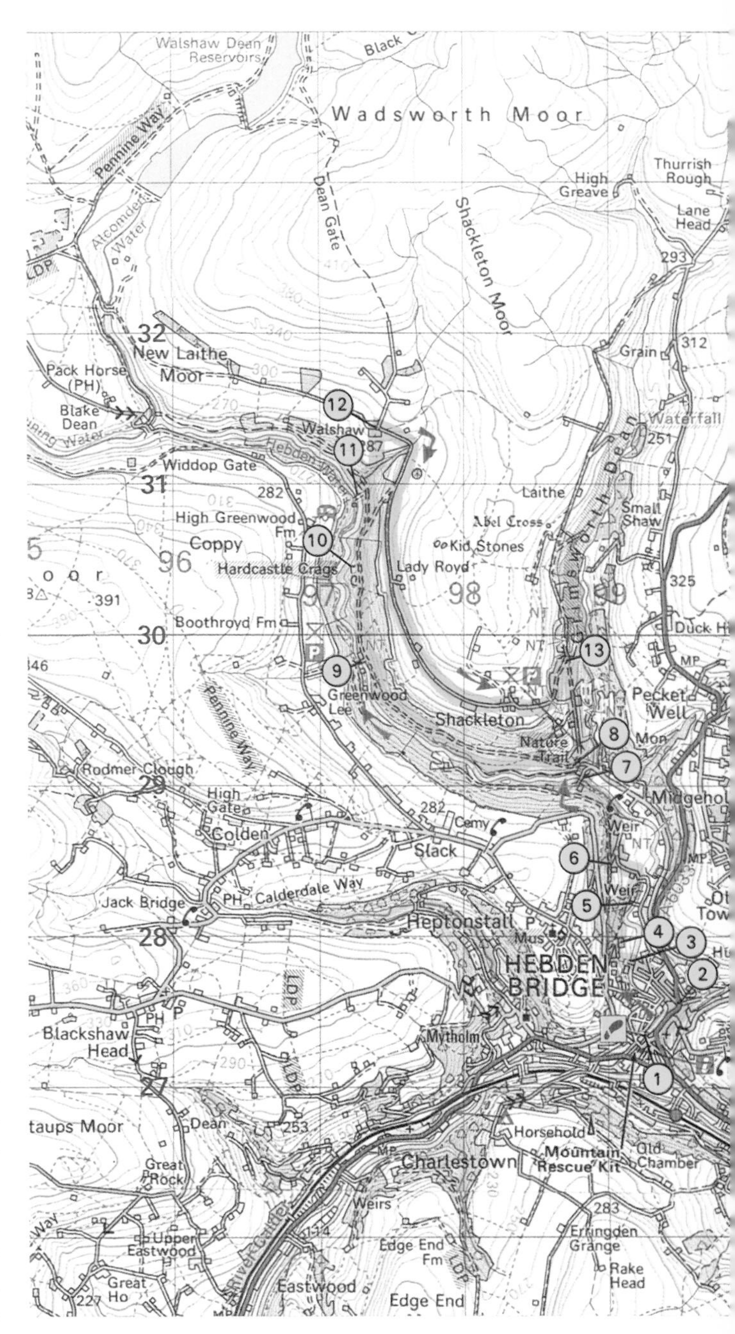

Royd (where there was a school for the children of these high farms) and Shackleton before swinging north to enter the woods, then sharply south (987298)[13] down Crimsworth Dean and back to the car-park under Hardcastle Crags. From here you walk slowly up the years from the natural marvels of the woods and high moors towards man's own more recent endeavours along the valley floor.

River Wharfe

OS 1:50,000 Sheet 98
10 miles

Although this walk follows the head waters of the River Wharfe upstream, for most of its length it runs not in Wharfedale but up the lesser known valley of Langstrothdale. This area was settled by the Norse invaders, and the syllables of their tongue are reflected in the lovely names of the settlements along the river banks – Hubberholme is the flat land by the water where Hubba set up home, and Yockenthwaite the clearing made by Eogan. There are no mills here, and farming is the only industry – though Buckden, the start of our walk, knew wild times when the miners from nearby lead delvings came in every so often to spend their earnings.

The River Wharfe takes its name from the Saxon *guerf* or swift, and its waters still hasten over the limestone pavement which forms their bed. Over the centuries they have smoothed and eroded the limestone into hollows, cups and ledges which force the water to curve sharply from bank to bank. Each side rise the steep slopes of Langstrothdale, lined with stone walls and dotted with old stone barns. Dippers, swallows and herons feed along the river, while from the hilltops comes the bubbling call of curlews. Langstrothdale is peaceful – so much so that even on cloudy days there are cars parked along the riverside road, whose occupants set out deck chairs in which they can do the crossword and drink Thermoses of tea beside the soothing rush of the water. On Sundays in summer the river is full of children dashing through the shallows and spraying water over each other – 'Blackpool by the Wharfe' is the locals' name for it. The Dales Way long-distance footpath runs along our upward route, but we return to Buckden by high-level paths overlooking the dale which are unfrequented even in high summer.

The 'buck' in Buckden harks back to pre-Conquest days when Langstrothdale was a vast hunting forest, so thickly wooded that it was said that a squirrel could go from the dale's head to Buckden without setting foot on the ground. Buckden village was founded by the Norse settlers as a dwelling place for the foresters. The staunchly Catholic Percy family held sway here until Tudor times, when the new ruling house cast them into the outer darkness; then the Cliffords took over in Langstrothdale. The Wharfe looks shallow and innocent enough in summer, but in winter it can turn in a few hours into a swollen monster capable of swallowing anything in its path. The village of Starbotton, two miles down the valley from Buckden, was completely destroyed in a disastrous flood at the end of the seventeenth century, after which Buckden built its bridge.

Walk down to the bridge from the car-park at the northern end of the village (942774). On the far side a wooden fingerpost marked 'Hubberholme – Dales Way' points the route along the river bank under Rakes Wood. After half a mile a stone wall accompanies the path up to the road[1], just above Grange Farm (932780), where you turn right and walk along to the George Inn[2] (926782) by Hubberholme bridge. The pub was once the vicar's residence, and is the scene of a remarkable auction every New Year. Its origin was charitable, the nearby 'Poor Field' being auctioned off to raise money for the poor of the parish. The vicar and churchwardens entered the pub in solemn procession, and a lighted candle was placed on the bar. The clerics retired to the parlour to receive the bids made by the locals in the taproom. The bidder who had made the highest offer by the time the candle went out was judged the winner, after which a feast and singsong were held. The ceremony still takes place, though nowadays it is a professional auctioneer rather than the vicar who takes the bids.

On the far side of the pack-horse bridge is the low, wide Church of St Michael and All Angels[3]. It contains a wonderfully carved and painted rood loft of 1558, which somehow escaped the edict of Queen Elizabeth I that all such symbols of popish idolatry should be

The limestone bed of the Wharfe eroded into cups and hollows below the Scandinavian-looking long, low farm buildings at Yockenthwaite.

destroyed. Perhaps the Percys saved it – their badge is featured among the carvings. Pews and chairs in the church were made in the works of Robert Thompson at Kilburn, North Yorkshire, and many of them carry his trademark, a carved mouse. A fellow carver remarked to Thompson one day while they were making a church roof that they were as poor as church mice, whereupon Thompson set to and carved his first mouse on the spot. Later he reflected on how in time mice could unobtrusively nibble away the hardest wood, and saw a parallel with the work of his modest business tucked away in the North Yorkshire hills. The little mice became the symbol of his craft, and appear wherever he worked in churches and other buildings all over the country.

When the vicar was living in Littondale, three long miles away to the south-west, he would ride on a white pony over the hills to take services at Hubberholme. The parishioners prudently waited until they could see the white dot of his steed on the hilltop before ringing the church bell to summon the faithful to worship.

The path curves round the end of the church to a wooden fingerpost marked 'Yockenthwaite – Dales Way', from which it runs beside the Wharfe through fields of close-bitten grass where the stone barns stand squarely against wind, weather and the centuries. One near the path (918784) is dated and signed 'JT 1804' over the door, but this was probably inscribed after a rebuilding – the Langstrothdale barns are several hundreds of years old. Those at Yockenthwaite (905790), along with the long, stone houses, were built in the seventeenth century, and make a fine contrasting group of grey stone against green hillside when seen from the far side of the valley.

The path passes the farmhouse by a fingerpost marked 'Deepdale & Beckermonds – Dalesway', and continues along the northern bank of the river past the stone circle of a Bronze Age burial site[4] (898795). The stones are not upstanding monoliths like those at Avebury or on the Cornish moors – these are stubby, weather-beaten lumps, half buried in the ground. The faint arches of strip fields laid down by the Angles who settled here run up the valley sides. The buildings at Deepdale echo this Scandinavian influence, too, in their length and lowness. Below them you cross the river on an iron girder bridge[5] (892797) to follow a rough cart track up to Beckermonds, another group of strong, solid houses and barns, well spaced from its neighbours at the remote top of Langstrothdale. The name probably signifies 'mouths of the becks' from the Green Field and Oughtershaw Becks which meet here to form the River Wharfe (874802).

Cross the footbridge[6] and then the pack-horse bridge[7] to return to Yockenthwaite. The route back can be varied by walking along the motor road, from which you can appreciate the tenaciousness of the ash trees by the river. Their solid mass of roots grip the rocks even where the earth beneath them has been completely flooded away. At Yockenthwaite you climb up beside the farm to a wooden fingerpost marked 'Cray & Hubberholme', pointing up the slope to a cart track running above Rais Wood. Ruined barns and stone walls stand along a limestone pavement eroded into lumps like fallen tree branches, which forms the lip of the valley. The path runs through the neck of Rais Wood and turns northward above the remote and beautifully placed Scar House[8] (921789), looking down Wharfedale over Hubberholme and Buckden. Quakerism took a strong hold here in its early days, and crowds of local people came up along this path to hear the preaching of one of the founders of the movement, George Fox.

The 2,000-foot hulk of Buckden Pike is in view ahead as you turn your right shoulder on Wharfedale and walk down to the White Lion Inn at Cray[9] (941791). It's a friendly and inexpensive pub, serving good beer and food to the weary traveller.

Opposite the pub you ford the Cray Gill at a fingerpost 'Footpath to Cray Bridge ½ – Buckden 1½'. A steep scramble up the slope brings you out[10] (944791) onto the old main route above Rakes Wood where the coaches lurched along the limestone shelf in the days before valley-bottom travel was safe. This track, a quiet green road nowadays, has seen 2,000 years of activity. It was built by the army of Caesar Agricola as a military road, and has a number of massive stone gate posts to witness to its great age. It runs above the dale for a mile before dipping down[11] (940780) through Rakes Wood to the car-park at Buckden.

The fields of Langstrothdale are dotted with these old stone barns, their roofs steeply pitched against winter snows.

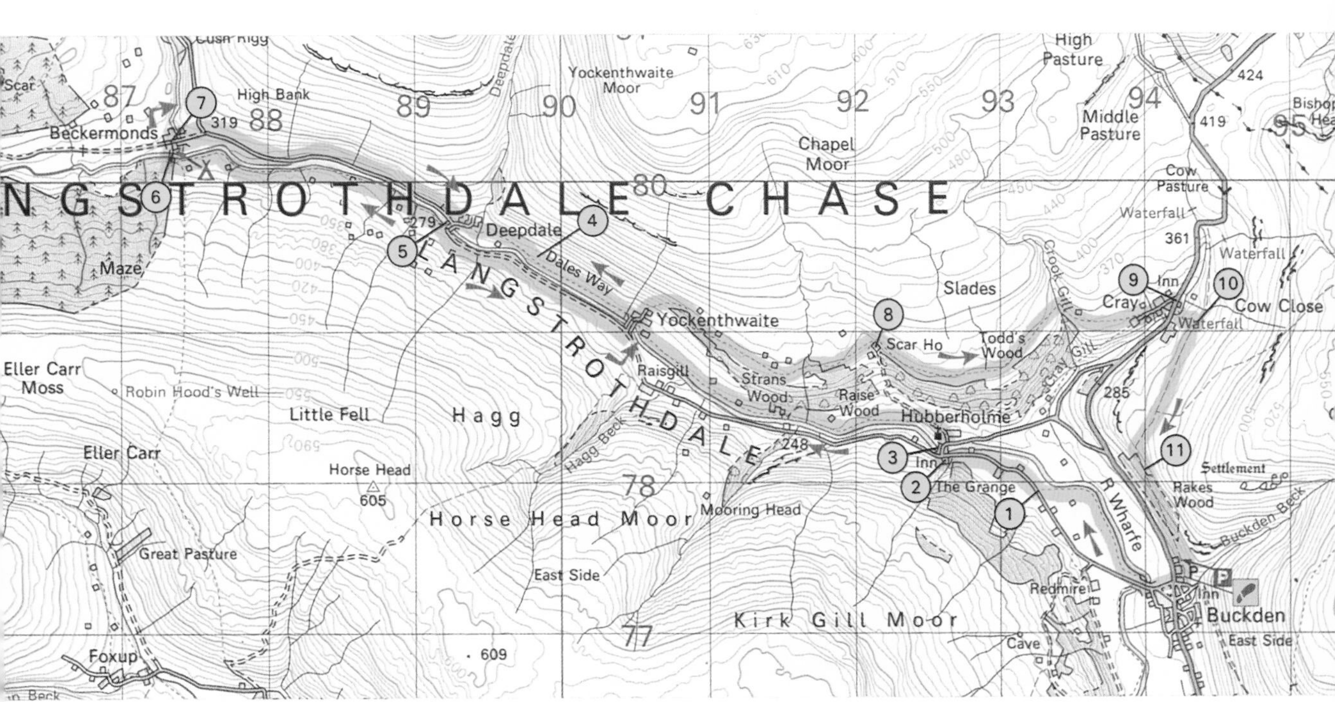

River Murk Esk and West Beck

OS 1:50,000 Sheet 94
4 miles

Two moorland railway lines dominate this walk, both closed and then reopened – one for steam trains, the other for walkers. The steam line is the North York Moors Railway which runs north from Pickering to meet the British Rail system just beyond Grosmont Station. Since it was reopened in 1973 the steam railway has been an enormous success; that would have pleased the Father of Railways, George Stephenson, who built the original line back in 1836. The track that was laid out under his supervision came to a sticky, not to say gory end, and now runs as a pleasant riverside footpath below the clanking, panting, superbly-restored locomotives that pull tourists and locals slowly along the North York Moors Railway.

At the level crossing by Grosmont Station (828053) – pronounced 'Grow-mont' – a signboard marked 'Footpath to Loco Shed and Goathland' stands at the entrance to the path, which runs up to cross over the top of two tunnels built side by side[1]. The smaller of the two, 119 yards long, is just tall enough to give passage to the horses that were the railway's tractive power from 1836 for the next eleven years; the larger one beside it was built when steam locomotives took over in 1847. Grosmont was the centre of a large-scale iron-working industry, with its own furnaces for smelting the locally-mined ore until larger ones were established on the coast further north. One hundred thousand tons of ore went every year by rail to Whitby to be shipped round to the furnaces on Tyneside. The North York Moors line was an important link in the railway network, giving through communication between the fishing port of Whitby and the markets of London. Unfortunately, as we will see later in the walk, it had a fatal flaw.

From the top of the tunnels the path turns left through a kissing gate at a yellow arrow waymark and green 'public footpath' sign to run beside the railway, with the locomotives, cranes and wagons of the North York Moors Railway (NYMR) on the left and beyond them the Murk Esk river, flowing in a series of gentle curves through the trees. The air is full of the sour, exciting smell of steam, coal-smoke and oil. A large colony of orchids grows by the path, apparently unaffected by this pollution.

Soon the railway line swings away, and the path on the trackbed of the original line runs ahead to pass Esk Valley[2] (823042), a terrace of cottages built for the ironstone workers which looks as if it might have been transplanted complete from a Durham pit village.

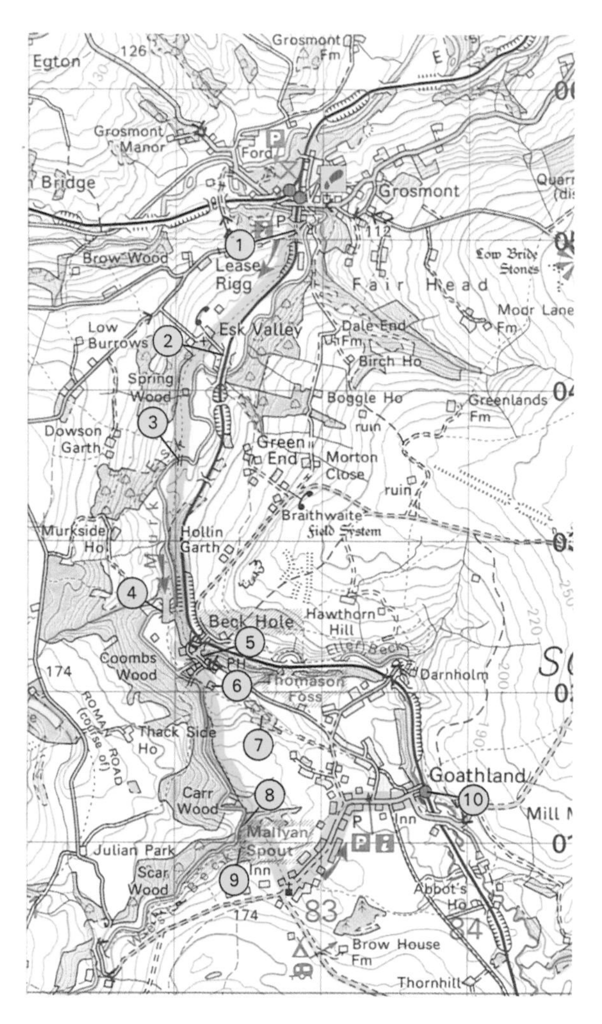

Beer, groceries and afternoon tea are all on sale in the Birch Hall Inn at Beck Hole.

The disused line passes between the cottages and the Esk Valley Methodist Chapel, built in 1902 for the workers here, and enters the woods which echo with the efforts of locomotives on the NYMR away to the left. It crosses the Murk Esk by a footbridge[3] (820035) which rests on the boat-shaped piers of a demolished railway bridge, and runs on through steep-sided sheep pastures overlooked by red-roofed farmhouses standing on the brow of the valley. The Murk Esk, now on the right of the path, has all the characteristics of a moorland river – shallow, noisy and bounded by mossy boulders and trees whose roots stand clear of the banks, the soil washed away by floods.

The old railway line curves away to cross the river – the bridge has gone, but the buttress still stands against the far bank, its stone blocks half hidden under nettles and saplings. The path keeps to the left bank of the river by trees which have been undisturbed for many years.

The disused line recrosses the river on a low, moss-grown arched viaduct[4] (819025), beside which our path comes to a sign pointing to the right and marked 'Public footpath to Egton Bridge – Egton'. Go straight forward here to reach the hamlet of Beck Hole, a string of old stone houses leading to a bridge over the Eller Beck[5] (821022). An ironworks was in production here between 1858 and 1864, employing 200 men, but after its short life the place slipped back again into peaceful obscurity. On the far side of the bridge is a remarkable pub, the Birch Hall Inn. You can buy a pint by way of a little hatchway and drink it in the tiny, dark taproom, decorated with old photographs of local quoits teams on the smoke-browned wallpaper; or take tea and cakes in the morning or afternoon, or buy provisions over the counter in the shop section of the building. On the wall outside hangs a rather superior pub sign, an oil painting of Beck Hole – it should be good, as it was painted by Algernon Newton, RA.

Just above the pub, turn right through two gates to reach Incline Cottage[6] (822020), the former station on the old line. From the gate ahead the Beck Hole Incline[7] rises at a gradient of one in fifteen for three-quarters of a mile, a damned nuisance for travellers in Victorian days until a tragedy occurred which led to its closure, and then the abandonment of the whole Grosmont to Goathland line and the building of the new railway. From 1836 a four-ton water tank at the top of the incline hauled up the wagons on hempen ropes, descending as the wagons rose to be emptied out when it reached the bottom; then in 1847 a steam engine and wire cables were installed. The incline had been constructed so that the railway company could avoid the expense of tunnelling under Wheeldale Moor, and was always a source of delay; but it sufficed until the evening of 10th February, 1864, when the wires suddenly snapped as the last train of the day was ascending the incline. The guard, Joseph Sedman, tried frantically to slow down the plummeting carriages, but they went on gathering speed all the way to the bottom. Here beside the station they overturned, spilling out the passengers. Two were killed, and thirteen injured. It was a devastating blow which forced the immediate closure of the incline, and therefore the whole line. Work on a new section between Grosmont and Goathland went ahead so quickly that within fifteen months the new link was established and the old line reverted to undergrowth and slow decay.

Go over the stile opposite Incline Cottage to climb steep steps to the top of the ravine, at the bottom of which runs the West Beck. The path descends to river level and comes to a wooden fingerpost[8] pointing left to Goathland and forward to Mallyan Spout[9] (824010). This seventy-foot waterfall pours down a rocky cleft at a bend in the beck, constantly soaking the dark green mats of moss clinging to the rock face. The bed of the beck is piled with flat tables of rock, large blocks of which lie under Mallyan Spout where they have fallen from the wall of the ravine.

Back at the fingerpost, a seemingly interminable flight of wooden steps eventually reaches the Mallyan Hotel at Goathland (827007). This is a real moorland village, where sheep graze the rough grass, sedge and heather of the common between the scattered houses. Witchcraft was a potent force here – everyone knew that the best way to force a witch out of hiding was to pierce the heart of a cow with pins and roast it on the cottage fire at midnight. The witch would be given away by her shrieks of agony. Goathland had its own family of witches, of which Awd and Young Nanny Pierson were the most notorious.

Deep in the woods the Murk Esk sparkles under a disused bridge that carried the original line of railway from Pickering to Grosmont.

Nowadays the Goathland Plough Stotts continue the rural tradition; t'Owd Man, t'Owd Woman, Isaac, Betty and the Madgy Pegs in horns and blackened faces dance, sing and pull the plough which in rougher times would dig up the garden of misers too mean to contribute to the collection. It's a form of the Plough Monday ceremony held in January in most parts of the country, but in August here. The Plough Stotts ('stotts' are young bulls, or rampant young men) are much in demand at local folk festivals, exporting this very specialized ceremony far and wide.

From the hotel, turn left up the village street for the best part of a mile to reach the station[10] (837013), where you board one of the restored carriages of the North York Moors Railway to be pulled by one of their splendid locomotives back to Grosmont.

River Esk

OS 1:50,000 Sheet 90
8½ miles

There are so many wonderful riverside walks in the Lake District that it's an almost impossible task to choose just one. This ramble up Eskdale does have several advantages, though – you reach it by steam railway; it's gentle enough to be done as a family walk, yet penetrates far up one of the wildest valleys in the Lakes; there are no stiff climbs or heart-stopping scrambles up sheer mountainsides; and, best of all, it rises to superb views of Bow Fell, one of the highest peaks in England, and of Scafell Pike, the highest of all. If you have time and energy to spare, you can extend the walk at its northern end and give yourself the pleasure of standing above everyone else in the kingdom. As on all long walks in the Lake District, good boots, waterproof gear and a map and compass are essential. There are boggy bits, and stony bits, in these eight miles; a sunny morning at Dalegarth doesn't necessarily mean a sunny afternoon higher up the valley. Even if everything is clear, the map and compass will help you to identify the fells and peaks around you.

The miniature engines and open carriages of the Ravenglass and Eskdale Railway, known affectionately as 'Ratty', bring you up from the Cumbrian coast to Dalegarth Station (173008), the terminus of the line. The little railway was opened in May 1875 to carry iron ore from the mines above the village of Boot down to the ships at Ravenglass. When the ore ran out there was granite to be transported seaward, and when that became uneconomic in 1953 the tourists still came flocking, carrying the railway on from strength to strength.

From the wooden café-cum-station turn left along the narrow road to the lane on the left (175008)[1] that leads to Boot and the Burnsmoor Inn. The village makes a charming picture, scattered in whitewash and granite under the flank of Great Barrow. Opposite the turning to Boot you go right along a twisting, walled lane that leads down to the seventeenth-century St Catherine's Church on the north bank of the Esk[2] (175002). There are no other buildings near

Rowan berries make a bright splash against the green and grey of the Esk at Doctor's Bridge.

the little church, which stands alone facing the river. Some well-preserved eighteenth-century gravestones are in the churchyard, and a notice on the door reminds visitors to close it against the sheep. Inside, the church is plain, low and quiet, conducive to meditation which can quickly turn into sleep on a warm afternoon!

From St Catherine's you turn left along the river bank for a delightful mile up to Doctor's Bridge. The river curves between rose-tinted blocks of granite, overhung with rowan trees whose delicate white flowers or scarlet berries give this stretch a special charm in spring and autumn. Ahead up the valley stands the steeply stepped profile of Birker Fell, a prelude to the far grander fells higher up the river. Soon you come to the twin girders of a bridge that once carried

Lining Crag
Allen Crags
785
910
Great End
6
759
Esk Hause
Tongue Head
Lingmell Crag
647
Lingmell
Round How
Long Pike
Corridor Route
Broad Crag
Tongue
Angle Tarn
885
Rossett Pike
Hanging Knotts
Esk Pike
Ore Gap
Ill Crag
7
977
Hollow Stones
SCAFELL PIKE
Little Narrowcove
Mickledore
Lord's Rake
Broad Stand
Mountain Rescue Kit
964
Dow Crag
Yeastyrigg Crags
BOW FELL
902
Great Slab
Pike de Bield Moss
Bowfell Links
5
SCA FELL
CUM
06
Waterfall
Cam Spout Crag
NT
Gait Crags
Green Hole
Three Tarns
Great Moss
815
Slight Side
762
05
Long Crag
Long Top
Scar Lathing
Quagrigg Moss
Adam-a-
High Scarth Crag
445
Silverybield Crag
Throstle Garth
04
10
Waterfalls
Black Crag
Whinscales
Heron Crag
03
Yew Bank
499
Mosedale
11
Brock Crag
Eskdale Needle
Hard Knott
549
Stony Tarn
Waterfall
Yew Crags
02
Border End
522
Rake
Weir
Gill Bank
Eel Tarn
Great Barrow
12
Taw House
River Esk
9
Hardknott Pass
393
Eskdale Mill
Hows
Paddock Wray
13
Brotherilkeld
Boot
Birdhow
8
Hardknott Fort
MEDIOBOGDVM ROMAN FORT
Black Hall
1
Inn
Hollins
Inn
76
01
Penny Hill Fm
Wha House Fm
DALEGARTH STA
Armont Ho
18
137
4
3
Low Birker
20
Crowhow End
22
23
Castle How
2
Demming Crag
Birker Fell

ore trucks from mines south of the Esk to Dalegarth Station and the 'Ratty'. Bear left here through a gate into a walled lane that becomes a path along the hillside leading down to the slender stone arch of Doctor's Bridge[3] (189008). Over the bridge is a track leading away from the clear green waters of the Esk towards Penny Hill Farm[4] (194008), where ducks, geese and hens wander freely in the fields and the dogs are divided into two camps – friendly and unconfined, or savage and caged up.

A rutted cart track leads over the fellside towards the rock face of Birker Fell, whose stony sides bulge downwards in steps like a fossilized waterfall. The view to your right over the river valley opens up into a great left-hand sweep of green slopes with the pointed head of Bow Fell, almost 3,000 feet tall, closing the top of the valley. The flank of Bow Fell[5] drops to the watershed saddle of Esk Hause[6], then rises to the sharply-outlined summit of Scafell Pike[7], at nearly 3,200 feet the roof of the English world. These remote, unworkable high fells stand in dramatic contrast to the green grass and long stone walls of the cultivated strip far down in the valley bottom.

The path crosses a beck on a wooden footbridge and runs down to the road at the foot of Hardknott Pass[8], up which cars crawl in agonizing first gear round the zigzag one in three bends. Just up to your right is the Roman fort of Mediobogdum or Hardknott Castle, built in its eagle's eyrie position some time in the second century. Turn left over a cattle grid, then right into the drive to Brotherilkeld Farm[9] (213014), originally built by Cistercian monks from Furness Abbey as a grange farm to supply their community. In the early years of this century Brotherilkeld was famous among walkers for its hospitality and huge teas.

From the farm the path passes a bridge over the Esk, put up to commemorate a climber, Dick Marsh, who was killed near here in 1964. It crosses a wide pasture freckled with dandelions and soon leaves the fields for the wilder surroundings of the upper valley. Yew Crags above you on the right sweep ahead to Yew Bank, while to the left Brock Crag is followed by Heron Crag; all these rocky brows and their screes leading the eye forward to the classic mountain shape of Bow Fell, symmetrical up to its very peak. The one yew tree that pre-war writers noted growing on Yew Bank is still there, buffeted by winter storms but clinging on grimly to its precarious hold in the stony downfall. Below the crags the Esk runs in a long strip of boulders, its tributary becks soaking the turf where lichens and bright-green mosses flourish.

Esk Falls[10] (226037) tumble down from Esk Hause along a rocky channel a couple of miles above Brotherilkeld, where the river bends sharply to the left at its confluence with Lingcove Beck. The beck also comes in a series of falls down its cleft from Bow Fell, and where the two streams meet there is an old pack-horse bridge which carried the ponies and their bundles on the high road from Eskdale over into Langdale. Writers have made great capital out of this lonely and beautiful place, though the patriarch Baddeley's rather bald description simply states that the Esk Falls 'are as perfect little pictures of wild mountain-torrents as can be imagined.' My personal favourite, HH Symonds, spread himself to better effect in his wonderfully bossy, didactic and entertaining book *Walking in the Lake District*, published in 1933. 'The longest and grandest cascade in all Cumberland,' Symonds enthused, 'a generous half-mile of colour and sound.' An advocate of cold plunges in freezing becks and a stern chastiser of charabancs, litter and girls in shorts and zebra-striped stockings, Symonds knew all about how to get across the Esk below the falls:

> *'There are one or two opportunities for the jump heroic; and, what is more, grand swimming pools. And this reminds me of a third way of crossing deep water: bathe first, and carry your clothes with you.'*

Brrrr! Unless you really want to try a shivering dip or a jump heroic, you can cross more sedately over the stones in the river bed – though not in times of spate. Once on the other side you turn left and walk back down the valley, looking forward and up to Harter Fell and its accompanying ridges and peaks. The height and sweep of Yew Bank and Crags are seen to full effect as you splash your way over the bogs down to a stone wall under Brock Crag[11] (220026). Bear right here up the side of the hill, keeping the wall

Grass, rock, water and silence – the keynotes of Upper Eskdale.

on your left and following it above the river past the thin white strand of the waterfall in Cowcove Beck (213021). From here a firm and well-marked track runs down to Taw House Farm[12] (211016) and the little box-like cottage of Birdhow[13] (205011) before meeting the road (202009) to Dalegarth Station and the 'Ratty' ride back to Ravenglass.

Sylvan's Pictorial Handbook to the English Lakes, published three years before William Wordsworth's death, summed up the River Esk for the Victorian adventurer:

> *'The Esk is a beautifully transparent stream, with a rough stony bottom, whose wooded banks, lofty fells, and numerous falls which the river makes in its course, present a variety of picturesque scenes, which the artist and the lover of rural scenery cannot fail to admire.'*

I will leave the last word to HH Symonds, though, cutting through all that overblown nonsense with the breezy assurance, 'You shall find for yourself that it is a good land.'

River Eden

OS 1:50,000 Sheet 85
1:25,000 Sheets NY 25/35 and NY 45/55
3 miles

Carlisle Castle[1] looks business-like – and it has needed to be down the centuries. Although today's English/Scottish border runs some ten miles north of Carlisle and puts the city firmly in the grip of the Auld Enemy, there were a brief couple of decades back in the twelfth century when the Scots claimed it for their own. Since that time the city has regularly changed hands in the token form of possession of the castle. The army holding the castle held the town as well for their respective rulers.

Carlisle has always been recognized as a prime defensive spot; the Romans had a fort at Stanwix on the north bank where the River Eden loops in front. When a thousand years later the Normans had to subdue resistance to their invasion, Carlisle was the obvious place to build a castle – near the sea, defended by the snaking river and positioned to be able to strike into the Scottish and English hills or to repel attacks out of them. The castle was begun by William II, and had a red sandstone Norman keep put up when King David of Scotland took over the city in 1136. It was his reward from Henry II for supporting Queen Matilda against Henry's predecessor Stephen. The walls of Carlisle came to symbolize the defiance of this often embattled city, standing as they did for over 700 years. They were breached regularly by Scots and English, but each succeeding occupier thought it worth repairing them. During the Civil War when General Leslie had finally captured the castle from its starving defenders after a nine-month siege, he sacrificed the west aisle of Carlisle Cathedral for building blocks for these walls.

A cobbled causeway over the castle moat (397562) passes under the arch of the sandstone gatehouse with its portcullis, opening into a large courtyard surrounded by military and civilian offices. The King's Own Border Regiment has its HQ in the castle, and the whole place still carries a strong military flavour. Another pointed arch through an inner gateway leads to the cobbled square under the towering, dusky-red keep inside which you can see the scrawlings, gougings and graffiti done by prisoners 600 years ago. The strength of those enormous walls kept out the best endeavours of Robert Bruce in his flush of success after Bannockburn, and they kept in Mary, Queen of Scots for a couple of months in 1568. Bonnie Prince Charlie made Carlisle one of the high-

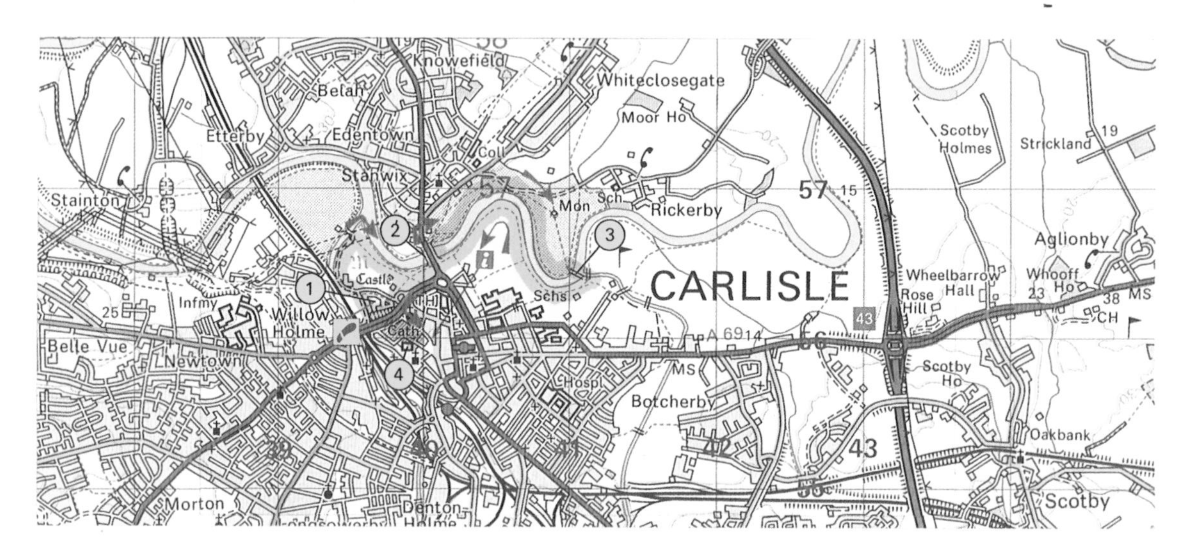

Broad bend of the River Eden under the Stanwix bank.

spots of the '45 rebellion when he rode in on a white horse, 'wi' a hundred pipers' to fanfare him, and proclaimed his father King from Carlisle Cross. The darling of the Scots was soon in retreat, leaving behind 400 Highlanders as a garrison in the castle. They made a tasty after-morsel for Butcher Cumberland, following the feast of slaughter at Culloden.

Leave the castle gate and turn right along Castle Way dual carriageway, taking the first on the right (396561) which runs down towards the River Eden beside the west wall of the castle. In this wall is the little doorway known as the 'Sallyport', built so that defenders could rush out and take attackers by surprise; but it provided a surprise itself for the English occupiers in 1596. Through this door crept Lord Walter Scott of Buccleugh and a small number of men, having forded the Eden on a dark and rainy night, to rescue one of Buccleugh's men lying in chains in the castle dungeon. By all accounts William Armstrong, known as 'Kinmont Willie', was a rough and ruthless fellow, but he was evidently worth risking life and limb for. Making a tremendous row so as to appear ten times their number, the Scots burst into Kinmont Willie's cell, loaded him chains and all onto the back of a giant named Red Rowan and made good their escape across the Eden – unpursued by the governor of the castle. Perhaps he was not too keen on a running fight in the dark and rain – more probably he was glad to be rid of an embarrassing guest: for Kinmont Willie had been captured on a declared day of truce between the Queen's men and the moss-troopers, thus putting 'Bold Buccleugh' in the right as far as local balladeers and story-tellers were concerned.

On your left as you walk down beside the castle are two other institutions that brought fame to Carlisle – the brewery and the railway. Theakston's potent brews, made in the red-brick brewery, can be drunk in many of the city's pubs. Carlisle was the scene of an experiment in which the state took over the pubs to cut down on drunkenness among munitions workers during the First World War. The pubs continued in state ownership until recently, known to outsiders as 'alcoholic post offices' but regarded with pride by many locals. The state still holds on to the railways, however, presiding over their steady decline from the high peak of Victorian glory when eight lines served the city. You can still travel to Glasgow, Dumfries, the Cumbrian coast, Penrith, Newcastle and Settle (just), but the famous Waverley Route to Edinburgh and the obscure little line to Silloth on the Solway Firth have vanished.

At the end of the road (395563) bear left onto a tarmac track around the perimeter of the castle park, walking forward at the bottom through the trees to reach the path by the bend of the river and looking across to the large houses of Stanwix peeping from their trees. To the right the castle fills the skyline, the long slate roofs of its buildings giving it the appropriate look of a cross between a prison and a barracks.

The Eden ran until the nineteenth century in two separate channels, one under the Stanwix bank and the other on the castle side. On the meadow under Stanwix there was a great cattle market to which drovers would bring beasts from Scotland and northern England. Goods also came to the city from Port Carlisle on the Solway Firth via a canal opened in 1823 which joined the Eden to the west of Carlisle. This was one of those speculative ventures of the early nineteenth century, born of the optimism of the Industrial Revolution and dying when that boom died.

Soon the riverside path goes under the A7 road bridge[2] (400566), built in 1932; beyond the bridge you climb up to your right to cross the river and walk down into Rickerby Park. This fine stretch of parkland, which sheep and cows share with the canoeists, fishermen, joggers and dog-walkers of Carlisle, was bought by the city as a monument to its citizens killed in the Great War. The wide curve of the river bends north and south, giving a striking view over the terraces, schools, office blocks and chimneys of Carlisle. The glass box of the Civic Centre stands tall over the city and its ranks of brick terraces built for the railwaymen and textile workers who crowded into Carlisle in its Victorian days of activity. It's hard to see in today's compact, friendly little city the place where for centuries it was dangerous to step outside your door for fear of both English men-at-arms and Scots raiders.

Where the Eden begins to bend north again you cross the river on a handsome girder suspension bridge[3] (412565), opened in 1922 by the Earl of Lonsdale as another memorial to Carlisle's war dead. The official obelisk in Rickerby Park, shaped like a square factory chimney, is less impressive than these practical monuments of park and bridge. On the far side of the Eden, turn right to walk back around the bends of the river and under the A7 bridge again. A path here crosses the castle park diagonally to meet Castle Way at the eastern corner of the castle. An underpass opposite the gatehouse goes below the dual carriageway to bring you out at the bottom of Castle Street. Half-way up the street Carlisle Cathedral stands modestly on the right[4] (399559), a small sandstone Norman church with many treasures inside and a wealth of history stretching back nearly 900 years.

Tall, round Norman arches give the interior of the cathedral a sense of space and light which belies its small size. Some of these arches in the south aisle have been squeezed upwards into misshapen curves by settlement when the cathedral was still new. The barrel roof over the nave is glorious in blue with gold stars, and in the choir there are misericordes under the seats from the early fifteenth century of eagles, saints and grotesque beasts. The Judgement Day scenes in the tracery glass of the east window were made about fifty years earlier, and the piers of the choir nearly 200 years before that. Their capitals show medieval husbandmen and women performing the tasks appropriate to all twelve months of the year – harvesting, sowing seed and so on. Other special treasures include a wonderful Flemish altar piece of 1505, bursting with lively figures, showing the Passion with two lurid pink robbers writhing on their crosses each side of a pale and calm Christ; and a head on the column of the south choir aisle nearest the east window, supposed to be a likeness of King Edward I. Carlisle had no cause to love Longshanks, the feared and hated Hammer of the Scots, and some mason whose sympathies obviously lay north of the Border has made a splendid job of distorting the monarch's face into a twisted leer of haughty bad temper. Perhaps it brought a little light relief to the Scottish prisoners locked up in the cathedral after the '45 rebellion to await their chains, dark cells and hempen nooses.

Sandstone stronghold – Carlisle Castle's forbidding keep.

River Wear

OS 1:50,000 Sheet 88
1:25,000 Sheet NZ 24/34
$1\frac{1}{2}$ miles

This walk around the peninsula stronghold of Durham City may be the shortest in this book, but it's also one of the most densely crowded with historical interest and contains enough striking views to melt your camera shutter. Two hours are not really enough to enjoy all the treasures of this short spit of land rising over a hairpin bend of the River Wear.

A few years ago Durham City was a smoky, dirty old town of crowded terraces and steep little cobbled streets. Nowadays it has smartened up, closed many of its most attractive streets to traffic and become a centre for tourists. Its glory is shared between the castle and cathedral, standing side by side on the top of the central peninsula and looking down over the river to what remains of the old city. The terraces are still there, running in herring-bone strips up the slopes from the Wear, smelling of smoke from coal fires and dotted with tiny pubs and corner shops; but the emphasis of the city has shifted from industry and coal-mining towards the life of its university and the influence of tourism. The new ring road leaves the centre of Durham untouched; new and old have been successfully blended together in a city which is thriving,

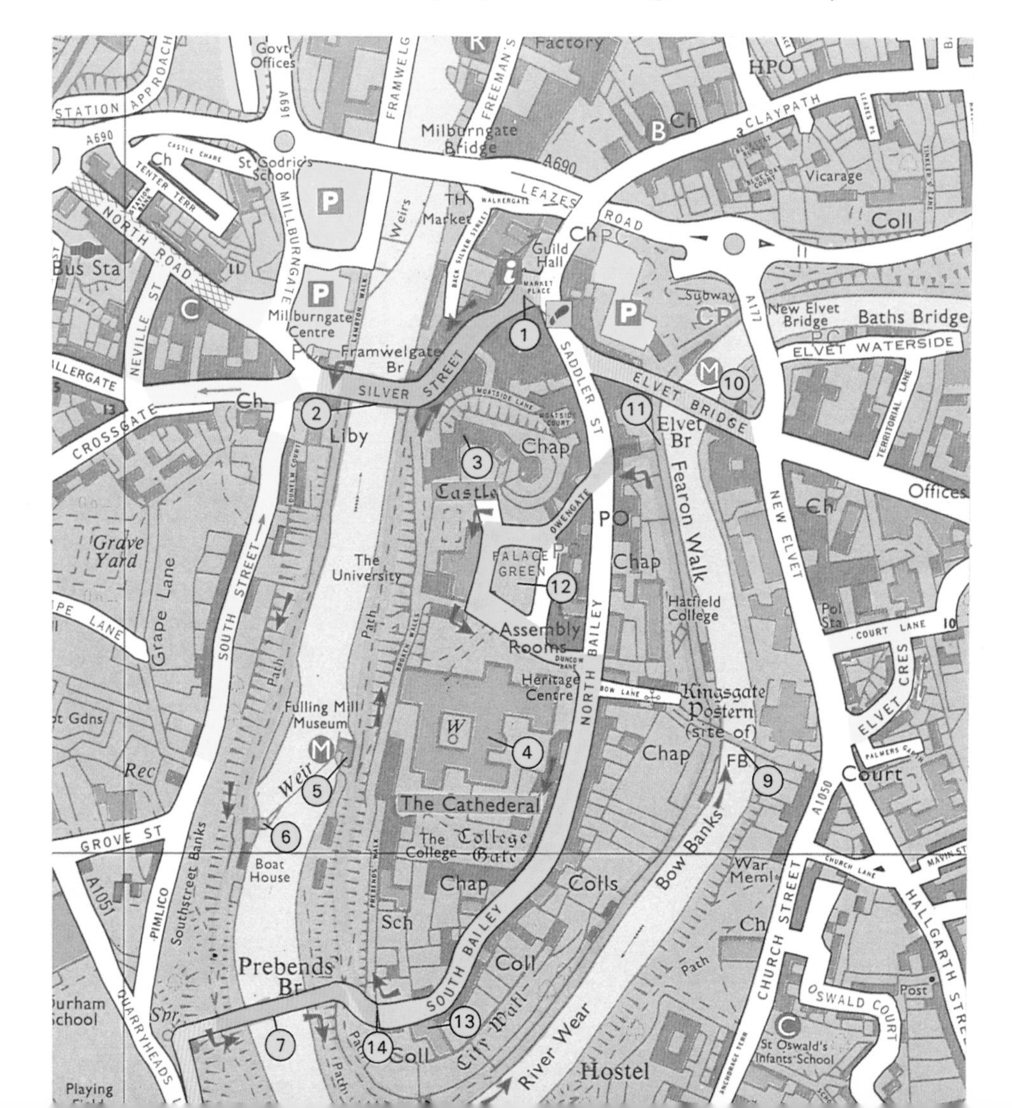

Looking downriver from the middle of Prebend's Bridge to the cathedral towers and Framwellgate Bridge.

unlike so many of the depressed and jobless towns of the north-east.

The market place in Durham[1] (274425) used to be a motorist's nightmare, with narrow medieval streets converging on an overworked policeman gesturing from a control box in the centre. It has recently been pedestrianized, and is once more a pleasant place to stroll. Dominating the square is the verdigrized equestrian statue of Charles William Vane Stewart, 3rd Marquis of Londonderry, a politician, military man, Lord Lieutenant of Durham and founder of Seaham Harbour a few miles south of Sunderland. The statue was put up in 1861, seven years after his death, one of the earliest experiments in copper electro-plating. The marquis sits resplendent in a frogged uniform, his curved sabre dangling from the saddle and a brave cockade streaming back from his busby. His stallion, pawing the ground and impatient for the charge, is splendidly equipped in the nether regions; but the sculptor, Raffaele Monti, was reputed to have forgotten to include a tongue in the horse's half-open mouth. Local legend says that he killed himself from shame when the omission was pointed out to him – but it didn't really happen. Either a tongue was slipped in later, or that horse has a very large stone lodged in its throat.

From the market place walk down the curve of Silver Street onto Framwellgate[2] Bridge (272425), rebuilt in the fourteenth century on the foundations of the original bridge of 1128. From the middle you look upriver to the first of the notable views of castle[3] (273423) and cathedral[4] (273421). The castle battlements and twin towers of the cathedral's west front, high above the river, are reflected in its water and make a great dark block of the east bank. A flight of steps in the left-hand pier at the far end of Framwellgate Bridge leads down to a path beside the Wear which passes the 'Coach and Eight' bar and runs along under the trees. Beside the long weir which bars the river you look across to the classic view, painted and photographed countless times, of the cathedral towering over a stone-built mill[5] whose river frontage rises out of the water. This is the Jesus Mill, its name derived from the use to which its profits were put – the money went to build the altar in the nave of the cathedral. It dates back at least 500 years, and has been used in the past for fulling cloth and shaping lead. Nowadays it houses the university's museum of archaeology.

You pass its sister mill[6] (once used for grinding corn) standing beside the path above the weir, and walk on to cross the Wear over the three tall arches of Prebend's Bridge[7] (271419). It was built in 1776 to replace an earlier timber bridge washed away by floods, and stands under the weather-beaten old outer walls of the castle defences. These run at the top of the bank as you descend to the path on the inner curve of the river and walk on to reach a little building sheltering under the beeches and horse chestnuts[8] (273418). Palladian columns and portico front a plain stone shed – a grand entrance to a modest sanctuary. A famous figure in Durham's history lived on the site where this folly now stands. He was Count Boruwlaski, a Polish emigré who came to live in Durham at the turn of the nineteenth century and died in his house here on the river bank in 1837, aged ninety-seven. The Count was easily recognized as he walked the streets of the city, for he was less than four feet tall.

The path runs on above the boathouses of the university's rowing clubs towards Kingsgate Bridge[9] (276421), built in 1963 and making a sharp contrast with its slim Y-shaped concrete supports to the solidity of the older stone bridges. Beyond it on the far bank of the river stands Dunelm House, the students' centre, followed by the plain face of the English Department's buildings; then the Wear is spanned by Durham's oldest bridge. The pointed arches of the twelfth-century Elvet Bridge[10] (275425) are dark and narrow, tricky to negotiate in a punt from Brown's boatyard just beyond it if you have had a skinful of Samuel Smith's Old Brewery Bitter in the 'Swan and Three Cygnets' on the lower end of the bridge.

Before reaching Elvet Bridge turn to your left up a narrow walled alley of steep steps, called a 'vennel'[11], which climbs up through a low archway into North Bailey. Turn left here, then bear right up cobbled Owen-gate to reach Palace Green[12] (273422). This was the nerve centre of the medieval city, covered at that time with a ramshackle huddle of taverns and shops which served the cathedral, and the castle in its early years; though once it had been completed they were razed to avoid the risk of fire. The castle stands on its mound to your right as you come out of Owen-gate. Its dramatically forbidding keep is a Victorian replacement for the original fourteenth-century one, which was added to a twelfth-century gatehouse and the Great Hall built by Bishop Bek a hundred years later. Like most other castles within raiding distance of the Border, it was built to keep the rampant Scots at bay, and is perfectly sited for defence with the Wear on three sides and a tiny neck of land on the north. No wonder neither Scots nor Danes ever succeeded in taking it. The military based in the castle came under the orders of the Bishop of Durham, and this fusion of church and state saw Durham safely through the worst of several centuries' wars. In 1836 the castle was given to the university, which had been founded four years before, and remains in their possession and in use as one of their colleges.

Over Palace Green stands Durham Cathedral, the finest and most complete Romanesque church in Britain. From its demonic lion's head sanctuary knocker to the glowing rose of its east window it's a box too full of treasure to be picked over by this writer. You will have to explore for yourself among the dog-tooth arches, tombs, monuments and carvings. Here lie the bones of St Cuthbert under a plain slab marked simply 'Cuthbertus'.

The shepherd lad who became Bishop of Lindisfarne, the inspired orator who chose a hermit's life on a tiny island with the seals and seabirds, did not finish his journeyings when he died. The body that showed no signs of decay when his monks opened his coffin in 698 AD, eleven years after his death, was fated to wander with them for more than a hundred years, taken from Lindisfarne in 875 to save it from the marauding Norsemen and carried wherever they went. Finally in 995 they were vouchsafed a vision, telling them to lay their saint to rest at Dun Holme. Here they brought him, and in 1104 buried him, still whole and uncorrupted, behind the altar. Even then St Cuthbert did not lie easy; he was dug up and reburied when the original shrine was destroyed during the Reformation, and unearthed again in 1827, a skeleton in a silken shroud with a bishop's cross

The three slender arches of Prebend's Bridge loop across the Wear above the mill weir.

lying on its breast. The cross, together with many other of the cathedral's treasures, is now in the cathedral's museum.

From Durham Cathedral you walk down past Abbey House into South Bailey, following the route of William the Conqueror's horrified gallop. The story goes that the proud invader tried to open St Cuthbert's tomb and see for himself if the saint's body was really still there in the flesh. Whatever he saw scared the king so terribly that he leaped onto his horse, fled across South Bailey and down Bow Lane, across the Wear and on southwards, never drawing rein until he was safely across the Tees.

Turn right down South Bailey, passing the colleges of St Chad's and St John's and the little Norman church of St Mary the Less, which contains a memorial to Count Boruwlaski. At the bottom of South Bailey is St Cuthbert's Society[13], the university's celebrated institution for those unclassifiable and unclubbable students who don't quite fit the mould. Beyond 'Cuth's' you pass through the tall arch of the Watergate[14], built in 1778 to replace an earlier gate in the castle walls, and turn right at the near end of Prebend's Bridge. From here it's a short walk past the archaeological museum at Jesus Mill back to Framwellgate Bridge and the market place.

Coldgate Water

OS 1:50,000 Sheet 75
4 miles

The Cheviot Hills are a byword among long-distance walkers. Not for their remote beauty or their great stretches of lonely high-level walking – though they offer both of these in the miles of border country along which they lie – but for their wetness, their sticky black peat that can infiltrate the most watertight pair of boots, and the grinding final leg of the Pennine Way that crosses them to finish this marathon. Twenty-nine bloody awful miles of barren upland nothingness have somehow to be got over in one aching slog, on feet already bruised and blistered into raw meat by nearly 250 miles of walking: no escape routes, no pubs, no refreshments of any kind, no roads, no joy whatsoever – only the prospect of a free pint, courtesy of A Wainwright, in the Border Hotel at Kirk Yetholm, the end of the agony.

Fear not, reader! This short and beautiful walk along the Coldgate Water shows you the other, softer face of the Cheviots where their northern flanks come down and merge into the Milfield Plain by way of Happy Valley. It is a suitable name for the lovely curving cleft under steep banks cut by a river of many names – the Harthope Burn in its higher reaches on the sides of the Cheviots, Coldgate Water through the valley, Wooler Water as it wriggles around the feet of the hills, River Till as it flows across Milfield Plain to join the Tweed on the Border.

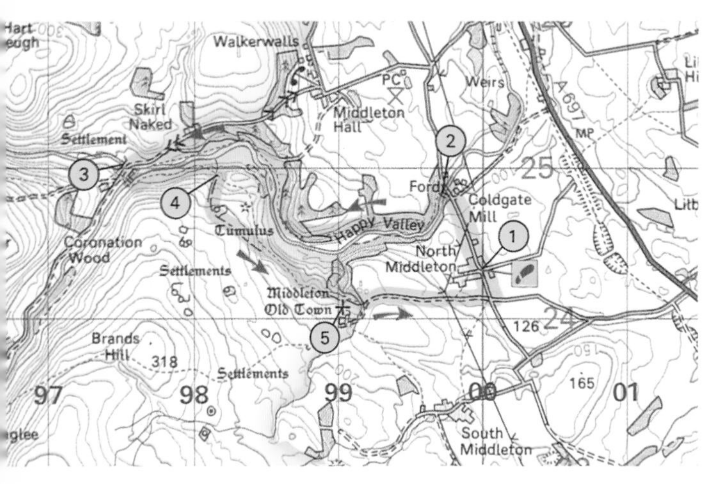

Our walk begins at North Middleton[1] (000243), three miles south of the small market town of Wooler. There are three Middletons within a mile or so in the Cheviot foothills – North and South Middleton, and Middleton Old Town. They were sizeable places in the Middle Ages; there were two large houses here, owned by the Rutherford family and fortified against the frequent raids mounted by the Scots from across the border. North Middleton at the turn of the nineteenth century still had a pub, three farms, a chapel and a number of cottages, but it had declined from the days when it was part of the estate of the Earl of Derwentwater. He backed the Jacobite cause in the rebellion of 1715, and paid for his mistake by forfeiting both his estates and his head. Nowadays the hamlet consists of a fine house behind tall beech trees, a trim old stone farmhouse with a walled garden and a couple of cottages, lying between rolling land of pasture and cornfields and the higher, harder outlines of the Cheviot Hills.

From North Middleton a narrow lane runs down to a ford over the Coldgate Water[2] (997248). Set back on the right is Coldgate Mill, now a private house, which ground corn until the 1920s. Back in 1302 the miller here, one Norman, was involved in a drunken fight that nearly put his neck in the halter. He had an argument in the tavern with his drinking companion, John Scott, which led to a chase over the fields. Norman was cornered by a ditch and lashed out with his stick, smashing John Scott's skull and killing him. Luckily he received the royal mercy when his plea of self-defence was accepted.

Cross the river by a footbridge above the ford and turn left along the water into Happy Valley through a plantation of Scots pine, spruce and larch. Tall aspens stand as a screen for the conifers, the shimmering light green of their constantly rustling leaves contrasting with the dour, dark immobility of the pine branches. Otters have been seen along the Coldgate Water hereabouts; the river and woods of Happy Valley are also a refuge for kingfishers, siskins, redpolls and those best friends of the bird world, goldcrests and long-tailed tits. The river can be violent in spate, however, as you can see from the way the banks are reinforced by stones bound together with wire mesh. Even in tranquil summer the water rushes forcefully over its stones and fallen branches.

The path leaves the trees to curve with the Coldgate Water around a long right-hand bend on a flat table of floodland. To the right and left are steep banks, and ahead an arc of hillside that forces the river to sweep round its base. The heathery tip of Brands Hill rears above and beyond this enclosing wall, known as Old Town Braes, above which Middleton Old Town once stood. The houses of the medieval settlement have crumbled away, but there are still lumps and bumps of foundations to be seen in the grass of the bank. The valley narrows and steepens as the river swings from west to north, then west again, opening up a view of the 1,000-foot Hart Heugh capped with a stone peak. The path climbs into a jungle of bracken and gorse, then drops again as the Coldgate Water begins to curve southwards. The northern ramparts of the Cheviots rise steadily ahead, deeply cut by their streams – their heart of granite is surrounded by a soft shell of lava from volcanic times, easily worn and moulded by moving water. Weathering has given rounded depths to these small valleys, which fill with shadow in the early evening long before the sun has left their upper slopes. Go over a stile into the lane which crosses a tributary of the Coldgate Water, the Carey Burn, by a concrete footbridge[3] (975250). Just upstream are the piers of its predecessor, torn down and washed away by a winter flood.

Now the river has turned through more than 180 degrees and leads into the steep-sided valley of the Harthope Burn. Rising to 1,450 feet, Cold Law stands hunched at the far end, closing the perspective. The road runs up the valley, a favourite route for walkers setting out to climb 1,800 feet to the summit of The Cheviot, the highest point in the range. The view from the top is like a good malt whisky – strongly flavoured with peat and water.

After crossing the Carey Burn, turn left over a stile at a wooden fingerpost and cross the Coldgate Water on a footbridge. The path goes up wooden steps in the bank into the bracken and runs on a ledge wide enough to take a sheep and not much more. Soon it turns sharp right away from the river[4] (981250) and climbs up through the harebells and heather, following yellow arrow waymarks. The view from the top of the bank, fifteen miles over sills, peaks, ridges, ledges and fields to south and west, justifies the steep haul up. From here the path swings left along the edge of the hillside, then skirts around the southernmost point of Happy Valley high above the bends of the Coldgate Water among the trees.

In Happy Valley.

Seen from up here, the site of Middleton Old Town[5] (990240) is knobbled with trenches and mounds of old walls and the remains of the buildings. This eastern side of Brands Hill holds evidence of earlier settlers, too – there are at least ten hut circles from the time of the Roman occupation. The path follows the course of a

lane, sunken and sheltered by aged, gnarled hawthorns, to pass below an old barn and the square foundations of one of the Old Town's buildings. From this point the waymarks bring you back to North Middleton over a burn and down a stony track with some large boundary boulders – waymarks of 1,000 years ago.

Flat wedge of flood plain sliced out by the Coldgate Water under the slopes of Old Town Braes.

SECTION SEVEN

Scotland

River Tweed

Water of Leith

River Falloch

River Devon and Dollar Burn

Moness Burn and the Birks o' Aberfeldy

River Dee

River Lair

River Spey (The Speyside Way)

River Tweed

OS 1:50,000 Sheet 73
7½ miles

'Ye maids o' high an' low degree
Frae Meggetdale tae Thornielee,
Kilt up your coats abune the knee
An' ower the hills tae Peebles.
As Beltane time comes roond each year
The exile, stirred by mem'ries dear,
Wad gie a wealth o' gowd an' gear
Tae spend a day in Peebles.'

True 'Gutterbluids' of Peebles (those born in the town) come back home from as far afield as Canada and Australia for the annual Beltane festival. There are hundreds of 'Stooriefeet' or dusty-footed strangers, too, who come to see the pipe bands, the Riding of the Marches, the jig performed in the High Street late at night and after a day's malted refreshment by the Beltane Cornet, and of course the crowning of the Beltane Queen. The Victorians revived and cleaned up the old pagan festival, but it still gives the inhabitants of staid Peebles an excuse for a wild week. The junketings have been shifted from the original Feast of Beltane, 1st May, to the week ending with the third Sunday in June; and this is really the best time to do this walk along the Tweed.

The town was founded around Peebles Castle, which was burned several times and was often the centre of those immense blood-lettings which tainted the Border country through the centuries. Peebles grew rich on wool and tweed, and fat on salmon and trout from the river. Nowadays the castle site by the bridge is occupied by the Old Parish Church of 1885, whose tall crown steeple, pierced with openings, is a landmark for miles around. Our walk begins at the church, from which you walk over the Tweed Bridge[1] (250403). Parts of the bridge date from the fifteenth century, and there is a fine view from the middle looking upstream over the wide river towards Neidpath Castle. The lamp standards on the bridge feature tritons like those on the Victoria Embankment in London.

On the far side of the bridge walk down the steps on your right to the riverside path in an

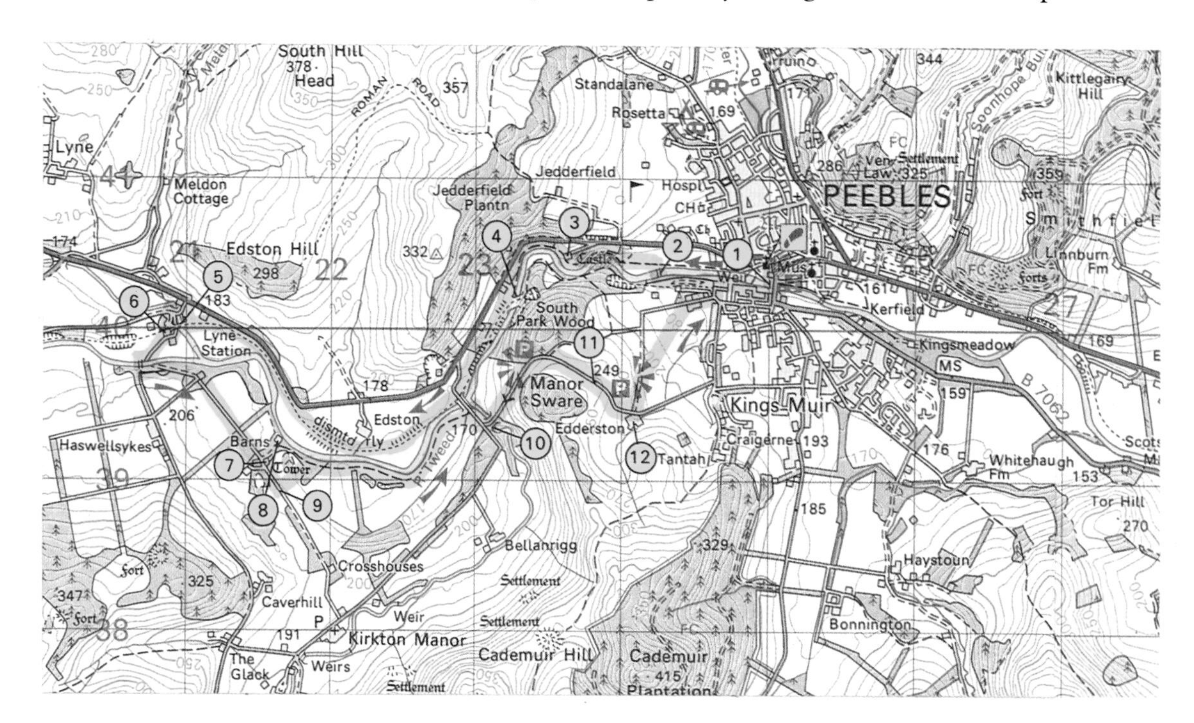

avenue of lime trees, passing the long bow of the weir above which the Eddleston Water joins the Tweed – a good place for local boys to pull eels out of the pools. The Tweed turns rapidly from brown to steely grey on cloudy days – not uncommon hereabouts! Rowan bushes are planted by the path, which soon crosses a tubular girder bridge[2] (242404) onto the north bank. The tree-covered slopes of the valley close in as you walk westward among Scots pines to a famous view forward to the tall block of Neidpath Castle[3] on its rock above the river. One of the Romantic Rocks by the water still has the rusty bolts which once held a diving board – hearty cold plunges in the smoking Tweed for early rising Victorian Scots. The path leaves the trees and runs below Neidpath Castle (237405), which is open to the public from Easter until early October. A side track leads up from the river bank to the castle.

Neidpath Castle was built in the thirteenth century, a fortified house rather than a conventional castle; Sir Simon Fraser, one of the early owners, once enjoyed three victories over the English in the same day. It passed eventually into the hands of the Douglas family, whose most notorious member was 'Old Q', the 4th Duke of Queensberry. He was a rake, gambler, womanizer and hard drinker, with a fine 'damn-your-eyes' attitude which led to his having all the woods by the river cut down – some say to spite his nephew. He earned a stinging poetical slap from William Wordsworth:

> *'Degenerate Douglass! thou unworthy Lord*
> *Whom mere despite of heart could so far please*
> *And love of havoc (for with such disease*
> *Fame taxes him) that he could send forth word*
> *To level with the dust a noble horde,*
> *A brotherhood of venerable trees,*
> *Leaving an ancient Dome and Towers like these*
> *Beggar'd and outraged! . . .'*

Never mind, William! The Forestry Commission are doing their best to put things right with their dull green battalions.

Chunks of masonry from the gaps in the castle walls lie beside the path, which crosses over a stile into woodland of chestnut, oak, lime, sycamore and wych elm, as well as the ever-

The single arch of Old Manor Bridge near the confluence of Tweed and Manor Water.

present pines. Ahead, the Tweed is spanned by the arches of the railway bridge[4] (232402) that carried passengers on the Carlisle–Glasgow line from 1864 until 1950. The original architect's model is supposed to have been carved from a turnip. A waymarked stile and steps lead up on to the disused line, on whose crunching ballast you walk past silver birch, rowan and wych elm which harbour long-tailed tits. The waymark symbol of the 'Tweed Walk' which you are now following is a dipper, and the little brown birds with their white shirt-fronts can be seen standing on the stones in mid-stream and skimming up and down the river below the old railway.

The path rises under a quarry to meet the road bridge at the confluence of Tweed and Manor Water (229395). On the far side of the road is a piece of railway jetsam to bring a smile to the faces of connoisseurs – one of Francis Morton's Patent Liverpool wire fence tighteners, which still stand bravely outfacing wind and rain all

Mist over the broad arches of the bridge that spans the Tweed below Barns House.

over Britain's network of disused lines. Wild strawberries grow on the old railway, which runs below Edston Farm with a view across the river of Barns House. The river takes a sweep to the south, while the railway path goes on over the rough grey ballast to a waymark[5] pointing the route down the embankment and bearing right up a field edge to the road (210401). Turn left over the Lyne Water and left again under the old railway to pass Lyne Station[6] (209399), now a private house, designed on the same low, compact lines as the local farmhouses. The road runs down to an old ford over the Tweed: cross by the footbridge a few yards upstream (207398) and turn left along the bank to reach a cottage (211397) at the entrance to the half-mile-long drive to Barns House.

The drive ends at Barns Tower[7] (216391), a tall, grim fifteenth-century stronghold built by the Burnet family. In those days on the Borders architecture had to be strong and solid, if not beautiful. Barns Tower is about twenty feet square and forty tall, with tiny windows and observation slits high up in the stone walls – a block-like, unyielding statement of defiance. An iron grid seals the door, which is marked '1488' – this inscription was probably put there much later. The window over the door carries the initials WB and MS. William Burnet earned the nickname 'Hoolet' or 'Owlet' on many a bloody night raid thieving his neighbours' cattle. MS stands for his wife, Margaret Stewart.

John Buchan set his romantic novel *John Burnet of Barns* around this gloomy, atmospheric old tower. The Georgian Barns House[8] (built between 1773 and 1780) a short distance away (217392) is less of a fortress, but still a square-jawed, formidable building. Those Burnets had a thing or two to prove.

Walk on down the drive for a couple of hundred yards to a waymarked stile on the left[9], from which you follow a stone wall down to the river (219391). Turn right here and walk back to the bridge, where our route diverges from the Tweed Walk by turning right and then first left over the Manor Water by Old Manor Bridge[10] (231393), a single arch span built in 1702. The road rises to a view back up the valley of the Tweed, then forward from the car-park and picnic place[11] (238397) over Peebles and the hills beyond. 'Unforgettable,' urged the Gutter-bluids of Peebles. 'You must go and see it. The finest view in the Borders. Don't miss it whatever you do.' I'm sure they were right – but Scottish mist is a great reducer of great views.

The road winds down to Edderston Farm[12]

(241393), which has one unusual feature – a tall factory-style chimney. An enlightened lord of the Wemyss and March estate experimented with a steam engine here, which ran a thrashing machine and a milk sterilizing boiler, and powered other farm implements. The building of the farmhouse cost the estate's factor his job when the bills were added up.

Opposite the farm entrance, bear left off the road through a gate, keeping a fence on your left over the hillside to reach another road by the pens of Peebles Auction Market (243402). Turn right here, then left down South Park West to the south bank of the Tweed (247403), which you follow back to the bridge in the centre of Peebles.

Water of Leith

OS 1:50,000 Sheet 66
$4\frac{1}{2}$ miles

The Water of Leith was clean enough in the seventeenth century to be quoted as a suitable measure of 'cleane rynand water' for a standard pint. Running fast and in an accessible valley on the south-western outskirts of Edinburgh, however, it was an ideal source of power for milling, and soon a long line of mills – snuff mills, paper mills, grain mills, saw mills, flour mills, lint mills – stood almost wheel to wheel along the river's corridor, extracting power and pouring their waste materials into it in a poor exchange. The villages of Balerno, Currie, Colinton and Slateford formed the vertebrae in this industrial backbone. Juniper Green, between Currie and Colinton, came into being entirely due to the mills along the river.

The branch railway from Slateford to Balerno, opened in 1874, brought further prosperity to the string of villages in the shape of transport for the products of the mills, and weekend trippers who could reach the countryside quickly and cheaply from the centre of Edinburgh. Since the closure of the railway in the 1960s, it has been converted to a walkway which runs for most of its length within sight and sound of the Water of Leith, now slowly recovering from centuries of industrial pollution.

You can park by Balerno High School in Bridge Road, just off the A70 Lanark road. Above the school a notice marked 'Public walk to Slateford' points through a gap in the wall (163668) down to the Water of Leith Walkway, a clear path surfaced with stone chips. The red-

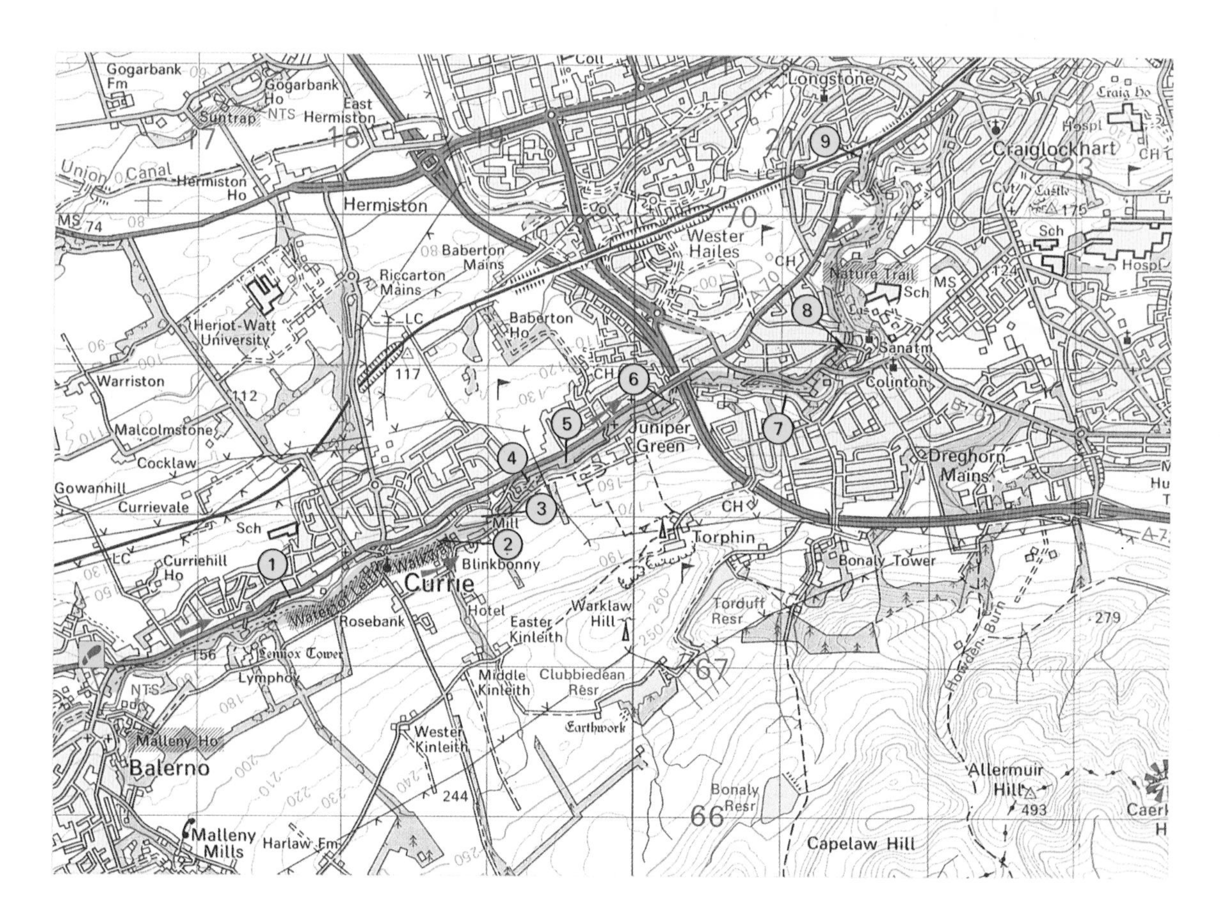

The Water of Leith surges over Kinleith Mill weir, as smooth and shiny as polished metal.

brown water of the river is seen between the ash and wych elms to the right as the path runs by a retaining wall, constructed like a honeycomb in separate cells which have been filled with pebbles to give plants a firm grip. Sweet cecily, like a delicate version of cow parsley, grows in clumps beside the walkway – if you crush the feathery leaves between your fingers, they give off a strong smell of aniseed. Also growing along here in the shade of the trees are fringecups, tall plants with fringed petals in spiky heads. They occur along the western seaboard of North America from California right up to Alaska. The ones by the Water of Leith must have escaped from nearby gardens, and thrive in the damp, shady conditions.

Soon you pass the red corrugated-iron barn and stone farmhouse of Kinauld on your right (173672) – there was a 'waulk' or fulling mill here as early as 1376, and a distillery in 1845 – they could get their peated water safely from the river this far upstream. The path crosses the river on a railway bridge and comes to the square red-brick wall of a tannery on the left[1] (175674), the former Balerno Paper Mill which promised in its 1788 advertisement that 'such gentlemen as please to favour them with their orders may depend on having the different kinds of paper of the best quality and on the most reasonable terms.' Purple meadow cranesbill grows beside the walkway as it enters Currie village past the rough stone blocks of a retaining wall to the right; the mountaineer Dougal Haston lived here as a boy and used to practise his climbing skills on this wall. They paid off in 1975 when he found himself on the summit of Everest during Chris Bonington's great expedition. The air in this tree-lined section is cool and heavy with water, and the rocks of the railway cuttings drip and trickle.

The approach to the station site at Currie is flanked by wild rose bushes and the large, heart-shaped leaves of Japanese knotweed. The old railway crosses over the Poet's Burn[2] (187678), named after the local poet James Thompson, which rushes down under the path to a weir and the crumbling wooden gates of the 'lade' or mill race for Kinleith Mill, just downstream. Before you reach it, you pass a colony of giant hogweed. Don't touch the leaves, especially on a sunny day – they can give you bad blisters, as local lads have found out when they use the hollow stems as peashooters. The derelict hulk of Kinleith Mill lies to the left[3] (189680), a sad shadow of what was the largest mill in the villages whose 280-foot chimney towered above the houses of Currie. Rusty railway lines embedded in concrete show where the mill sidings brought the wagons full of paper onto the branch line until the mill's closure in 1966.

The path recrosses the river; from the bridge you can look down to your right on the arches of East Mill Bank Mill[4] (192682), which ground barley until it was burned down in the early nineteenth century. Next comes the red-brick Woodhall Paperboard Mill on the left[5] (195683) – still turning out packaging – the site of Juniper Green Station, and then the grey bulk of Curriemuir Grain Mill[6] (202687), also still in business. From here you walk under the tall Edinburgh bypass bridge and past the weir of Mossy Mill to reach a road at Colinton. Turn left to cross the river and go down a tarmac path to the left of West Mill[7] (212688), home of Scott's Porage Oats till 1971. Their famous packet with its muscular shot-putting Highlander still brings a hearty tang of Scottish heather to pallid southern breakfast tables, but the oats are now milled across the Forth at Cupar. West Mill houses the Forth River Purification Board.

Colinton station site is set with old mill-wheels and crossed by an old sandstone viaduct. Beyond it gapes the oval mouth of Colinton Tunnel[8] (214692), built on a tight curve, and now illuminated with electric lights – a benefit the locomotive crews never enjoyed. Walk through the echoing tunnel, past a mural of a tank engine painted on the wall – can you see daylight at both ends simultaneously? The grey carboniferous stone of the cutting on the far side of the tunnel splits easily into flat slices, in which fossilized fragments of leaves can be found. Sweet woodruff grows here, a head of tiny white four-petalled flowers sticking up out of a ruff of seven or eight spiky leaves. German wine producers use it today for flavouring; in medieval times it gave a sweet savour to stews, and a scent of hay to linen.

As you approach Slateford, there are cherry trees growing wild on the railway embankment – fruit of the stones thrown out of carriage windows by day trippers of long ago. The path

crosses over the dual carriageway of the Lanark Road[9] (215703), with a fine view to the north-east of Edinburgh Castle on its hill above the city. Just up the road is a bus-stop, from which a 43 or 44 bus will take you back to Juniper Green and Balerno.

A row of arches in an ivy-draped wall is all that's left of East Mill Bank Mill.

River Falloch

OS 1:50,000 Sheet 50
9 miles

The River Falloch has had a hard struggle to reach Loch Lomond, and is still fighting to get there. A glance at the map shows its easiest course, from its source on the slopes of Beinn a' Chroin, north to join the River Fillan at Crianlarich. Somewhere along the line – probably after one of the Ice Ages – it found its northward path blocked and had to make a tight and unnatural right angle bend to the south-west. The result is a happy one for the walker – five miles of falls, cascades, pools and bends as the Falloch bulldozes its way through the glen to the north end of Loch Lomond.

Our walk begins and ends on the West Highland railway line, which accompanies the river throughout. The most convenient return journey to the starting point – unless you have an accommodating driver to hand – is by rail, which brings with it the bonus of enjoying the walk in reverse from the carriage windows. The railway, forging its route along the hillsides over spectacular viaducts and embankments, is a testimony to the energy and toughness of the navvies who hacked it out with pick and shovel in the last years of the nineteenth century. The present-day locomotives are decorated with a picture of a white Scottie dog, an appropriate symbol of faithful service and determination. When winter fills these glens with snow and chokes off all road communication, the West Highland line is proud of its tradition of struggling through.

Derrydaroch Farm, isolated in the bottom of the wide, lonely Falloch Valley.

The route beside the River Falloch lies along part of the West Highland Way, which runs for ninety-five miles from Milngavie on the outskirts of Glasgow, beside Loch Lomond and over the wild wastes of Rannoch Moor to Fort William under the shadow of Ben Nevis. The Way, Scotland's first long-distance footpath, was opened in 1980 and attracts walkers from all over the world. Two words of warning – you need to check up before starting on the times of trains from Crianlarich back to Ardlui, and you need to be properly equipped for hill-walking. The path is rough, boggy and stony, and when mists descend is no picnic. Good strong boots, rain wear and emergency rations are essential. A sunny day may mock these precautions, but bad weather and tiredness will have you blessing them.

From Ardlui station (317154) it is a long two miles by road to the Drovers Inn at Inverarnan (318184) – but if you want to travel back at ease, they have to be faced. The views are compensation – the northern end of Loch Lomond peters out into a morass of reeds thronged with ducks, the 1,900-foot peak of Cruachan Cruinn[1] rears ahead, and the Ben Glas Burn[2] tumbles in white skeins of water down its dark gully beyond the river on your right.

Fiarach
652
Beinn Dubhchraig
977
Creagan Soilleir
Crùachan Cruinn
Crianlarich
Hotel
Mountain Rescue Post
Kirk Craig
Inverardran
Keilator
188
Craw Knowe
464
Old Military Road
West Highland Way
Waterfall
586
Fionn Ghleann
Allt Fionn Ghlinne
Es Eonan
Buck Craig
Hawk Craig
Grey Height
685
Glen Falloch
Creag a' Bhuie
Lochan Dubh
Derrydaroch
Clach na Briton
Coire Ordren
Sròn Gharbh
708
Coire Eich
Coire Earb
Falls of Falloch
River Falloch
Stob Glas
708
Troisgeach Bheag
Glen Falloch
Weir
An Caisteal
995
Coire a' Chuilinn
Stob Creag an Fhithich
Ben Glas
Meall Mòr nan Eag
621
Glenfalloch Lodge
Beinglas
Inn
Inverarnan
Waterfall
Meall nan Tarmachan
Beinn a' Chroin
Lochan Beinn Chabhair
Beinn Chabhair
931
Ben Glas Burn
Carn Liath
Garabal
Creag Bhreac Mhòr
Blarstainge
Paflan Hill
663
Waterfalls
Dubh Lochan
Cnap Mòr
164
Cruach
511
Sidhean a' Chatha
West Highland Way
Stob an Fhithich
419
Bealach nan Corp
Hotel
Pier
Ardlui
Garristuck
Ardleish
Ferry
(summer only)
Beinn Ducteach
Meall Mòr
747
Stuckendroin
Cairn
Doune
Stob nan Eighrach
613
Glen Gyle
31
32
34
35
36
37
38
39
1
2
3
4
5
6
7
8
9
10

A quarter of a mile past the hotel at Inverarnan[3], cross the wide, peat-stained River Falloch by a footbridge (319187) and turn immediately right to walk round the edge of a field. At the far side you join the West Highland Way by one of its waymarks, a white thistle emblem. The path runs behind Beinglas Farm[4] (321186), whose window frames and doors stand out in pillar-box red from the green slopes. Late primroses and early foxgloves are sometimes in flower together on this section of the route, which threads its way through groves of oak, birch and wych elm above the river. Through the trees you can see the slim girders of the viaduct which carries the West Highland line over the Dubh Eas. The hillsides are heaped with mossy stones among the bracken, and with black-faced sheep.

Above Glenfalloch Farm[5] the river sheds its placid mask and charges in white and brown sheets down a narrow, twisting gully choked with slabs of rock. You cross the channels of side streams by wooden footbridges, or squelch through sodden peat where the water trickles down on the surface. The path leaps up from the grassy river bank to the open hillside, then down again, challenging the ankles as it undulates.

The Falls of Falloch[6] lie hidden away in their cleft below the path; their crashing noise tells you where to diverge and look for them. Dorothy Wordsworth, walking here in the summer of 1803, was overwhelmed by Glen Falloch's noisy waters:

> '... *we sate down, and heard, as if from the heart of the earth, the sound of torrents ascending out of the long hollow glen ... it was everywhere, almost, one might say, as if 'exhaled' through the whole surface of the green earth. Glenfalloch, Coleridge has since told me, signifies the Hidden Vale; but William says, if we were to name it from our recollections of that time, we should call it the Vale of Awful Sound* ...'

Above the Falls is a good viewpoint from which to appreciate the efforts of the train crews as their engines grunt up the incline with passengers or long loads of goods. Soon the battering sound of the falls dies away to the rustle of shallow water over stones, and the path enters a wide, desolate valley with mountain peaks all round. Mountain

ash trees stand singly by the path, carrying either white blooms like elder flowers or red berries, depending on the season. The electricity pylons, bearing their vital cargo high above bog and rocks, are far more intrusive in this remote setting than the blue and yellow engines on the railway. In 1845 there was a battle here between rival factions from the Caledonian Railway and its rival, the Scottish Grand Junction. The surveyors from the Caledonian ended up being thrown into a ditch by their opponents.

A zigzag rough road leads to Derrydaroch Farm[7] (351218) – 'The grove of the oaks.' You cross the river here, and turn right into oak and silver birch on a very rough and marshy path. Rowan and alder, thickly hung with lichen, grow above the river. The railway line crosses under the road to the left, and soon the path swings up to go under the railway by a tunnel less than five feet high[8] (359226). On the far side

The Falls of Falloch, Dorothy Wordsworth's 'Vale of Awful Sound'.

it crosses the A82 and climbs up to a track running north-east (358228). This was one of the military roads built by soldiers after the '45 rebellion, and it makes purposefully straight for Keilator Farm[9] (370243) – well, not quite straight! On the far side of the glen are a number of pine trees standing tall in ones and twos – all that remains here of the mighty Wood of Caledon which grew after the last Ice Age to cover all the Central Highlands. These survivors somehow escaped the axes and the fires which cleared the forest for agriculture.

From Keilator Farm you walk up Bogle (Goblin) Glen beside a stone wall to a ladder stile (374248) which gives access to a Forestry Commission plantation. Here the West Highland Way climbs on over the shoulder of the hill, but our route follows a signpost to Crianlarich down between the trees to the A82 road where you turn right to reach the village.

Crianlarich in Gaelic is Crithionnlaraich – 'the place of the aspen.' It was expanded from a tiny farming community by the railway, whose lines from Glasgow to Fort William and from Perth to Oban meet here. No love was lost between their employees, and the two stations in the village – Upper and Lower – hardly communicated until nationalization put an end to pride and prejudice. Nowadays only the Upper station remains[10] (384250). It boasts a famous tea-room patronized by railway travellers, walkers and the local boys and girls who gather here in the evenings to chat and giggle. If you have not refreshed yourself in one of Crianlarich's hotels, you can restore the tissues and put your feet up before catching the train back to Ardlui Station.

River Devon and Dollar Burn

OS 1:50,000 Sheet 58
8 miles

This is a walk in two moods – the first a cheerful stroll beside the placid River Devon, the second an exciting scramble up the spectacular glen in which the Burns of Sorrow and Care meet at the foot of Gloom Hill to form the Dolorous Burn.

From Tillicoultry, a little paper-making and woollen manufacturing town at the foot of the Ochil Hills, you walk by Devon Valley Railway to Dollar. Join the path by turning down the A908 road from the centre of Tillicoultry for 200 yards, then left onto the old railway line[1] at a sign: 'The Devon Way' (921967). The line has been converted into a footpath which runs beside the meandering River Devon, well surfaced and provided with picnic tables, benches and interpretative notice boards. The Devon approaches and shies away constantly during the three mile walk, at one place bending so acutely that the resultant ox-bow has formed itself into a complete circle like a watery doughnut[2]. Flat potato fields and grazing meadows lie each side of the river. The main interest of the railway walk lies in the great green wall of the Ochils to the north, rising over 1,000 feet above the valley; and in the multitude of flowering plants that find safe haven on the old line. Splashes of colour brighten up the grassy sides – the yellow of broom, buttercups, coltsfoot and moon daisies; pink dog roses, stocks, campion and ragged robin; the purple of rhododendrons, vetch,

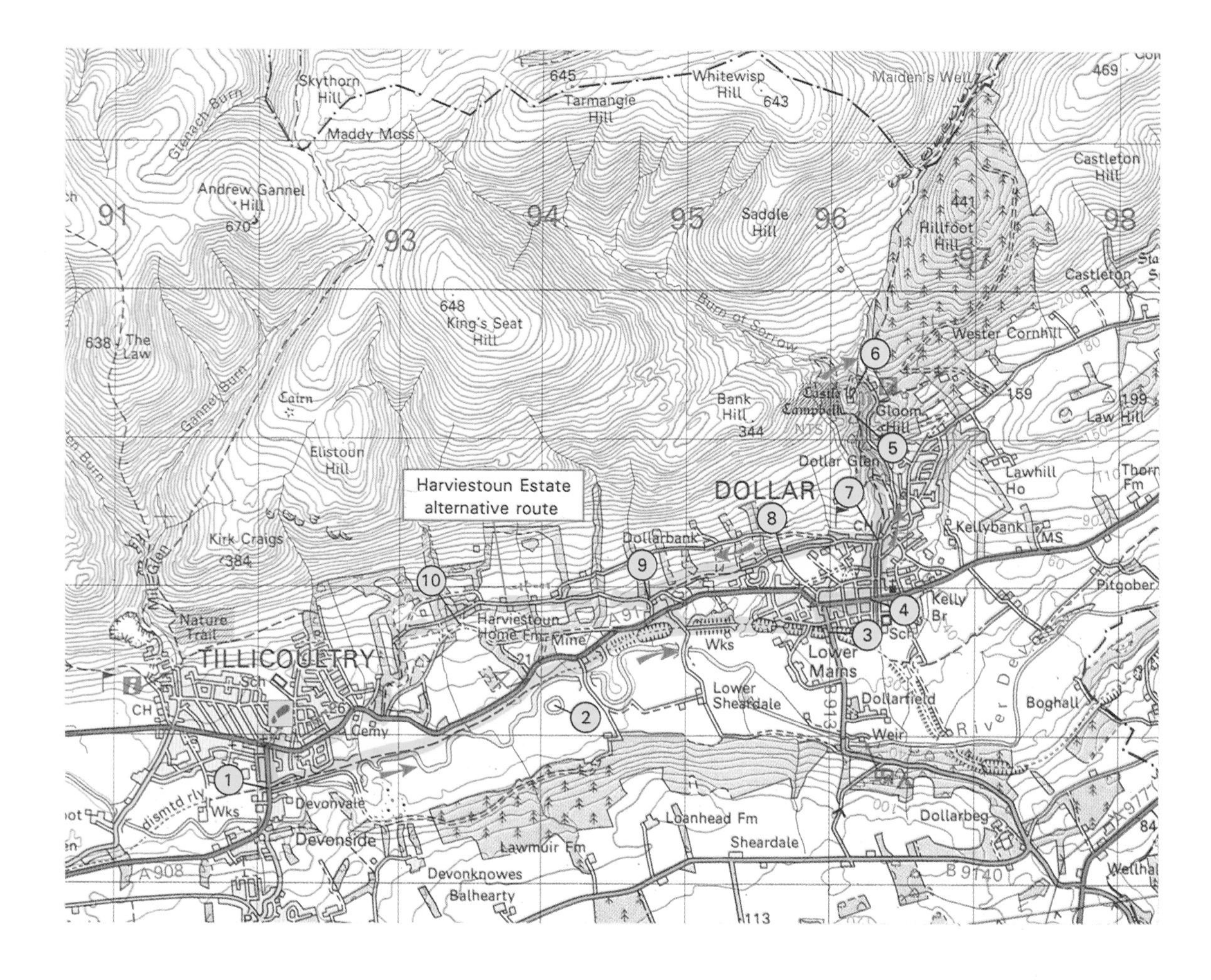

Looking up Dollar Glen to Castle Campbell over the tree-tops.

dame's violet and cranesbill; blue speedwell and bluebells. The old railway arrives in Dollar under two bridges, at the second of which[3] (960977) you climb up the embankment to the road and turn right to reach the A91. Turn right again here for half a mile to the stumpy little clock tower in the centre of Dollar (963979), and left up West Burnside[4], following Castle Campbell and Dollar Glen signs. Dollar is best known for its academy, founded in 1819 on the money left by John M'Nab, a herd-boy from the town who had made good in the Navy. The academy lies just to the left of West Burnside, while to the right the Dollar Burn comes down beneath little stone bridges to join the Devon.

At the top of West Burnside, cross the burn and turn left up the signposted path into Dollar Glen (963984). As you come out of the trees you can see Castle Campbell sitting in the collar of Bank Hill and Gloom Hill above the glen. The castle is a property of the National Trust for Scotland, and open to the public. To reach it you follow the track over Mill Green and into the wooded glen, where it rises quite steeply on a rocky, sloping ledge which can be very tricky in wet conditions. The unguarded edges drop more than one hundred feet in places to the bottom of the chasm, and in some parts the path is less than three feet wide. A series of wooden footways leads to the most exciting part of the climb – the narrow slits in the black, dripping rock through which the burns of Care and Sorrow tumble down to the place where they meet and mingle to form the Dollar Burn[5] (962992). The best climb is to the left up the side of the Burn of Sorrow, between sheer rock walls eight feet apart and fifty or sixty feet tall, shaggy with moss, nettles, bracken and ferns, that literally tower above you. At the far side the burn sluices down a double fall, slanting like the shining black lips of rock that enclose it at an angle of seventy degrees which increases its battering noise and makes this an awe-inspiring place.

Steps lead up to a high-level path which emerges to cross the burn and climb up to Castle Campbell, or Castle Gloum as one of its captives styled it[6] (962993). Perched on its rock with precipices on three sides and the mountains at its back, the castle is stark, strong and grim. The great tower was built in the 1490s, a stack of cold stone chambers linked by a spiral staircase and pierced by small windows eight or ten feet thick. What winter must have been like in there one shudders to think. There is a superb view from the top of the tower; no enemy could approach from the hills to the north without being spotted, while to the south a defender could spy over thirty miles of country. The southern side of the castle, built later, has larger windows and a less military feel, but the cavernous rooms and unadorned rough stone walls still speak of feuds, fear and defence. The castle belonged to a Douglas who had the honour of being stabbed by the Scottish King James II. Sited where it is, and built in an age of border battles, murder and other family vendettas, it must have witnessed a string of terrible events unrecorded and long forgotten. The doom-laden names of those nearby burns and hills – Sorrow, Care, Gloom and Dolour – carry a whiff of the dark history which inevitably gathers around such a fortification in such a place. Montrose attacked it in 1645, but couldn't take it (he burned and ravaged the surrounding country to make up for his failure); the Macleans, supporters of Cromwell, fired it with burning arrows in 1654 while the inmates were out looking for food. A century later it was a ruin:

'Oh! Castell Gloom! thy strength is gane,
The green grass o'er thee growin',
On hill of Care thou art alone,
The sorrow round thee flowin'!
Oh! Castell Gloom! on thy fair wa's,
Nae banners now are streamin';
The howlit flits amang the ha's,
And wild birds there are screamin'.'

From the castle gate go down steps to the right to return to the confluence of the burns of Care and Sorrow, and on down to the bridge at the head of West Burnside. Turn right here up Back Lane[7] past Dollar Golf Club and the academy. The lane runs behind Dollar and soon bends to the left, with a notice of No Through Road ahead[8] (957983). Ignore this and keep ahead on a rough path through the trees, which comes out at a T-junction of lanes[9] (947979). To the left the road drops down to the A91 and the old railway line, which can be followed back to Tillicoultry. The road on the right climbs up past Harvies-

toun Castle[10], visited several times by Robert Burns, and on between tall parkland trees to drop into the eastern outskirts of Tillicoultry. This road is not a public right of way, but the owners of the Harviestoun estate are sympathetic to walkers who keep to the paths and follow the country code.

The Burn of Care comes jetting down under the trees.

Moness Burn
and the Birks o' Aberfeldy

OS 1:50,000 Sheet 52
2 miles

> *'Bonnie lassie, will ye go,*
> *Will ye go, will ye go:*
> *Bonnie lassie, will ye go*
> *To the Birks o' Aberfeldy?'*

> *'Now summer blinks on flow'ry braes,*
> *And o'er the crystal streamlet plays,*
> *Come, let us spend the lightsome days*
> *In the Birks o' Aberfeldy.'*

Bonnie lassie or laddie, you are in for a treat when you climb up the Den of Moness from Aberfeldy to the great falls by which the Moness Burn tumbles down from the moors to join the River Tay. Robbie Burns certainly thought so in 1787; though another great poet, Robert Southey, couldn't wait to get away from Aberfeldy when he was here in 1819 – he thought it 'a place which might preferably be called Aberfilthy, for marvellously foul it is.' Aberfeldy has cleaned up since then, and now caters for the tourists with a host of shops, hotels and bed-and-breakfast places.

The walk up the Birks o' Aberfeldy starts from the car-park by the bridge half a mile south of Aberfeldy, where the A826 road crosses the Moness Burn (855487).

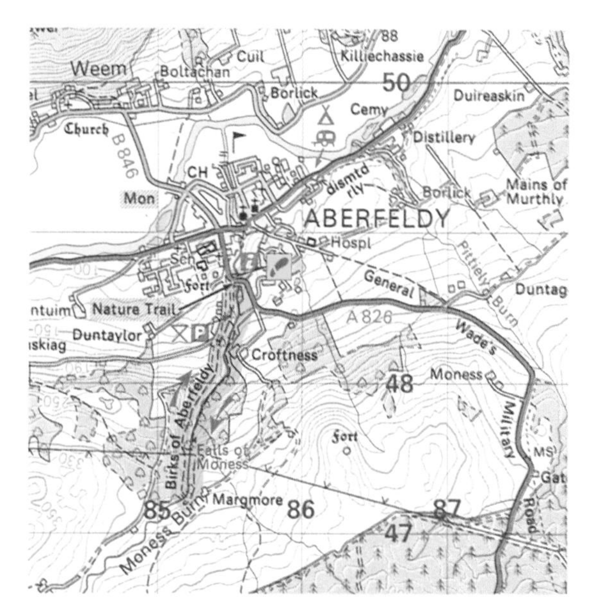

The path leads up the east bank of the burn into a picnic area where you can pick up a Nature Trail leaflet. Numbered posts along the route refer to explanatory sections in the leaflet, which makes a well-informed companion on the walk.

Cross the burn by a footbridge and turn right up the path, which climbs up above the water through oak, ash, birch and hazel.

> *'The little birdies blythely sing*
> *Or lightly flit on wanton wing,*
> *While o'er their heads the hazels hing,*
> *In the Birks o' Aberfeldy.'*

A long list of 'little birdies' is given in the Nature Trail leaflet – the tree cover and inaccessible lower reaches of the glen give good shelter to a large variety of bird and animal life. In fact, Burns spotted his 'birks' or birches at Abergeldie, but thought Aberfeldy would sound better in the poem. The burn makes its noisy way through, round and over an obstacle course of boulders and flat plates of rock in the bed of the glen. The drop of 450 feet from top to bottom of the burn is achieved over a series of falls and cascades, paralleled by the steep upward course of the path high above. Suddenly the valley narrows to squeeze the Moness Burn into the Lower Falls, a cataract leaping down below trickling side streams where the falling water over slippery black rocks makes an ideal environment for the damp-loving ferns, mosses and liverworts. Wooden walkways lead up above these side falls beside a large birch tree that overhangs the sixty-foot drop to the Moness Burn. Daring folk like George Buchanan (10.7.68) and J Reith (1986) have carved their names for posterity on its trunk – risking a

dramatic death plunge as they did so.

Concrete steps go down to a viewpoint over the Middle Falls, which completely fill the glen as far as the eye can see. Over 200 yards long, and one hundred feet high, they come racing down to the final pool in which the sodden trunk of a fallen tree, stripped by water-power of its bark and branches, is slowly dissolving under the jet of the burn.

'The braes ascend like lofty wa's,
The foaming stream deep-roaring fa's,
O'erhung wi' fragrant spreading shaws,
The Birks o' Aberfeldy'—Middle Falls.

Top Falls leap into space. Don't linger here with a full bladder.

'The braes ascend like lofty wa's,
The foaming stream deep-roaring fa's,
O'erhung wi' fragrant spreading shaws,
The Birks o' Aberfeldy.'

The path goes on climbing, fringed by Scots bluebells with their turned-back petals. Soon the surge of the Top Falls can be heard as they trample the rocks beneath them. Close your eyes and it sounds like a giant launderette – accurate, though not too poetic. Burns, unburdened with irreverent modern images, had a more lyrical idea of the Top Falls:

'The hoary cliffs are crowned wi' flowers
While o'er the linn the burnie pours,
And rising weet wi' misty showers,
The Birks o' Aberfeldy.'

There are glimpses of the moorland ridge ahead as the path swings round to cross the footbridge directly over the top of the falls, plunging down in a long, thick spout into the pool below. Dorothy Wordsworth, sightseeing here with brother William, was evidently able to climb down beside the pool to marvel at the sight of the falls roaring down at her:

'They tumble from a great height, and are indeed very beautiful falls, and we could have sate with pleasure the whole morning beside the cool basin in which the waters rest, surrounded by high rocks and overhanging trees.'

I have to report that the sight from the middle of the bridge of that powerful jet of water shooting out into space between one's legs is a great diuretic.

The path on the far side of the Moness Burn slopes down uneventfully back to the car-park, though if you are lucky you may see a red squirrel clinging tight to the trunks of one of the Birks o' Aberfeldy.

River Dee

OS 1:50,000 Sheet 44
3½ miles

An old woman suffering from a nasty and painful disease started the whole thing off; and a young woman madly in love with her husband and with Scotland set the seal on it.

Half-way through the eighteenth century Ballater was not even on the map. A couple of farms scratched a living from the strip of fertile land where the River Dee bent in a wide horseshoe at the feet of the hills; otherwise the river valley was an almost deserted wilderness of bog, rough grass and heather. On every side the hillsides sloped up to a high skyline which effectively cut off communication with the outside world. Drovers' tracks ran over the tops of the fells, and one of General Wade's new roads came down to river level by the manor house at Balmoral a few miles to the west; but the lonely spot under the 'Rock of Oak Trees', Craigendarroch, remained unvisited and unknown.

Scrofula makes you itch – itch until you have scratched off most of your skin, unless you can find a cure. Exactly how that old lady in about 1760 came to roll in the marsh at Pannanich, a couple of miles downstream, will never be known. The popular theory is that she was led to her curative wallow by a dream. Anyhow, wallow she did, and emerged from the bog filthy but free of her affliction. Word got about, the marsh waters were tested and found to cure a number of unpleasant illnesses besides scrofula. A small spa came into being, a fashionable resort where Scottish gentlefolk could relax, enjoy music, dancing and flirtation, and take the waters. There were many such spas all over the country at that time, and Ballater stayed a local affair for nearly a century. Then in 1848 the young woman and her husband arrived in the Highlands, and adored everything they saw. Four years later they bought up the old manor house at Balmoral and a large slice of the surrounding countryside, knocked down the house and built in its place a great baronial castle, more suitable to the needs of the Queen of the realm and her Consort.

The arrival of Victoria and Albert in the district took the little spa and shook it into new life. Ballater sprouted more houses, hotels and shops, acquired a spanking new turnpike road in 1857 which brought in royalty-seekers from the south via Aberdeen, and developed that profitable connection with a branch line railway in 1866. Money poured in with the visitors who would happily gamble on a few weeks on 'Royal Deeside' in high hopes of the ultimate jackpot – a glimpse of the royal couple on street, road or railway.

Nowadays Ballater still thrills to those occasional moments of contact with the Royal Family, especially during the Highland Games at the Braemar Gathering in September which are always attended, as everyone here knows, by one or more of the family from their base at Balmoral Castle. The traditional field-sport of 'Royal-spotting' still brings visitors to Ballater, but today most holiday-makers are intent on the superb hill-walking, fishing, climbing and general savouring of the Highlands offered by these miles and miles of hilly open spaces along the River Dee. Ballater is full of shops whose

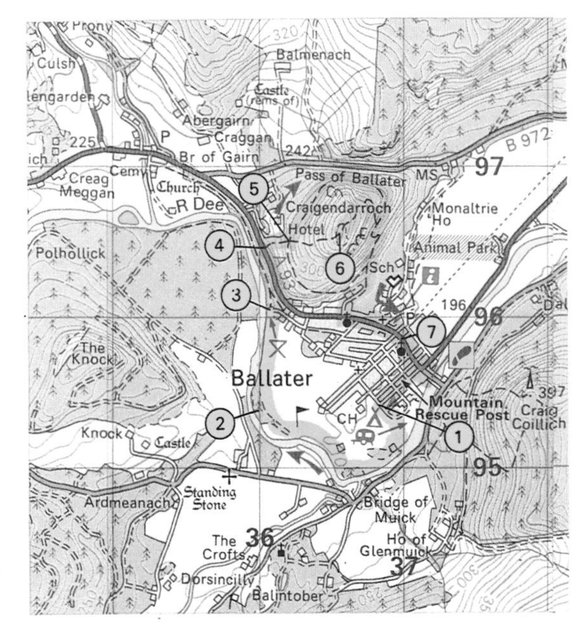

View from Ballater's golf course across the Dee.

windows display tartan, tweed, fishing tackle and sporting guns; and you certainly won't have to look far to find one of those enormous Scottish high teas – cakes, pastries, meat dishes, jam, chips, scones – to fill the corners after this short but strenuous walk beside the river and up over the Rock of Oak Trees.

Thomas Telford built a large number of bridges in Scotland at the height of his powers around the turn of the nineteenth century, but the 'Muckle Spate' of 1829 proved too drastic at Ballater even for his workmanship. He was in good company, however; many a Scots bridge-builder had already tried his hand here, and each successive structure was swept away by the rising Dee, swollen with springtime rain and melting snow. The present bridge, where we start our walk (372955) was opened by Queen Victoria in 1850 and has kept its four pink granite arches intact through more than a century's floods, helped by specially-constructed islands of stone in mid-river which break up and divert the full force of the spates.

Walk up the street towards the spire of Glenmuick Church of Scotland, behind which the arched swell of Craigendarroch Hill rises over the stone buildings of Ballater. Take the first turning on your left into Dee Bank Road – just up the main street on the left is a sporting shop whose windows contain a snarling, striped Scottish wild cat and a large black capercaillie, its crimson eyebrows touched up with paint, revolving on a turntable like a plump and clumsy fashion model. The stone terraces of Dee Bank Road lead down past the Ballater Youth Hostel to a T-junction[1] (368954), where you turn left to go down a fenced path between a caravan park and the town's golf course to the river bank (370952). Turn right here on a narrow path which winds between broom and blackberry bushes in the rough lower edge of the golf course. (Remember to keep well away from the flying balls, and to freeze if someone is playing a shot nearby.)

The Dee, wide, shallow and stony like a good fly-fisherman's river, flows in a saucer of steeply-etched ridges, clothed with Forestry Commission pines terminating at the top in collars from which rise the bald heads of the hill peaks. It is a scene straight out of a tourist brochure –

rippling river, purple heather, conifers, sharp mountainous outlines, golfers and fishermen. Craigendarroch Hill is the focal point to the north, its purple-grey, craggy face in full view amidst a thick covering of oaks. These old trees are survivors of the great forest where Scotland's own kings went hunting long before Victoria's forebears took a grip on Caledonia.

The path runs through thistles, knapweed, white foxgloves and harebells growing in the dense scrub to reach the river's edge in a grove of Scots pine[2]. The far bank of the river shows evidence of the flood-prevention efforts of succeeding generations – breeze-blocks, bricks and stone slabs holding the earthen wall in place against the flood level of the Dee. A stretch beside the river leads to a stile by the tenth green (360957)[3]: don't cross over, but turn to your right away from the water and walk up the side of the golf-course with a hedge on your left to a grove of silver birch trees. At a T-junction of paths in front of a wooden fence, turn left over another stile and through a copse to reach the A93 Braemar–Ballater road, where you turn left (363960). Half a mile along the pavement and past the Darroch Learg Hotel brings you to a steep, smooth track[4] (360965) running straight up the side of the hill just before the Craigendarroch Hotel and Country Club. With a stone wall on your left, mount this track until you come to a junction of paths 150 feet up from the A93[5] (362965), where you turn left to walk round the back of Craigendarroch Hill.

The narrow path runs among white and purple heather and the bright-green leaves of bleaberry (try the purple berries – sharp and mouth-watering if picked at blackcurrant size), dipping in and out of stands of Scots pine whose tall, slim trunks rise to dark-green ruffs of foliage thirty feet into the air. Between the trees there are far views over the purple, tan and olive heads of the hills beyond the river, before the path rounds the flank of the hill and threads its way along a precipitous hillside high above the Pass of Ballater. On the far side of the pass jagged sides of sheer rock stare you in the face, rearing above the narrow defile through which all traffic had to pass before the road to the south was built. From this peregrine's viewpoint you can well imagine what effect the winter snows had on life in this district in those days.

The path zigzags up the side of the Rock of Oak Trees, turning back on itself and forwards again to reach the summit at 1,250 feet[6]. If you haven't spotted a capercaillie lumbering away across the bleaberries, the view from the top of Craigendarroch makes up for it. Ballater lies away below to the south, a grey huddle round its church spire cradled by the River Dee – but the best is to the west around Balmoral. In 1848 Queen Victoria proved her mettle by climbing all the way to the top of Lochnagar, whose 3,750 feet stand clear of all contenders as a magnificent gatepost for the blue ridges of the Cairngorms beyond. A treat in store – back in Ballater you can buy *The Old Man of Lochnagar*, a children's entertainment written by her great-great-great-grandson.

Returning from the heights to the path, you drop down between the oaks and pines. The bleaberries and sphagnum mosses peter out as you reach the drier and more sheltered side of

Looking from Craigendarroch Hill over the Pass of Ballater.

the hill, to be replaced by the toothed leaves and spiky flower-heads of wood-sage. At the bottom of the hill turn right out of the trees onto Craigendarroch Walk, which leads to the A93 Braemar Road (366960). Turn left here to cross the bridge over the old railway[7] (370959), closed in 1966 after a hundred years of operation. The Deeside line was regularly used by the Royal Family during their journeys from Buckingham Palace to Balmoral; but even royal patronage failed to save it when the Beeching accounts were added up. It still serves the travelling public, however; no wheels turn along its level trackbed, but the boots of walkers keep it clear along the sections at each end of the line – Aberdeen to Peterculter in the east and Cambus O'May to Ballater in the west – that have been converted into walkways.

If you have had enough tramping, however, turn left over the bridge into the restored station building in its neat coat of crimson-and-cream paint. The Information Centre will tell you all you want to know about Ballater (and Balmoral) – and the restaurant will serve you a high tea to send you waddling on your way through the town and back to the river bridge.

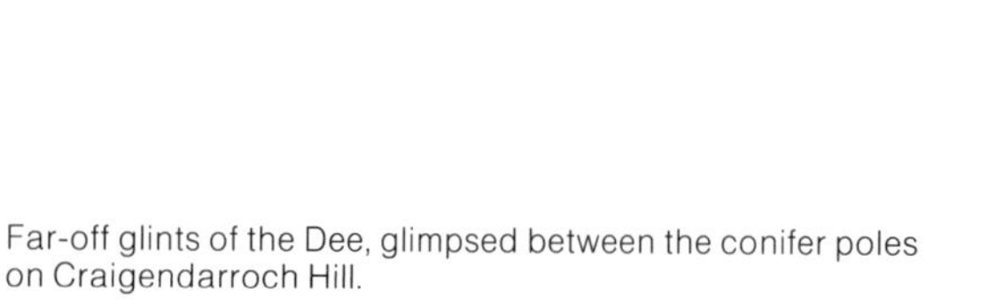

Far-off glints of the Dee, glimpsed between the conifer poles on Craigendarroch Hill.

River Lair

OS 1:50,000 Sheet 25
6 miles

When the Dingwall and Skye Railway opened up the north-west coast of Scotland to railway traffic in 1870, the trains passed tiny Achnashellach by without stopping. There were not enough potential customers in the locality to justify the building of a station; it took the influence of Viscount Hill to achieve that, and even then the little halt under the mountains started life as a private facility for Achnashellach Lodge. Nowadays you can alight from the train here[1] (003484) to tackle the steep climb up a rocky pass beside the River Lair to the high and bleak moorland plateau in a bowl of mountains where the river flows from Loch Coire Lair – one of the most striking river walks in Scotland.

Before you leave the station, however, pause for a moment to picture the gloomy evening of 14th October, 1892. A driver and fireman have just uncoupled their locomotive from its train and shunted it away, leaving the carriages on the gentle slope of the incline in the care of a brake van. The weight of carriages and passengers slowly but surely overcomes the adhesive power of the brake, and the whole train begins to slide quietly away down the slope. At the bottom it has worked up enough momentum to continue up the next incline for a few hundred yards, the travellers inside chatting or staring out of the windows in blissful ignorance of their dangerous situation. Meanwhile, back at Achnashellach station, the station-master is peering down the line through the gathering darkness, wondering where his train has gone. He swings round and shouts at the engine crew, telling them to something well go and fetch those carriages. Driver and fireman put their locomotive into reverse and set off back down the track – while below them the stranded train is just beginning

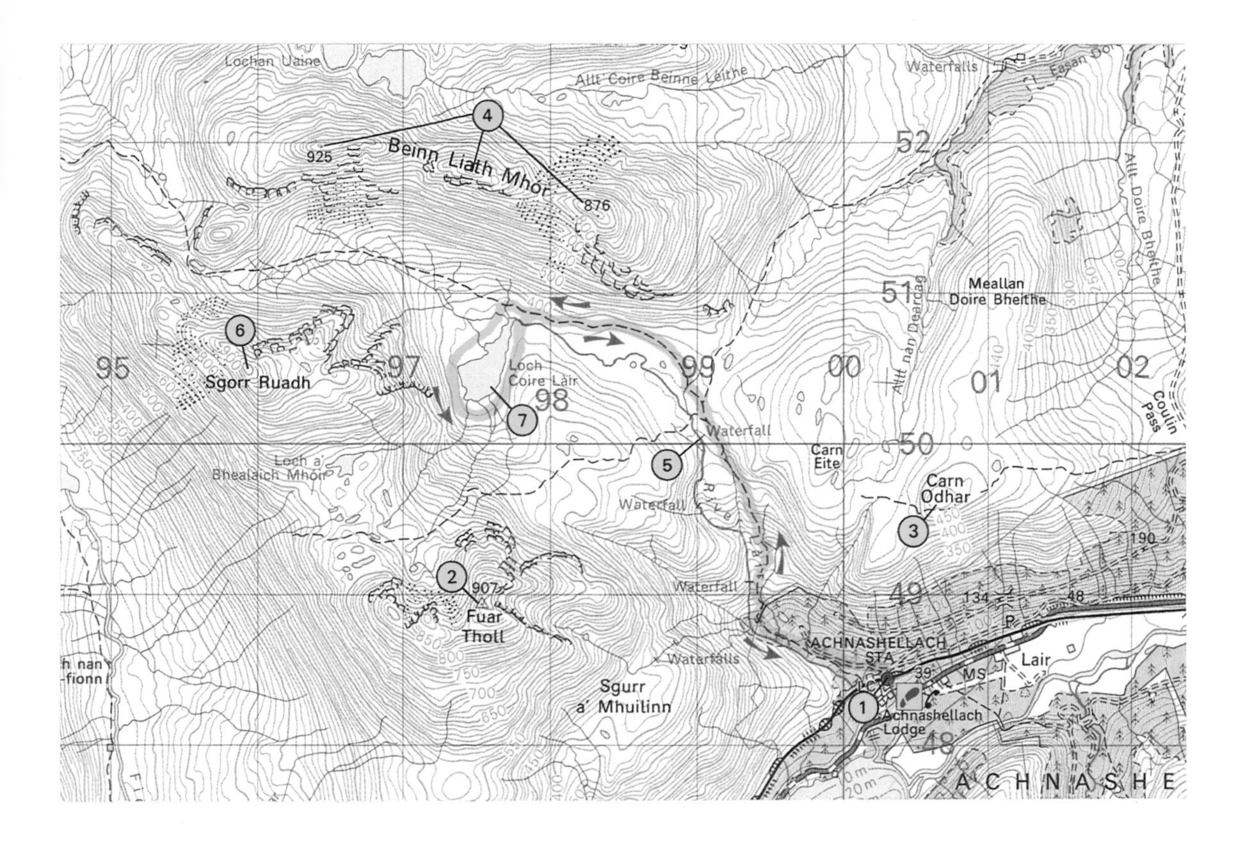

its forward roll from the opposite incline. Down in the dip between the two slopes, engine and train are reunited – crunch! When the dust has settled, eight badly injured passengers are on their way over the bumpy Highland roads to hospital and scores of others are demanding an explanation of the wretched station-master. Real-life drama, and perhaps the only bit of excitement this backwoods railway station ever saw.

Achnashellach has the unhappy distinction of being one of the wettest places in Scotland – six feet of rain fall here every year. If you are lucky enough to arrive on a dry day, however, the view up the valley of the River Lair is sufficiently majestic to take your breath away even before you have started the stiff climb. Over on the left the great purple shark's tooth of Fuar Tholl (The Cold One)[2] rises above the tree-tops, almost 3,000 feet of piled strata sloping as they soar up to a sharp peak against the sky. Carn Odhar (The Dun Hill)[3] on the right forms the other side of the saddle of mountain which holds the gully of the descending river. The path climbs up from the north side of the railway station for a few yards, then turns left on a forest road to wind upwards through Scots pine and Sitka spruce on a bed of black, waterlogged peat. The rough road ends beyond a stand of seventy-foot spruce (997488), from which a very boggy, narrow path bears to the left and mounts to a fence.

The rushing sound of the River Lair has been growing louder as you climb among the trees, and beyond the fence a few steps off the path to the left will give you a view down into the deep and narrow gorge through which it tumbles. A small but lively burn sluices down over rock shoulders to the right of the stony path[5], which carries you up among tussocks of rough grass towards the lip of the defile high above against the skyline. Oaks and mountain ash grow in the sides of the cleft, while beyond the rim ahead rise the three heads of Beinn Lath Mhor (The Great Grey Mountain)[4], the tallest of which towers over 3,000 feet. The heads are joined by saddles from which long arcs of scree sweep down until they are cut off from view by the rock wall above you. Cloud shadows moving across the screes turn them from grey to dun and then to silver.

Keep going up, winding in and out of narrow vees of rock scored across with the scratches left by those sturdy generations of hob-nail boots that climbed this path before modern composite soles outdated them. A little pass, littered with loose boulders left behind by the retreating Ice Age glaciers that formed this landscape, leads over the collar of rock (991501) and up to a splendid view into the plateau of moorland where the River Lair has its origin. Away and up to the left stands Fuar Tholl; ahead, its neighbour Sgorr Ruadh (The Red Peak)[6] – another craggy shark's tooth, sharply outlined – and to the right the long ridges of Beinn Lath Mhor. The silence is immense; but a shout will bring long echoes out of the towering rock faces. The river curves its way under these great wardens through the peat and heather, and beside it runs the narrow path undulating back and forth under outcrops of rock, laboriously making its way forward to snake up the pass between Sgorr Ruadh and Beinn Lath Mhor and over the top into Ben-Damph Forest. Legend has it that a postman used to cycle along this unforgiving track down into Achnashellach to visit his lady-friend. The power of love!

Loch Coire Lair[7] lies hidden from view behind a flank of moor; like Bunyan's Christian you must plod on along the track with faith as your spur until you are right under the stepped flank of Sgorr Ruadh – then comes the reward as the pear-shaped lake suddenly appears to the left (977988), lying dark and glittering in the hollow which you could have sworn a step before was dry and barren. The little loch is fed by burns which come down from the heights as white threads of water in shadowy clefts. You can complete the outward trek by walking round the lake – but this entails fording the River Lair up to your ankles at least, and a tiring trudge through deep heather and sticky peat bog.

Returning to Achnashellach down the steep, stony path, let your eyes wander at ground level. Here are gleaming green mosses, and dark velvety ones as smooth as a teddy bear's ear; fly-devouring sundews and pale purple orchids; cotton grass and yellow bog asphodel of the acid wetlands; dwarf birch and flat mats of coniferous plants; dragonflies and tiny frogs. Somehow

Dramatic cleft of the River Lair's rocky gorge.

The jewel at the end of the climb – Loch Coire Lair in its remote upland setting.

they all survive when the snow fills this high valley and the bitter winds and rains of winter bite into everything that lives up here. However superb the mountain peaks, it's a desolate scene that they overlook – but, in that secretive way in which nature operates, life does go on.

On reaching the stone wall at the tree-line again, you can avoid the boggy path through the trees to the left by keeping to the much clearer, stony one that skirts between the edge of the wood and the top of the river gorge. This runs down to arrive at a gate onto the railway line beside the old Station House, which stands in the middle of a most beautiful garden.

NB Thousands of ramblers every year enjoy this spectacular climb by the River Lair, which is included in the Scottish Tourist Board's booklet, Walks and Trails. *Just how they make the connection between the platform of Achnashellach railway station and the beginning and end of the walk, without either flying over the railway tracks or infringing the terms of the large red trespass notice by the line, must remain one of those unexplained Highland mysteries – like what the Scotsman wears under his kilt!*

River Spey (The Speyside Way)

OS 1:50,000 Sheet 29
30 miles

NB Return journey: unless you have a willing chauffeur, this has to be by bus (Ballindalloch–Aberlour–Elgin–Fochabers), involving several changes *en route*.

This long and beautiful walk into the hills of Speyside is all about two of Scotland's most celebrated delights – salmon and malt whisky. A lip-smacking ramble, reader – we'll start with the salmon and keep the water of life for later.

The Spey must be just about the best-known salmon fishing river in Scotland, and the Speyside Way, opened in 1981 between Spey Bay and Ballindalloch, puts you within sight and sound of thigh-deep fishermen for the whole thirty miles. They stand in the middle of the fast-flowing water, whipping their long lines to and fro before landing the flies with pin-point accuracy upstream of their prey. Salmon of up to sixty pounds have been taken from the Spey as they make their annual pilgrimage back to their parent river from their deep sea cruising grounds.

At Spey Bay, where the river meets the sea, a thick bank of shingle has been thrown up as the river switches course among the stony spits in its mouth. The Speyside Way begins at Tugnet, a suitable name for the wind-swept fishing settlement where salmon were (and still are) netted from the water. By the car-park stands the old ice house[1] (349654), built in 1830 with three vaulted chambers which were packed with ice collected in winter from ponds dug for the purpose near the shore. The ice, which lasted in these insulated chambers throughout the season, was used to pack the freshly-caught salmon for their journey southwards to Billingsgate. Nowadays the ice house contains an exhibition on the life and work of the settlement here.

Across the river mouth are the houses of Kingston-upon-Spey, founded in 1784 as a ship-building centre. Wooden ships were built here up till 1890, when iron hulls and their new technology made the old vessels obsolete. Just inland is Garmouth, a sea port trading in timber from the forests upriver until the Spey formed a new mouth and shingle bar and strangled the business.

The walk runs south on the east bank of the wide, island-dotted river, towards the disused Spey Viaduct of 1886[2] (346642) which brought the railway from Elgin across the Spey to the fishing towns of the Banffshire coast. The viaduct is 950 feet long, to allow for changes in the course of the fickle river. Nearby are the shallows known as 'Cumberland's Ford'[3] where the Butcher of Culloden crossed with his men on 12th April, 1746 on his way to deal with Bonnie Prince Charlie and his upstart Jacobites. This is a strange landscape, half salt and half fresh water, where oystercatchers and gulls compete for the fishermen's leavings on the scrubby, thistly islands of shingle that divide the various channels of the Spey. The river can gain terrible force in winter and during the spring spate, tearing down bridges and demolishing houses as it rushes down from the Cairngorms. In 1829 the Great Flood raised the Spey more than fifteen feet above its accustomed level and smashed down almost every bridge between the mountains and the sea. At the height of its spring spate the Spey comes exuberantly alive; you'll probably find yourself, as I did, whistling one of those leaping Strathspey dance tunes as you walk along.

The Speyside Way is well marked with helpful white thistle symbols and yellow arrows, useful higher up the river; but here at the mouth the path is easy to follow, running behind dense groves of alder and pine which screen the river, then curving right-handed to join the east bank (347630). The tidal flow of the Spey forces some currents seaward, some inland, and those in between into eddies and whirlpools. There is the constant sound of the shuffling of water over shingle and the screeching of the gulls wheeling above. Each side are flat fields of barley, leading away southwards towards the low hills which frame the taller peaks beyond. Heather, broom

S P E Y
Kingston
Tugnet
Mus
Hotel
Spey Bay
Garmouth
Corskie
Ashfield
The Links
Sand Pits
Nether Dallachy
Connagedale
Cemy
Essil
Speyside Way
Laighhill
Hill of Garmouth
Bogmoor
Landing Strip
Upper
Spey Fm
New Mains
Newton
Byres
River Spey
New Stynie
B 9015
Romancamp Gate
B 9104
Stynie Glebe
Cemy
Church
Den Fm
Stynie
Redhall
Mosstodloch
Cowfords
dismtd rly
Gordon Castle
Cross
Balnacoul Wood
Crofts of Dipple
Fochabers
Hotel
Dipple
Millhill
Cairnend
Graveyard
Leitch's Wood
Ardcanny
Blackhall
Wood of Conerock
Back Burn

Burnside of Dipple
Westerton
Ordiquish
Slorach's Wood
Ordiequish Hill
Auldearg
Culfoldie
Inchberry
St Marys Well
Craiglug
Scotch Hill
Craigs of Cuildell
Mains of Orton
Newtack
Hill of Cairnty
Orton Ho
Whitehillock
Haugh Island
Slackbuie
Speyside Way
Mains of Cairnty
Backshalloch
Woodside of Cairnty
Woodhead of Cairnty
Cairnty Croft
Garbity
Orton
Delfur Lodge
Burghnamary
Boat o' Brig
Wood of Dundurcas
Collie Fm
Distillery
Bridgeton
Newlands
Kirkhill
Church
Auchroisk
Crofts Fm
Dundurcas Fm
Castle (remains of)
River Spey
Knock More
Aikenway
Works
Ben Aigan
Arndilly Fm
Wood of Arndilly
Haughs
Arndilly Ho
LDP
FC

and gorse grow beside the path, which skirts a long plantation of mixed conifers to reach the B9104 road[4] (347605). Turn right here beside a stone wall over which are tantalizing glimpses of the roofs of Gordon Castle[5].

The chiefs of Clan Gordon used to rejoice in the title of 'the Gudeman o' the Bog': they lived in the middle of a wide tract of marsh called the Bog o' Gight, or Windy Bog. Then in the eighteenth century the 4th Duke had the area drained and shed his ancient nickname. He was an energetic improver, who from 1776 onwards built the town of Fochabers (pronounced with the accent on the first syllable – *Foch*abers) which you reach a mile upstream. There had been a little township of Gordon retainers within the castle grounds, but when the 4th Duke decided to extend his family home the settlement was

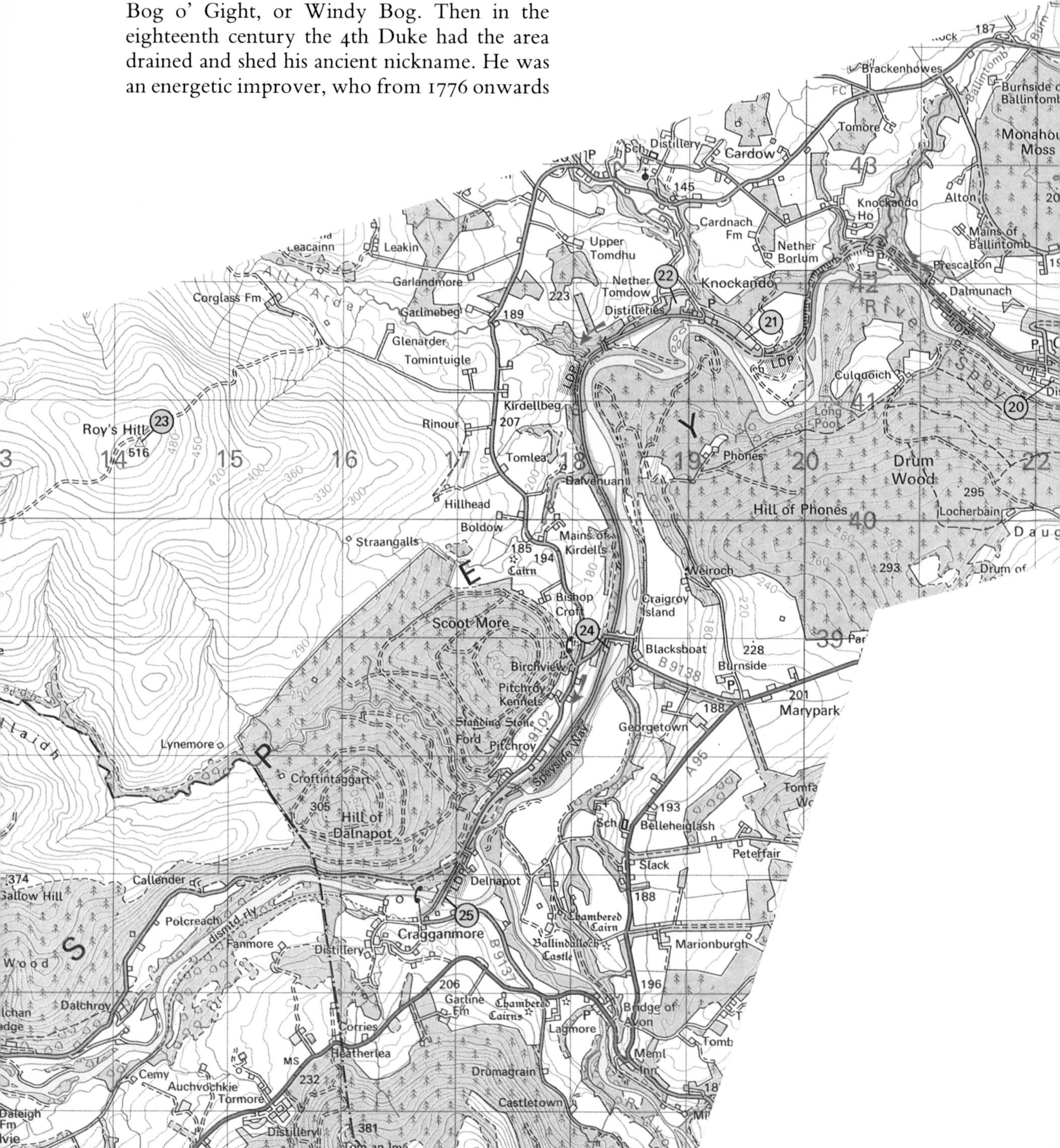

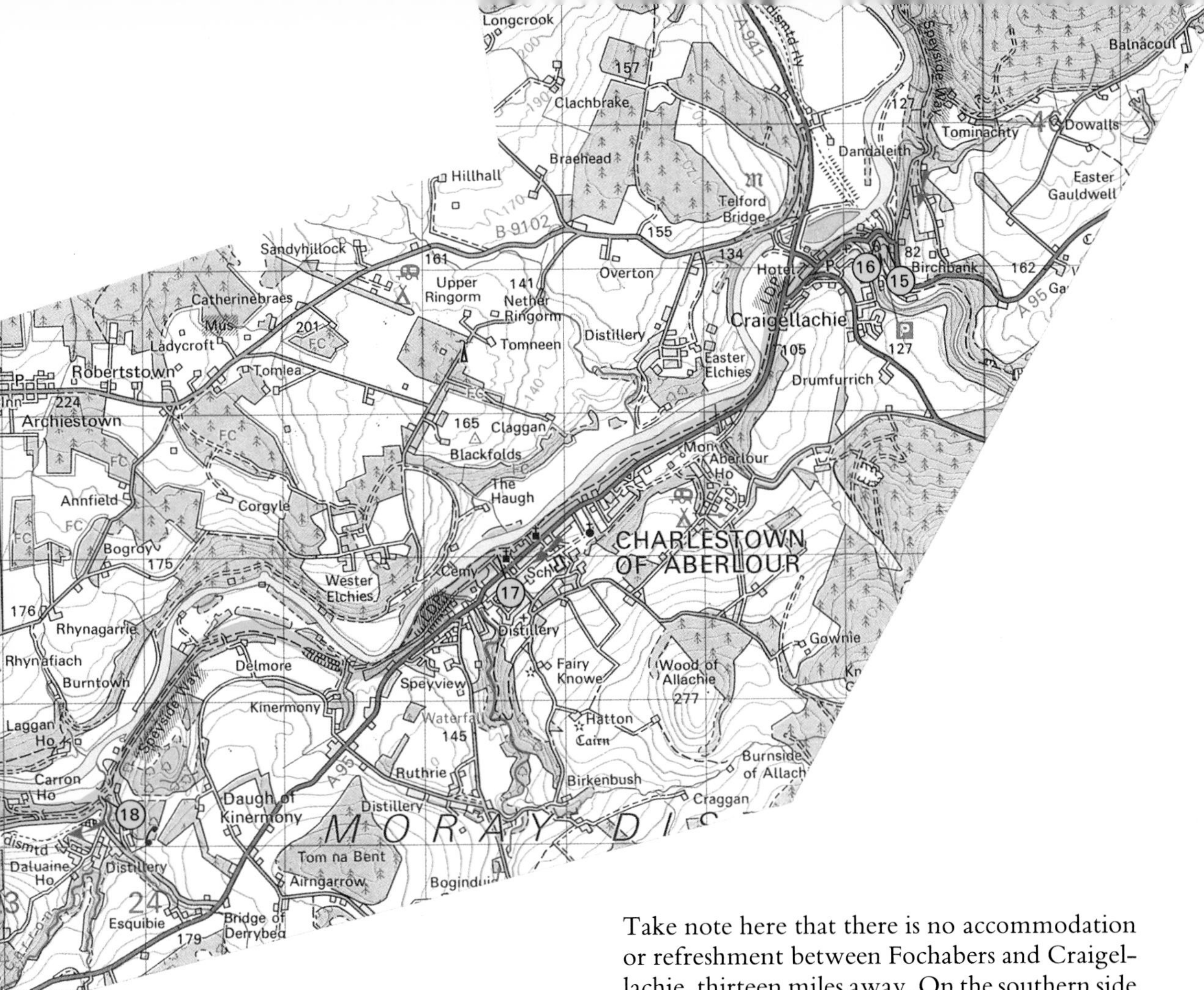

simply demolished and a new one laid out further away on a grid plan. The Gordons were all-powerful in the district, but one son of Fochabers must have blessed the day that he threw off the imperious yoke. The 4th Duke decreed that all schoolboys in his town must submit to an identical haircut, which was too much for young Alexander Milne. He evaded the ducal bull by emigrating to America, where he made spectacularly good. In 1846 he had the last laugh, leaving $100,000 in his will for the building of a new high school independent of the castle and its incumbent.

The Speyside Way enters the outskirts of Fochabers under two road bridges that stand side by side over the Spey[6] (341595) – a modern one, functionally planned, and a beautiful old structure of weathered yellow-stone arches and a lattice girder bow. The waymarks lead you around the edge of the town, whose pubs and shops can be quickly reached by side turnings. Take note here that there is no accommodation or refreshment between Fochabers and Craigellachie, thirteen miles away. On the southern side of Fochabers the path dips down into a dingle, where the waymarked post appears to be pointing over a gate into a field. It isn't! Go along the fence at the bottom end outside the field, climbing up through banks of bracken to reach a narrow road below a farmhouse[7], where you turn right and keep to the road for the next four miles and more. It climbs up to run along the lower edge of the great Wood of Ordiequish, with fine views to the west over the gleaming bends of the Spey, the widely spaced farms among their large cornfields and the purple tops of the ever-mounting hills inland.

The road reaches a wooden signboard marked 'Speymouth Forest – Earth Pillars Viewpoint' – turn right here for a short detour through the trees to a wonderful prospect[8] (336564) north up the Spey, running in the centre of the view far below around the islands. Beyond it stand the first really mountainous peaks, heaping away out of sight into the outlying ranges of the northern Grampians. The 'Earth Pillars' of the noticeboard are tall red needles rising up out of the trees, hard hearts of packed earth left behind as their soft shells were gradually washed away by rain.

The road runs on from the noticeboard to drop by some of the steepest hairpin bends I have ever seen to cross a burn. On the far side you climb just as steeply up to the isolated farm of Culfoldie[9] (337559), past which the road enters a remote, quiet stretch of larch and Scots pine, heather, moorland and wind. The occasional seagull from Spey Bay makes its way this far inland, its raucous screaming contrasting with the musical trilling of curlews. Pass the abandoned black-eyed farmhouse at Mains of Cairnty (327528) and drop downhill to a view over the twin bridges at Boat o' Brig, one railway and one road, below which the Spey curves southwards around the feet of Knock More and Ben Aigan.

More hairpin bends bring you to the bridge[10], under whose arches you walk (319517) past a dog kennels with scalps and horns of stags displayed on the sheds. Turn right at the road and immediately left up a stony track which bends round Bridgeton Farm[11] (319512) and climbs up into the trees of Craigellachie Forest. From here on the Spey valley is glimpsed intermittently between the tops of the Scots pine, larch, spruce and silver birch. Forestry is big business locally, and together with the Speyside whisky distilleries employs a large proportion of the local workforce. The Forestry Commission track through the trees is green and heathery, covered by a soft flooring of pine needles where it passes under the trees. It climbs steeply up to level out high above the valley, where it begins a series of curves[12] along the contours and round the hillsides which negotiate a succession of tumbling burns. At certain points the view back from the curves stretches north as far as Spey Bay and the steely blue line of the sea nearly twenty miles away. Lichens form a secondary forest of their own near ground level. The path straightens out at last, and drops down to a road[13] (291483) which passes the splendidly baronial pile of Arndilly House[14] (291471), built in 1750, and descends to the small and smoky Fiddichside Hotel[15] (293451) beside the bridge over the River Fiddich on the edge of Craigellachie.

Craigellachie (accent on the second syllable – Craig*ell*achie) is Clan Grant country. They gave the name Craigellachie to their rallying point, a rock near Aviemore thirty-seven miles deeper into the mountains, and gathered there for war, shouting their dreaded battle-cry 'Stand fast, Craigellachie!' Some of the clan diversified into distilling, and the village of Craigellachie relies on its whiskies – the Macallan malt among them – as much as on tourism. Here the Spey is spanned by a bridge built by Thomas Telford in 1815, which withstood the Great Flood of 1829 when all around it were toppling into the raging Spey. Telford's bridge carried all the road traffic across the river until 1973, when a new one took most of the weight off its ageing shoulders.

Cross the River Fiddich and turn left into the site of the old railway station[16] (292451). The Strathspey Railway, along whose line the Speyside Way now runs, was opened in 1863 to bring trippers from Aberdeen into the Grampians and to carry freight to and from the remote mountain settlements. The trippers made good use of it, but there was never enough freight traffic to keep it in the black. Dr Beeching chopped it down, and for nearly twenty years it lay gathering weeds and rubbish until Moray District Council saw its possibilities and joined forces with the Countryside Commission for Scotland to clean it up for walkers. A spur runs south-east from Craigellachie Station for four miles to Dufftown, home of Glenfiddich malt whisky; take a grip on your thirst, however, and turn right under the road bridge to enter the southernmost section of the walk to Ballindalloch (during which you will pass three distilleries within the space of two miles – and right beside the line).

The old railway line, surfaced with black cinders and rich in broom, silver birch, ragwort and the tall pinky-purple heads of rosebay willowherb, approaches the Spey to run on a ledge between river and road below the A941 and on to a seventy-yard tunnel. This short shaft, an expensive nuisance to build, could not be avoided by the railway planners; the line of the railway was blocked by a spur of rock which ran straight down from the steep hillside above into the river, cutting off any hope of a bypass. On the far side of the tunnel the long, straight course of the railway continues beside the Spey to

Between the trees of Craigellachie Forest the view over the River Spey stretches north to distant Spey Bay.

Charlestown of Aberlour – or Aberlour, as everyone calls it hereabouts.

The town was laid out in 1812 by Charles Grant, one of three brothers who left their names marked on the district – Archiestown and Robertstown a couple of miles to the west bearing witness to the energies of the others. The long single main street of the town with its similarly-patterned houses bears all the marks of an estate settlement, planned and executed to one design – in some ways it resembles a coal-mining village in County Durham or South Wales. The Aberlour Hotel, half-way down the street, goes out of its way to make hungry and thirsty ramblers welcome – even when they arrive wet and filthy, having covered twenty miles in the pouring rain!

The Speyside Way leaves Aberlour through the old station area[17] (265430), neatly restored with smooth lawns running down to the river. You can take tea in the station building itself, or something stronger in the Station Bar behind. Cross a bouncy wooden suspension footbridge over the Aberlour Burn (262427) and carry on through undramatic but handsome riverside scenery of Forestry Commission hillsides thick with conifers and slashed by the dark diagonal bands of forest roads. Opposite the Gothic Laggan House the line passes the short, overgrown wooden platform of Dailuaine Halt[18] (237413), the name still just decipherable from the imprint of the metal letters on the nameboard. Some fine tall silver birch trees stand among the Scots pine, Douglas fir and larch as the line crosses the Spey to reach Carron by way of a combined road and railway bridge which carries the inscription 'McKinnon & Co. Engineers. Aberdeen 1863'[19].

The Imperial Distillery[20] (222412), producing blended whiskies, occupies a solid set of granite and brick buildings which were opened in 1897 beside Carron Station to give instant access to the railway network – malt in, and whisky out. From Carron the Speyside Way continues under Knockando House, hidden by trees above the old railway on the right, and passes the Knockando Distillery[21] (195415),

Yes, it really is this colour! A fly-fisherman casts across the Spey at Charlestown of Aberlour.

built like Imperial next to the railway. An old crane marks the site of the sidings which connected railway and distillery, though nowadays malt and whisky travel in opposite directions by road. The distillery is not officially open to the public, though the manager will cheerfully arrange a tour round the works for you. The single malt Knockando whisky is on the pale side, and has quite a bite.

A few hundred yards further on is Tamdhu Station (189417), restored by the adjacent Tamdhu Distillery[22] as an exhibition centre, where visitors are given an introduction to the whisky process (seasoned by a dram of the product) before being shown over the distillery. In another part of the old station you can buy a bottle of the golden and delicious single malt. The distinctive peaty flavour is infused with the whisky by smoking the barley over burning peat – Tamdhu is lightly peat flavoured, but some malts reek with its acid taste.

Now the Speyside Way begins its final run of four miles into Ballindalloch along the west bank of the Spey, still a wide and impressive flow over its stony bed. The bowl of hills that encircles the old railway rise on the right to the flat top of Roy's Hill[23], nearly 1,700 feet high. The walk passes the lattice-girder birdge with its line of flood arches taking the B9138 over the Spey, and comes to Blacksboat Station[24] (183389), a low granite building and a tall wooden goods shed now used as a hay store. The final approach to Ballindalloch Station is made over the Spey again by an impressive lattice-girder viaduct[25] (169368), with ornate plates over each entrance marked '1863 – C. McFarlane – Engineer – Dundee'. Beyond stands Ballindalloch Station (167366), the temporary terminus of the Speyside Way. There are plans to extend the route to Glenmore Lodge near Aviemore, thirty miles higher into the Cairngorms. What a walk that will make one day!

Index

Page numbers in italics refer to illustrations